Beyond the
House
of the
False Lama

Nancy—
Forward. Always forward.
Back is for the dead.
Make a gorgeous fuss...
Happy birthday—
George Crane

Beyond the House of the False Lama

Travels with Monks,
Nomads, and Outlaws

George Crane

HarperSanFrancisco
A Division of HarperCollins*Publishers*

HarperCollins books may be purchased for educational, business, or sales promotional
use. For information please write: Special Markets Department, HarperCollins Publishers, 10 East 53rd Street, New York, NY 10022.

HarperCollins Web site: http://www.harpercollins.com
HarperCollins®, ♠®, and HarperSanFrancisco™
are trademarks of HarperCollins Publishers.

FIRST EDITION
Designed by Joseph Rutt

Library of Congress Cataloging-in-Publication Data
Crane, George (George L.)
Beyond the house of the false lama : travels with monks, nomads, and outlaws / George
Crane. — 1st ed.
p. cm.
ISBN-13: 978-0-06-052441-8
ISBN-10: 0-06-052441-3
1. Crane, George (George L.)—Travel—Mongolia. 2. Buddhists—United States—
Biography. 3. Spiritual biography—United States. 4. Mongolia—Description
and travel. 5. Tsung-tsai, 1925– I. Title.
BQ948.R36A3 2005
294.3'092—dc22
[B]   2005046093

05 06 07 08 09 RRD(H) 10 9 8 7 6 5 4 3 2 1

For Siri

There was things which he stretched,
but mainly he told the truth.
            —Huckleberry Finn

Limited by space, a frog in a well cannot
understand what is an ocean;
limited by time, an insect in summer cannot
understand what is ice.
            —Chuang-tzu, poet, follower of Lao-tzu, 300 BCE

The universe is not only queerer than we imagine,
it is queerer than we can imagine.
            —John Wheeler, physicist

I understand noodles.
            —Tsung Tsai, Zen monk

contents

I
Beyond the House
of the False Lama

Autumn–Spring
2001–2002

You're bound to become a Buddha
if you practice
if water drips long enough
even rocks wear through
it's not true thick skulls can't
be pierced
a person just needs
a hard enough mind

—*Han Shan, T'ang dynasty poet*

"Last night your dead mama visit me. She floating like bubble," the Zen monk Tsung Tsai was saying. He spread his arms wide. "Like big orange bubble. And she very frighten for her son. So I need tell her, not worry. I am monk and truth is truth. Georgie almost my family."

My mama died five years ago. I hardly knew her and rarely think of her now. Her dark eyes no longer glitter as they did so long ago when she would say, "Before having you I should have died on the delivery table."

I tried to love her, but that I was her son frightened me. Still, when she reached that point where she no longer got out of bed, then no longer spoke or moaned or moved, my brother and I made sure she felt no pain or fear. The hospice doctor had given us control of the liquid morphine and dropper, and if she so much as twitched, I dosed her. Some of the clear syrupy dope would dribble over her slack lower lip to puddle on her chin. And always I had to fight the urge to lap it up like a cat.

Then my father died. Emphysema. Three packs a day had toasted his lungs. I didn't get there in time to say goodbye. He was in Phoenix. I was adrift in Manhattan. Neither of us had ever learned how to talk to the other. Death changed all that had been missed into guilt. "I should have been there. I should have been with him," I told Tsung Tsai when I returned with the news. "His nurse said that every time he spoke my name he cried."

"Georgie, write poem about your papa. Read. Remember. Give to me. I give to Buddha. He can give to your papa. Now you can say goodbye."

Daddy you taught me
what to look for,
how to pick
the sweetest corn.
Firstly find browned silk,
then peel back the husk.
Look for the small kernels
the not too yellow;
the pale,
the tender
got the sugar
and taste incredible.
A hot Sunday,
the family driving out of Chicago:
Illinois July prairies
and buying at the farmer stand
corn and homegrowns.
The fat red beefsteaks you sliced up thick
with salt and pepper,
with Russian black bread,
sweet butter.
We'd always eat in the kitchen,

your haven,
where you were happiest;
happy as a monkey in the moment,
that sane sweet moment.

Tsung Tsai waggled both hands enthusiastically thumbs-up. "But best you become Buddha," he said. "Best idea. Best stop this suffering. Become Buddha." He clapped once. "Become really."

"Become," I said.

"Of course. Must." He nodded. "Then no more suffer."

I looked at his bald monk's skull that needed a shave, and when his head came up I saw the thin white Chinese hairs sprouting at his chin. *Become.* I've spent the last twenty-five years of my life trying to *become,* and it hasn't been easy, because the man I am is always getting in the way. "Good idea. No more suffer," I said.

Nonsense. Pure drivel, I thought, remembering a friend who couldn't stop screaming.

One evening, I was still a new father then, sitting around the table after dinner, my daughter in my lap; her soft breath, her face tucked into my neck as friends told us, over coffee and dessert, of their only son's death.

"Eight years ago he fell off his bike, hit his head. Five days later he was dead. He was sixteen. I went comatose," he said.

"I couldn't stop screaming," she said.

Long after they'd left, that midnight, it began to snow. My family was sleeping safe for the moment. And so I sat, like an old man, wrapped in a blanket. He is huddled close to the fire, in a rocking chair, a notebook in his lap, pages fallen and scattered on the floor. Chin to chest, past the precious midnight hours, he snores—loudly, horribly—or snaps awake gasping for breath, for understanding; for a flash of last words.

"Life and death both of them are good," Han-shan wrote, using water and ice as examples. But life and death weren't, for my friends, both of them good.

life and death
both of them are good
but life I'd guess
is better.

"No good," Tsung Tsai said, his voice an appalled whisper. "Life sad. Necessary sad."

"It can suck."

"True. Very badly can suck." He bowed his head so that I couldn't see his eyes, and we sat there with dust motes dancing until we both were sure there was nothing more to say. Then I drove home in what was left of the light.

Fifteen years ago, shortly after I first met Tsung Tsai, his vitality and agility, his toughness and courage surprised me, and I wondered about his age. I knew he was older than he seemed, particularly for one who had lived hard and suffered. I wanted to look into the future, into the mystery of old age and death. He would be my measure, my Huck Finn already lit out for that territory ahead.

For as long as I could remember I'd sorrowed growing old, just as two thousand years ago a poet who called himself the Emperor Wu of Han did when he wrote this, in my loose translation:

the fall wind blows
frothy cumulus.
the grass browns,
leaves fall,
and wild geese fly south.
the last flowers bloom,

pansies,
chrysanthemums with their bitter perfume.
I dream
her lovely face
I can't forget
while on the river
a barge rides the current
dipping in whitecaps.
they play flutes
and drums;
the rowers sing
and I'm happy in the moment,
until that ancient sorrow reminds.
Just yesterday I was young.
and now I grow old.
I grow old.

I asked: "Tsung Tsai, how many years do you have?"

"When I'm dead I'm dead," he said.

I knew what he meant. A profound awareness of death led him to the peace of Buddha. It led me to fear and, greedy for sensation, to the desire to squeeze more from every moment; a voracity even for enlightenment. I had always been susceptible to misadventure and excess of every kind—an edgy anarchic Zen.

Give me more! More! I want! I want!

on top of graves
make love my darlings,
make love,
and while you're alive
have wine,
get drunk.

there are no second helpings
for the dead
know nothing of death,
nor of their life
that has passed.

The loss of breath and day; emptiness. A depressing spin when you lust for forever-consciousness. When you haven't come to terms with the very essence of Buddhism—that is, to be one who is liberated from desire, from all ideas of self, of life and death. And so I had at various times of transcendent life-looniness considered checking myself into a Zen monastery for a year. . . well then, perhaps a month . . . a week . . . a day . . . an hour . . . a minute. No, I want it all. All desire. Everything. I desire, therefore I am. Life is everything. Death nothing. I hate it. Fear it. Court it. It's life's most engaging option by far, ahead of love, sex, art, and nirvana.

c h a p t e r

2

The nirvana that is desire fulfilled was Spain when I was young. I was trying, without success, to finish a first novel, *Lonely Pine Tree with Bear Tracks Leading Up to It.* "That's a long title," was one editor's only comment. "Not a problem," I wrote back; "it's a short book."

And oh yes that glorious lust for life and art carries memories of my then *campo* neighbor, another old man, another teacher, that master of desire, the painter Rog Rogoway. Memories of how, after a day of trying to work well, we'd share stories, jug red wine, salted garbanzos, and bebop. "Never enough," was Rog's motto. "In the life of the ant, George, man is a dinner guest who came late and left early," he'd say, dancing without moving from the spot. "Just shaking his rubbery members like a deboned sardine, an octopus in the throes of ecstasy," was how Henry Miller remembered him in *Big Sur and the Oranges of Hieronymus Bosch.*

Rog was simply in love, with everything. He was all lust. And just when you thought another drink, another spout of wild words was too much, over the top, more than you could handle, Rog would raise his glass again: "Let's go too far, shall we?"

For fear of nonexistence I would, every once in a while, try to count, to quantify time, to add it all up—how much time is there in a second, a minute, an hour, a day, a week, a month, a year, the decades, the centuries, the millennia, a life passing. It was stupefying, a spiritual and philosophical moron's concern, which in fools is the purest of all emotions and the primal law that governs all of living; not love, not hate, not hope, but fear. Its universality is the cause of every abomination in the shitty chaos called human history. The trick is not to become unbalanced, punished, ruled by it.

For Tsung Tsai, of course, fear was never the appropriate response. "I don't believe afraid. Never," he said. "Please Georgie, you must be learning."

"I'm trying. I'm trying."

"Try is no good. Just *do*. True monk, he knows past, present, future. Knows his death."

"What a bore," I said, almost under my breath.

Tsung Tsai, who was cleaning his fingernails with a small flathead screwdriver, ignored me. When finished, he made a steeple with his fingertips. "Too much attachment. Very foolish," he said.

"What about you, Tsung Tsai? Are you never foolish?"

I'd heard the rumors—all from women—at Woodstock's de facto town crier and rumor mill, the health food store Sun Flower and the farm stand Sunfrost. They'd corner me and whisper.

It was possible. He was fascinated with women. With vaginas. He thought fucking was medicine. *Big medicine. Very much.*

"Everybody have this problem. Even monk. Me too. But not so foolish as you. Georgie much more foolish than me. Almost crazy. Maybe kill by yourself." Tsung Tsai pushed a paper plate piled with saltines in front of me. "Have a crack. Eat. Good for you."

The light was uncertain. That September—it was 2001—had been seemingly colder, wetter than usual. Early on there had been snow. Raindrops blown from overhanging trees spattered noisily against the windows. I needed to get away from him. I was anxious and wanted to slow my breath. I walked as slowly as I could out into the yard and stood under the thick, twisted branches of what must be a centenarian catalpa, watching shreds of cloud run the horizon. Then I heard mockingbirds and saw them fly, but nothing else. I had no faith in reincarnation. The only future I believed in was unknowable; completely in the hands of chance. I was sure, unlike Einstein, that god does play dice with the universe. But still I bought Tsung Tsai's certainty more than the future foretold by any one of that legion of New Age airheads: the gurus, astrologers, tea-leafers, palm readers, or feces-sniffers. Some shut themselves up and meditate in solitude, some love wine, the joys of sex, and words; both are fine, both work, both are Zen; but some of these professional gurus, these fame and fortune hypocrites, are enemies of understanding. Monks' rooms, temples, churches, synagogues, and retirement homes all smell the same: not fecund, but rich with the disgusting, winey decay of flesh, of stagnant philosophy.

"Foolish," I would agree.

Tsung Tsai was still talking when I returned, as if I had not left the room at all. I stuffed a couple of cracks in my mouth.

"Georgie, still make meditation? Still do my exercises I show you?"

I grinned and with my mouth full of cracks spit a few crumbs answering him. "No. I'm afraid not. Just now I'm practicing the art of not trying, not knowing, just doing."

"Humpff," he snorted. "Strange. You also have this Zen education?" He looked at his fingernails. He shook his head again and again. "Very strange. Couldn't believe."

There is a Las Vegas Zen that I learned one night in the Desert Inn. I was betting without a system and hot on a winning streak. At the table next to me sat a round man, bald as a monk. He was wearing white high-waisted flash pants. A red alligator belt was notched above his beach-ball belly at a point just below his nipples, which peeked out of an unbuttoned red silk shirt. On his feet were Italianate tassel loafers, red alligator also, no socks. And he was talking to no one in particular.

"My name is Portnoy and I'm booking out of pocket. The numbers are small but I ride 'em to the tune of a grand a pop," he said. Then he twitched and jumped, graceful and nimble as a dancer, out of his chair and onto his toes, suddenly riled into action and shouting at the bank of monitors multicasting the day's games, his voice high-pitched and delicate as a schoolgirl's.

"Nothing's serious. It's nothing serious. Ryan's blasting a no-hitter through seven. Nothing's serious. Nothing in the universe; nothing but chance is serious."

The room went quiet. To the silent bank of game monitors blinking in their silent progress, Portnoy pirouetted, bowing to the odds, in homage to all the goddesses of chance. And in a voice now near to hysterical, he announced to one and all, "Lady Luck still sought."

Portnoy was a infamous klobiosh player.[1] A hustler who usually worked the twenty-four- to forty-eight-hour gambling marathons at the Russian baths—Chicago, Philadelphia, New York. The big-money games.

"We break every now and then for a *schvitz,* a steam and a rub. Cold cuts. Katz would deliver. You know Katz, don't you? No? You're kidding. You ever get to the City?"

The following month we met for lunch at Katz's Deli, on Houston Street, the Lower East Side, New York City. Hot pastrami piled three inches thick. He had his on rye. I had mine, Chicago style, on an onion roll. An order of fries to share. And seltzers. On the table there was also a bottle of ketchup, a jar of yellow mustard, a tub of sour and new dill green tomatoes, pickles. Chocolate egg creams to wash it all down.

"In the forties," he said, pointing, "all through the war there was a sign behind that register. Send a salami to your boy in the army. Those were the days." He admired and then took a huge bite out of his sandwich, making a *sluup* sound. Yellow mustard bubbled out onto his fingers, out the corners of his mouth. His eyes closed with pleasure. A brief grunt. A sigh. "Those were the days."

After lunch we parted. "See you," I said.

"The odds against are long," he answered after a belch and long pause in which he seemed to have figured it. And he was right too. He died within the week. Heart attack.

---

[1] A fast-moving, addictive, and subtle card game for two players (also known as klaberjass, clobby, clubby, kalabriaz, clobber, clob, klabiash) which, like poker, demands a fine strategic balance of techical skill, luck, reading an opponent, taking inference, and bluffing.

I can still hear him thundering like a rabbinical Tsung Tsai. "You can't beat the numbers, *boychik*. But still you gotta be an optimist. Any fool can be a pessimist; it takes no imagination, no guts. Remember that, *boychik*. Remember to remember that."

Now, twenty-some years later, after many deaths, many losses, I still don't know what luck means. What is good luck and what is bad is mutable. Nothing can be known with certainty. So, as always, as Portnoy said, "Lady Luck still sought."

Next afternoon I was back sharing noodles, tea, and philosophy with Tsung Tsai. I wanted to begin planning for our return to Inner Mongolia, where we had unfinished business.

Five—now almost six—years earlier, in late autumn, Tsung Tsai and I had traveled to Ula Shan, Crow Pull Mountain, on the southern edge of the Gobi Desert, on a quest to find the bones of his teacher and cremate them. In November, the day after Thanksgiving, we found his teacher's grave, but we were too late. We couldn't dig. The burial mound was frozen hard as concrete. Tsung Tsai was coughing blood. We were finished. Winter and Tsung Tsai's failing health forced us back to Hong Kong and then home. He wanted, I thought, to finish now what we couldn't finish then.

And then there was the lost temple. In North of Yellow River country, where we'd traveled in 1996, there are stories, persistent rumors, of a lost temple, undiscovered and intact, an ancient monastery located in the far southwestern Gobi, somewhere Beyond the House of the False Lama, near the Wolf Mountains. On that earlier trip, we'd made an aborted attempt to look for, if not the temple, at least the way to it, but were stopped by sand and season. And though Tsung Tsai was positive, I was skeptical, didn't think there was a snowball's chance in hell that the stories were true. Still, I was haunted by the sexiness of the idea, the possibilities, the movie romance of it: *Illinois Crane and the Lost Temple.*

It was time to return to Mongolia.

Tsung Tsai had other ideas. But first tea. Tea was always the first order of business. He was bouncing away from the stove, veering around the kitchen with a near-to-boiling cup of tea, filled to the brim.

"I need concentrated bring to you. Never spill." He laughed, the cup swaying, the tea sloshing. "I call this one very full kung fu. Really it is meditation," he said, setting the cup down on the table in front of me. Not a drop spilled.

The goal of meditation, literally the art of sitting and forgetting, is to abandon matter, be impervious to perception, discard self, abandon intelligence, and become one with the All. It was good work for romantics; for monks, poets, and slackers.

"You must be learn something," Tsung Tsai said. "Now I find you out. I find out. Drink your tea."

He stared with ostentatious seriousness, waiting for me to lift the cup. I leaned over, lips pursed, and sucked up half a cup, then looked up at him, hardly wincing from the heat.

"Not a drop spilled," I said, trying to hold back a smile. "I call this one slurping kung fu." I laughed then, snorting a spout of tea onto his kitchen floor.

"Aii, you make mess. Small mess," Tsung Tsai said, bending from the waist to wipe up my mess with a scrap of rag. He clicked his tongue. "People have mouth, must say something. But okay. No problem. Maybe meditation too hard for you."

"Maybe."

Tsung Tsai dismissed the idea with a flip of a hand. He turned his back to me, stirring noodles with chopsticks. "Everything cook so nice. Boil. Boiling time." He stared into the steaming pot. "Georgie, don't worry. You worry too much. You just need write. Always write. This is poet work. *Your* work. You are monk. Writer monk. You just need put together many-many good sentences. Sentences that like stone must be cut. And also simple. Simple is best, but not easy. Complicated is easy. But complicated no one can know. They just throw away. Like garbage."

Still stirring, he added, "Also you must remember philosophy. Philosophy very important."

"I'll remember. Though I think the best sentences, like the best poems, are met, bumped into like an old friend by accident and recognized, not made."

Tsung Tsai jumped out of his chair in a move that belied his age. He grunted. "Oh! Georgie, now you can begin a little bit. So good. Very truth. Truth like Buddha. Hard like iron. Delicate like lotus petal. Now you can think. Now. Oh yes, very concentrated you must be. Then you can find every sentence. Then you can meet poetry. Just simple."

"There was a man, maybe crazy," I said. "He hadn't spoken a word in more than thirty years. His doctors, finally bored with silence, thought to experiment, to try medicine. After only a few weeks the man spoke. 'Simplicity is best,' he said. It was all he would ever say. After a few months, bored again, the doctors stopped treating him. The man went silent again."

Tsung Tsai said, "Best idea."

Some years ago I had dead-ended in another sorry, but fortunately rare, survival job. "My boy is too heavy for light work and too light for heavy work," my father used to say. Proving him a prophet, I was proofing copy for the local weekly. On the masthead my job title was given as "Zen Services." Coolness was my cover. If art, as

Picasso described it, is the lie that makes us realize the truth, then the best journalism is the opposite. The poet on the other hand is like a baby, working with emotions that are without language, attempting to express what can't be expressed by words or silence. "Art and death are all I hope to discover here," wrote that brilliant fantasizer and self-inventor, Malraux. I had discovered neither. It didn't take too long for the work to drive me nuts, and there were times I lost the ability to read. Stories were meaningless, a succession of word blurs, not decipherable, so some weeks the word processor's spellchecker was the actual copy editor at the *Woodstock Times*. I told a writer friend that I had developed a distaste for words, a mistrust for writing.

> *I said,*
> *the moment turning,*
> *all that is left to write*
> *can be fit into a few*
> *simple declarative sentences.*
> *he said,*
> *the next step is silence.*

Still, writing—*cacoethes scribendi* (L.): that passion for scribbling blindly—was and is the closest I've come to having a home and acts as pivot for my nomadic inclinations. Writing and travel are the best things, the *only* things, that always work, that always make me feel connected, whole. With both, there is nothing to understand, nothing to explain, no family, no phones, no bills, no worries, no past and no future, just now and just movement.

I can be a nihilist, comfortable with the idea that nothing matters, that the universe has no meaning. Nada. Nothing. And writing is not a way of coming to terms with that meaninglessness, but a way of establishing relationships with life, a way of loving, a way of giving meaning. The story then is the essence of creation, the beginning of heaven and earth. The path to understanding.

In the beginning there must have only been the vowels; aa, ee, and oo; the sounds, like a drunkard's, would have been slow and slurred. Breathy.

with breath,
that's how the gods
tell the stories,
with breath.

"And remember more important," Tsung Tsai continued, "poem only need have question. No answer."

"I have no answers."

"So good," he said. "My thought is that one word more important than whole book. Oh very. Literature always like this. Life too."

I was finished with philosophy. I made the left turn. I asked, "When do you want to leave for Mongolia?"

"I don't know. You know my mind. Monk mind. You ask Tsung Tsai what time, what day, what month, what year, I can never tell you."

"Soon then?"

"Soon I can understand. Soon is best idea. Maybe in coming springtime we can just go. *Must* go. I have many things to do. I miss my mountain, my Ula Shan, so I write poem. Later Georgie, you can make translation." With that, Tsung Tsai put down his chopsticks and turned, settled into himself, and sang, his voice sweetened with mysterious vowels, rapid arpeggios, glides, and semiquavers.

ravines
boulders in heaps
precipitous escarps
shattered ridges
treacherous riprap
cold caves inlaid in ragged cliffs
towering summits
spilling cloudscapes
frost flowers
in the valley
pinecone temples
tremble in the wind
on truth's road
a bell rings

"You know my purpose. My people like Tibet people, like Georgie people—Jews—blow like leaf round world. Now I must be return. I need burn my teacher's bones. Build *stupa*. Give original people[2] material to build temple. I *must*. This is my karma. My responsibility. If I do not, very bad for my life."

Tsung Tsai had returned to stirring noodles and was quiet for some minutes. I waited and watched the September sky turn winter slate. Some early insubstantial snowclouds showed in the west as the trees caught wind and bent. Then there were flurries. The twisted branches appeared etched, abstracted, disconnected, floating in air that was only a slightly grayer shade of gray.

"False winter," I heard Tsung Tsai say. "Strange."

---

[2] *Original people,* Tsung Tsai's term, is I believe a literal translation from the Chinese for "peasants," "farmers," carrying much the same freight, the same meaning, as the English idiom *the salt of the earth.*

it would be cold tonight;
exquisitely so.
clear and arctic.
I confess to fear.
I can feel the freeze through these walls,
aching;
aching like that first rush of mortality,
the rush that sees blood,
that imagines the clutch of heart;
the sudden explosion of pain,
the gurgle of lungs,
the subtle numbness,
the weakness of arm,
of knees,
the devastating paralysis
and then that final breathy sigh,
at last.

When I looked back Tsung Tsai was still bothering the noodles. He lifted a chopstick-load out of the pot, testing tenderness. "Also I love bagel. You show me this food. With cheese. Tomato. I can understand American food. But noodle better for me. If I eat noodle I don't worry anything. I become strong."

Tsung Tsai and his noodles reminded me of Popeye the sailor man, that 1950s cartoon weakling become muscular hero upon eating his spinach, at Saturday afternoon matinees, the movies for a quarter: the Mode Theatre on Broadway, Uptown, Chicago, Illinois.

I'm Popeye the sailor man
I'm strong to the finish
for I eat my spinach

I'm Popeye the sailor man
and I am what I am
and that's all that I am
I'm Popeye the sailor man

I was laughing. "Me too. Me too. Me too."

"Don't laugh, Georgie. You and me. We don't care. We are very danger men. How you say?"

I'm Tsung Tsai the Buddha man . . .

"Adventurers," I said, picturing Tsung Tsai in a pith helmet, big ears sticking out.

A few weeks later, when false winter had turned Indian summer again, Tsung Tsai would tell Mary Talbot, the writer who was interviewing us for *Tricycle,* "Georgie very danger man so now also I want him to get bone of lama who walk on water."

"Like Jesus," I said, when Tsung Tsai first proposed yet another bone hunt—as if the search for his teacher's wasn't enough.

"Exactly, he was also one," he said, nodding.

Tsung Tsai had hidden the relic bone almost fifty years earlier, just before he made his escape, walking at night for fifteen months across the heart of darkness, from Mongolia to Hong Kong. China was starving. In chaos. Two disastrous harvests in 1959 and 1960 and Mao Zedong's policies during the Great Leap Forward (1958 to 1962) had created the worst famine in human history. In the West, we tend to associate the greatest excesses and atrocities of Mao's China with the Cultural Revolution (1966 to 1976). The Great Leap Forward was far more brutal. The monasteries were attacked as feudal and reactionary, depositories of class and cultural disease. Old customs, old habits, old culture, and old thinking, the revolution decreed, must be destroyed. Fifty million would starve to death while Tsung Tsai walked. Perhaps another ten million more would die in the gulags or by suicide.

Tsung Tsai was tiptoeing in a stream of sunlight falling on the polished oak floor in the altar room of his Woodstock cabin. He kept pulling up his pants to keep his cuffs from getting wet, mimicking how the lama would walk on water. Every movement he made had a dancer's grace.

"He stand on water. Walk on water. Like baby jump, jump, jump."

And now, drunk with storytelling and standing next to his chimney, he pointed first at the bricks and then at the wiggling fingers of his other hand.

"For example, if chimney be my mountain, these fingers must be Georgie. Watch. I show you. Easy . . . easy . . . very easy," he mumbled repeatedly, while his Georgie fingers, "for show," climbed the brick chimney-mountain. "Here, under stone in this *cave,* I hide bone of lama who could walk on water," he said, sticking his finger in a poorly caulked crack—stand-in for the cave in Ula Shan, the cave below the summit of Crow Pull Mountain. "Communist only want break. Burn. Make mess. After, I must quickly go. Just run. Hide. They need be kill me, kill my teacher, my old brothers, just kill-kill-kill. Oh, Mary, so many. So suffering."

The cave where Tsung Tsai's teacher, Shiuh Deng, or Red Foot Truth, had lived for thirty years was cut into a narrow cliff, under a knot of boulders. Before Shiuh Deng, it had been occupied by another; Shiuh Guan, the lama who could walk on water, had wandered into Mongolia from Tibet toward the end of the previous century. His ashes and a shin bone relic rested against the rear wall of the cave, on a blunt stone shelf, where Tsung Tsai had put them and where he was determined to also enshrine the ashes of his teacher.

Tsung Tsai's eyes filled again as they always did with the memories. He grabbed his throat, pulling the corded crepe of skin at his neck in a gesture that was a commentary on all that was lost. Then, without missing a beat, he cleared his throat, covered his mouth, yawned hugely, and turned in a near-perfect pirouette. His right hand shot out and he pulled an imaginary relic bone from its Crow Pull Mountain cave, that cracked brick high on the chimney of his Catskill Mountain cabin. He clenched it beneath whitening knuckles an instant before spreading his arms and loosing his fingers wide to let it go to air.

"Can do. Can do. No problem. Lama bone Georgie can bring back to this country for show. Show to world. Show to you. Would you like it?"

"Oh yes." Mary nodded, turning to me. "Are you a climber?"

"Just a scrambler and a coward for heights to boot."

"Path to cave very high and ice come. Couldn't believe." Tsung Tsai pointed at me and mock trembled. "Do you remember, Georgie? Last time you too afraid. This time no problem. I think about it very much. You can take string."

I remembered. It was a treacherous climb up an icefall. I chickened out only fifty feet or so from the mouth of the cave, on the last almost vertical pitch, where I had an attack of acrophobic paralysis, an obsessive, slow-motion movie of falling.

"String?"

"Of course string. Just take and tie to stone; to any little tree. Then you can just climb. But Georgie, you must take nail steps because the way hangs over emptiness. And try not to shake. Fall and string catching you. No problem. Never hurt. Never die."

"I'm glad to hear it."

"Yes, very good. I dream it. Also I write Georgie poem. Words so pretty. Only Zen idea. Don't worry."

just climb
the winter path
long and deep
through mountain mist
and embracing rainbow rings
the green water
falling in ropes
falling
past pine, cypress, and silent jade
a sky of china blue locking
the white cloud steppe
the birds in spirals
soaring
the valley
there!
where the creek runs narrow
and where at noon
he waded the rapids
walking on water
and dancing
singing again and again
in awe
in awe behold the joy
the freedom of a monk

"I'm not worried," I said.

There was a pause. Tsung Tsai jutted his chin, dark eyes staring. "True? Really?"

"Really. True," I said. And it was, at the moment. I believe in poet magic, where saying and doing, cause and effect are one, and words are direction and destiny. It's the imagery. The images are real, even as all life is illusion. But sometimes the magic works and sometimes it doesn't. And so, still unable to walk on water, I was planning to pack, as insurance, an ice ax and crampons to go with my string.

"So good," he said.

"What about your teacher? Do you have permission to dig up his body? Cremate it?" Mary asked, pushing her tape recorder a little closer to the source.

"My teacher is in desert. I can bring him out."

She had the stare. She was rapt. And I knew just how she felt, what she was thinking. Of course she was catching, straight from the horse's mouth, his deep dharma, for everything he said carried that freight—spiritually profound, philosophically weighty, and full of portent. Innocence and sweetness. Always sweetness. And confidence. Absolute surety.

"Easy for me. Just simple. I tell Georgie many times, but still can't understand. Simple is the first foundation. The first philosophy. But not simple," Tsung Tsai said.

"So you have permission?"

Arms folded across his chest, he rocked, almost imperceptibly, back and forth from the waist. "This moment very hard for me to say yes or no. But I don't care them. Government don't give me his body. I have no choice. I'm not ask them again. I just take. Burn."

"Tsung Tsai," I began.

He knew what was coming. I knew what was coming back. We were like a couple of vaudeville comics. I was the straight man. We'd done this routine many times.

"I know, Georgie," he said. "I cannot climb. Too old. Too dizzy. But I think. I dream." Here he spun his hand above his head and whirred. "I need take helicopter. You and Tsung Tsai, Georgie, we can do it. Whrrr-rr, whrrr-rr. Circle. Circle. Then we can jump out. Not too far. We can do it."

"You still want us to jump from a helicopter?"

"Of course. This is my dream. I tell you many times. What do you say?"

I laughed. "Where will the helicopter come from?"

"Army can give to me. Easy. They have many-many. Chinese army rich."

"I don't think so."

"Sure. Very nice. I talk to them. I burn my teacher's bone. I say, Now I need go to high mountain. I just need you to fly me a little bit. No problem."

I managed to get two words out. "You think . . . ?"

"Think. Think. Think. I don't care think. *Think*. It is very stupid. Too stupid. Not good. Monk's mind is not poor. He is action. Philosophy is his power. He can do everything."

to remain sane,
be twisted
to become straight,
be bent
to become full,
be hollow

He flitted his hand past his nose. He paused a beat. "Can you see me?"

"See you?"

"Sure, me. Tsung Tsai. Monk."

"Yes. I think so."

He sighed. "Aii, Georgie. You *think* again. Nobody who can know, thinks. You cannot. You cannot see me. You see only shadow."

"Shadow looks like Tsung Tsai," I said.

He clapped. "Oh-kaay! Now you learning my situation. Wisdom mind not like computer. Wisdom doesn't need remember. Wisdom doesn't need think."

I am what I am . . . what I am . . .

Bingo. Action. My philosophy. *Exactly*. All my life I'd ignored people who told me the opposite. "Use your head," my mother would shout, practically slamming hers against the wall in frustration as my father nodded in agreement. Or it was my grandmother crooning, "Think, Bubala, think." Then it was teachers, friends, lovers, and wives. Even my daughter once or twice.

Think? Why bother? The only thing I knew was that I knew nothing and knew that that was the highest flight of reason. Knew that anarchic Zen, crazy wisdom, was the only wisdom I could follow; clown, trickster, jester, fool, poet, and monk. I was that Everyman, a *bonbu,* a foolish being wandering through an aimless samsaric life, trapped in the suffering-ridden cycle of life and death, of deluded consciousness, of desire and ignorance. And no different really from the purest saint, for since the way of Zen is process, Everyman's nature—enlightened and unenlightened consciousness—samsara, and nirvana are identical. The big Ah-ha! The only difficulty is that I, *Master Bonbu,* the foolish one, can't see my perfection, which must be present in every moment. Must be, I would guess, some *bonbu* insecurity complex.

"We'll get that helicopter," I said.

"Good. Be so special. First I take care my teacher. After you can get lama bone. Then we can find Two Wolf Mountain and the lost temple."

Among the northern monks of Mongolia, the strange legend of an intact 2,000-year-old temple—complete with statuary, paintings, tapestries, and libraries—hidden beneath the north face of Two Wolf Mountain had been passed down from master to disciple for as long as anyone could remember.

Tsung Tsai had first learned of it from his teacher, Shiuh Deng, Red Foot Truth. And then again from an old monk who had once wandered the western wilderness and claimed to have visited there, describing it in a poem.

hidden by mountains
by sand
a lost temple waits
wavering
ten thousand butter lamps
a stone jungle
madly entwined
vines, lotus flowers and buddhas
quicken

There are oddities here. And the lost temple—the idea alone is the epitome of scholarly romantic cool—would be another if the legend be true, since it is a lost world, leaving only traces in history. Buried, lost to time.

"Whole life I want to go to there," Tsung Tsai said. "Now I know how we can do it. Completely I know. We need prepare special truck. Carry very much water. Food. Everything. Now we can just go. Not like last time."

Last time, our first trip together, had taken place five years earlier. Last time Tsung Tsai had almost died; the mountain was too high, the path too hard, too cold; he was too sick, too old, and we were lost; there was a sandstorm. This second trip, I was determined, would be different: we would go by the numbers, find our way using Western magic—satellites instead of stars—using one of the palm-sized GPS receivers that can pinpoint a traveler's waypoint anywhere on the planet. Maps like dreams. Just follow the yellow brick road.

"My situation you must be know," he said. "If I do not try I must be die. Best die."

if I couldn't see
the flowers,
I'd prefer to die . . .

"Don't take him up any mountains," one of his students phoned to warn me when she heard we were planning to go again.

"I take him nowhere. He takes me. He doesn't take orders," I said. "Not from me. Not from anyone. He does what he wants."

"But he could die," she protested.

"Yes," I said. "He knows that. But he'll be fine. Don't worry."

I heard the click of the hung-up phone and waited, listening to the buzz of the open line. Of *course* he could die. My dear sweet old friend is seventy-six. His lungs are damaged. He could get sick and, coughing up blood, die. Pass into the unknown. Goodbye. *Namo Amitofu.* All praise to Buddha. I felt no guilt. Instead, desire and the strange pleasures of grief filled me.

"Your students don't want you to go," I told him.

"They are foolish. I have not finished my wheel. You look at me," Tsung Tsai strutted. "I become young."

"Great. Now we can go." I gave him a pumping thumbs-up. "And no—not like last time."

Last time was November 18, 1996: the southernmost edge of the Gobi Desert, approximately 42° north latitude, 109° east longitude—North of Yellow River country, the Chinese call it—north of the once wild, once ferocious Yellow River, which is fast dying. Meticulous reports of the river's torment, including detailed charts of flooding along its densely populated lower reaches, kept since the seventh century BCE, document the reasons: overpopulation, excessive water use, pollution, and most recently, global warming. Take heed: the desert is growing.

The morning was moonlit, pale and fluorescent. Off to the west, through the wavy plastic windows of our jeep, the spikes of scattered thorn shrubs glowed. We had started off before dawn, driving northward from Mouth of West Mountain through the dry pass that is the southeasternmost extension of the Winding Road, the vaguest and least known of the caravan roads, the opium-runners' way through the Gobi and Taklimakan deserts. Gun-gun, according to Tsung Tsai the best driver in Mongolia, drove, accelerator to the floor. Tsung Tsai rode shotgun, balanced on the jeep's narrow seat, legs folded lotus. I bounced around in back.

The sun rose for a long time. The road bent west a few kilometers beyond what was a dying village. The only signs of life were a few ribbons of stove smoke and a boy in a red quilted bunny suit squatting over a ditch. An hour later, at the end of an unspeakably bad road, the sun was blinding.

Around noon we came upon a donkey hauling a cartload of pig, so fresh-killed that rigor mortis had yet to set in, the clotting carcass flopping and quivering like Jell-O. The nasty stink that death makes was overpowering. Tsung Tsai covered his nose and mouth with his cap and chanted what I supposed was a dead pig mantra. I didn't ask about the missing driver.

Tsung Tsai was busy looking into the past. "Once have temple near to here. Then big yellow windy come and temple, every-thing—begging bowls, silver coins, even lamas—become sand." His face had turned the color of putty. He shuddered. "When I am young monk, five maybe six thousand lama worship here. Now only wind make sutra."

The jeep swayed and lurched over double ruts and washouts, humps and outcrops of feldspar, red oxide like copper, scraping the underside of the chassis. The mountains were invisible in the lin-gering dust. Topping a low rise, a wind coming up out of the Gobi by way of Siberia met us head on. And then a cloud like a bruise took out the sun.

"It is yellow-soil cloud," Tsung Tsai said. "Soon pebbles come."

In minutes it began to hail furiously, pea-sized ice exploding in the sand, the canvas top reverberating to the beat of a thousand drummers.

We stopped to wait out the weather. Tsung Tsai stuck an arm out the window and waggled a stern finger at the cloud. "Bad god air, monk is here. Don't make mess for me." When the clouds had dispersed, scattering east and south, Tsung Tsai waved goodbye to the departing storm.

"Impressive," I said.

"Hmmm," Tsung Tsai acknowledged. "Cloud god, I guess, knows what I say."

Tsung Tsai got out of the jeep, climbed the rise of a sandy ravine, and stood on a low mound, staring west and drinking hot water out of a black and red checkerboard thermos. Wind flapped the hem of his robes. To the west our universe was clear-skied and we could see a stone-pile travelers' shrine. About halfway up its eight-foot height, stuck in a niche above a scrawl of fading black ideograms, was a mud and straw idol. Anticipating my question, Tsung Tsai translated, "Spirit of god."

In the direction of the easternmost reach of the Wolf Mountains, the sky remained black and blue. Tsung Tsai sighted westward, staring straight down his outstretched right arm and two pointing fingers.

"Two Wolf is near middle of Dah Sha Moh, Big Sand Desert, that sometimes Mongolia people call Be-boh Liou Sha, Flowing Sand from North to South, or Moh Be-boh, Desert South of North. A little far. But not too far."

"*How* far?" I asked.

He took a breath and continued, ignoring my question. "We just need go to north a little bit. Then west until we come to Home of Not Too Real Lama. Two Wolf is close to there, in Valley of Slaughtered Armies. Very famous Sung dynasty general, name of Yang, with Mongolia fight there. But all his soldiers go down to dust. Mongolia kill them. General Yang also. He is bury there. You must find his burial mound. Near to here look for square stone that must be made at beginning of world. Behind this one is Two Wolf Temple. This is history. True history," he said, emphasizing this truth with a sweeping gesture of his still pointing fingers, which in the dusky light of afternoon made a luminous arc.

"How far?" I asked again.

Tsung Tsai shrugged. "Maybe one thousand Chinese miles. Maybe more. Who can know? We just need look a little. No person know my Two Wolf place. It is pure. No one touch. Never touch. Never break. I tell you straight, many things are bury in my Mongolia. Many places. Many things there are that you don't know."

It is a place where things can be hidden. Lost to the eyes of man. Even the ancient Greeks had thought their fathers, their gods, had come from these vast empty northlands beyond Olympus. There have long been stories: sightings of wind- and sand-sculpted ruins, of a great city—the legendary Shambhala perhaps—of walls and watchtowers, of golden temples and buddhas, of polished bones, incandescent and hard as iron, littering the sand.

The earliest references to Shambhala, the mythic kingdom of lakes and flowering parks, of saintly wisdom, are found in the Kangyur and the Tengyur, a set of more than three hundred volumes, the Tibetan canon, once lost for over a thousand years before coming to India in the tenth century. These texts tell of a lost civilization tucked away to the north, beyond towering icewalls, somewhere in the brutal heart of the desert. But, the books also warn, it is a dangerous journey that only a pure soul can make; all others will find blinding storms, empty mountains, and death.

"Do you know Shambhala?" I asked on a whim.

"I know very much. That means I can find."

"Shambhala?"

"Sure. There are many. Many good ones. Anything I can find. Even if I don't know where is *exactly*. But I think very difficult to go to there, even for camel, for truck. Georgie, you can go. You can try. Now is little difficult for me. Older. Age-y give me trouble."

Topping a low rise we came suddenly up on a dump truck. It was stuffed to capacity with a dozen or so white-robed men in peaked headdresses who were chanting and beating sticks; they sat around a coffin, two grass scarecrows, and a near life-size pagoda made of sun-flashing metal foil triangles—gold, blue, red, green.

"They give dead person place to live and friends to help him in shadow world," Tsung Tsai said.

The truck veered suddenly, maniacally skidding off the road, heading east over broken ground into country that dropped and rose toward a ridge of pale dunes.

After driving another hour into the western sun, we entered a country of dunes and rock; outcroppings of faults and anticlines glazed, trembling and veering in the warmer air rising. Slowly the road began to descend, stretching west over broken ground that dropped and rose toward a ridge of pale dunes, then disappeared. Blown away. Gone without a trace, though as recently as two days earlier it had been open, for that was when the weekly bus from the northern settlements—from Bayod Mod, Hail, Qog Qui, and Suj—had arrived at the railhead town known as Mouth of West Mountain.

Gun-gun and I would scout ahead, looking for tracks. The sand was still pocked by the hail blown past. There were no other tracks. I walked west, the curved bill of my baseball cap pulled low over my eyes. When I lost sight of the jeep, of Tsung Tsai, of Gun-gun, and could hear only the rush of blood in my ears, I sprinted, the sand grabbing at my boots, up a long, curving knife-edge ridge to the top of a sheer north-facing bluff.

A sky the color of pearl hung over a landscape in motion; sand rolling like the endless ocean; wild waves and breaking dunes; the frail scent of ozone in the air. There was no road. No trace of standing water since the last ice age. Nothing. There were no gods. None but the wind, the Yellow Flower, which is feral and constant. It blows from the northwest, out of Siberia and off the eastern face of the Himalayas, desiccating over the deserts and erupting occasionally (November through April) into a devastating sandstorm, the

Fengchenbao, the wind-dust-tempest. There is also the dusty Karaburan, the Black Wind that comes off the Gobi in the spring. Like the Harmattan in West Africa, the dust storms of central Asia, distinctly visible in weather-satellite photos as gigantic yellow blobs, are the result of rabid desertification in China and Mongolia. The Gobi is growing, and has been growing for more than two thousand years, twenty thousand square miles in just five years, from 1994 to 1999. The desert's steadily advancing edge now sits a mere 150 miles north of Beijing. So serious is the threat that the Chinese are planning to plant a series of greenbelt forests around the city—another great wall, a quarter-million-square-mile green wall.

The Yellow Flower wind in my face blew me back in time, to memories of another place, another desert. There is a wind like it in Arabia, the Red Wind or Sea of Darkness, which explodes out of the Sahara, filling the air with red dust, scorching dust that renders sweat and rain the color of blood.

I met it once.

It was 1971: Morocco was home to an underground world of expatriates—black sheep Euro-trash royals and wannabes, fading beats, innocent sad-eyed hippies, broken-down artists of every stripe, deserters, draft resisters, hustlers, spiritual pilgrims, adventurers, drunks, dopers, smugglers, womanizers, sluts, whores, freelancers, and failed writers. Except for the royals category, any and all of the above would have accurately described me. I'd spent the first part of that summer working Marrakech for stories with no luck (except for the finest opiated hash) and was antsy to move on.

The anarchist and radical iconoclast Yün-men, the ninth-century Zen master, was my philosopher hero, my spiritual main man. When he was asked, "What is Tao?" he said, "Go!" Another Ah-ha moment. Instant enlightenment. I was with him; absolutely.

I was certain that what he had in mind was *Go your way free, without attachment to how or where or to the results of your going. Do your thing and pass on.* It was not only right but necessary. He was the perfect teacher. The perfect fit. For back then *Go!* was my only Zen.

I had just finished reading the journal of Michel Vieuchange, a French explorer who, disguised as a Berber woman, set out on the night of September 11, 1930, from the River Massa, some twenty miles north of Tiznit in southern Morocco. With his native guides he planned to penetrate the territory of the dissident tribes and find the ruins of Smara, a great walled city that had been abandoned for centuries. Never seen by Europeans, even its location was uncertain. Perhaps a myth, Smara was known only as an oasis for fierce desert nomads.

Traveling for weeks through the desert, first on bleeding feet and later in a camel's pack basket, Vieuchange found his obsession but could only risk three hours there. A month later, on the return trip, he died of dysentery. His last journal entry reads something like this:

Nine o'clock, halt.
Valley opens facing black djebel;
steep sides;
big.
Weather clearing.
Stools—and stools
—watery.

Next morning I sold the last of my hash and hired a car, a Citroën, a beat Dos Caballos, and was on the road south within the week. It was hot and dry that year, even for summer; and in a Harmattan, the mother of hurricanes, a wind that is said to drive men mad, there would be stinging dust storms and a murder on the road to Smara, the Forbidden City.

It was close to two in the afternoon. The light was tepid. I never heard the shot. We were driving downslope into the wind when the driver's head exploded. His fingers had clutched at death, but the thick veins popping on the backs of his living hands had disappeared and the blanched skin glowed weirdly like polished marble. His shirt buttons had popped, exposing his belly button.

The Citröen came to stop on the road's soft shoulder. I rolled out of the car, crawled into a ditch, and burrowed in sand, hiding. Waiting for the next shot. Waiting for death. Waiting for I don't know how long. Waiting forever. Waiting until I could wait no more. The time passed quick and slow. The world went insanely silent; even the wind was mute. At my feet something that looked like an eyeball rolled.

His name was Ali.

The why and who of it was and will always remain a mystery. Mistaken identity—a shot fired in anger, a cuckold's rage, a family feud? Pure accident—a shot fired in celebration of a wedding or the birth of a first son; some kid playing with a new rifle, just a bit of target practice, a hunter's miss? A shot gone awry, just a terrible piece of luck, or murder? A crazed killer coolly taking aim, squeezing off the shot; a hard-on for the thrill of the kill, the thrall of ultimate power, the taking of everything a man was or ever will be?

There was no way I could explain a murder to the cops. I'd spend christ knows how long in some Moroccan prison hell. No way. Not me. He was dead. Beyond help. Garbage. I kicked his body out of the car. Dragged it by the feet to the ditch. Wiped up as much of the gore as I could manage and with bare hands shoveled a few inches of sand over his remains. I paused only to say, "Inshallah," as Allah wills it, over the makeshift grave before jumping back in the car and hightailing it back to Marrakech. I left the car, key still in the ignition, in an alley in the old quarter. I knew that it, like Ali, would quickly, without a trace, be gone. Without a single trace.

That night I celebrated. A feeling of utter happiness overwhelmed me. Every survivor knows this feeling: this mixture of freedom and entitlement, of power and irresponsibility. My beard was musk and my fingers, from petting her, whoever she was, smelled good enough to lick. I was drunk, ecstatic that the bullet had found Ali rather than me, that it was some other poor sonofabitch dead out there in the desert. And not me. *Me.* Me was alive. And life had gotten suddenly even more delirious. More delicious. Fickle chaos, luck; a couple of inches here or there—it's accident that makes the whole thing gorgeous. All of it. Eros pure and simple. Survival. I fell back on it. Gloried in it.

I have faith only in my passion for living, the instinct to search for that happiness which is only and always a flux, for in the succession of events that is a life, there is no stasis. What is happiness, serenity? Where is the dividing line between grief and joy? Where?

Survival. Simple as love and hunger, survival is what matters, more important than anything else, I wanted to shout. Listen, it's just about eating, drinking, reading, traveling, arting, playing, loving, and oh like happy little gods laughing. It's about passing through—goddamnit, simply growing old. Loving life hopelessly, I will go on as long as possible, if I am well, if it is good, if I am independent. I will finish this story and start another. I will endure until life is unendurable.

Though I might desire to be, among all those I love, the first to die. Though I might love death, might even welcome it when it comes. But not now, for now here's a napkin; forget the fasting, grab an egg roll.

My exhilaration died with the sunrise when I noticed I'd been pissing blood (from a kidney I must have contused, perhaps leaping from the car) against a whitewashed wall in one of the cloistered alleyways near Djemaa el-Fna, the great square below the minaret of the Kutubia mosque, where from dawn to long after dusk little booths sold meats and tea and sweets; where traders just in off the desert haggled; where beggars and scribes worked their magic; and where musicians, jugglers, acrobats, tumblers, conjurers, blind fortune tellers, monkey men, and snake charmers capered for the entertainment of all who passed; a *jinn*.

We are at war with the elements, with fear, capricious chance. So, as it turned out, that murder, that moment of random violence, was the beginning of my Zen education. It also saved my life. I'd planned to travel to Afghanistan with a freelance photojournalist, Thomas S., to research the opium trade. When my bloody kidneys kept me from leaving as planned, Thomas went on without me and disappeared. He was never heard from again. His body was never found. I spent my recuperation in a Marrakech guesthouse overlooking Djemaa el-Fna, self-medicating with opiated hash and sweet mint tea, and reading—over and over—the Tao. And discovering in it the inklings of understanding. Clues to the *way*. So it is that time, that death brought me surely, certainly to Tsung Tsai's door, to this here and now, from Morocco to Mongolia. From pathlessness to path seeker. *Inshallah* to be sure. *Karma,* hey?

Now, back in 1996, back in Mongolia, in this northern desert, the long shadows fell to the east. A sun-powered updraft out of the desert plain whipped cold dust into devils at my ankles. I shivered and, just as I had almost three decades earlier, turned and ran. I ran until I caught sight again of the jeep. Then I slowed to a walk and collected myself.

Gun-gun had returned before me. He was smoking a Golden Monkey and pacing, in slow, worried circles. Above his dark shades, a purple vein in his temple pulsed. Tsung Tsai sat as I had left him, settled into the front seat, eyes closed, asleep. He looked awful; tender, almost fragile.

"Tsung Tsai."

He opened his eyes and in one easy motion unfolded himself and stepped out of the jeep.

"Do you find road?"

"No, nothing. Sand."

He nodded. In the pause, I dug the map out of my pack, spreading it on the still-warm hood.

"Where is Two Wolf? We are here," I pointed. "Approximately."

Tsung Tsai looked at the map with disdain; maps bored him, while I had only to see a map to begin to plan some improbable travel.

I particularly loved ancient maps and charts faded, worn, and brittle with age and use; on their corners and along the edges are cherub heads, cheeks puffed out and blowing the direction of the prevailing wind across carefully rendered compass points. These maps conjure dreams, reveal desire more than direction—the ancient image of territory; they illustrate mysteries, propositions, theories, and rumors of topography, routes for invasion and trade, the half-mad ravings of travelers; the endless oceans teeming with great fish and sea monsters, their tails writhing in foam and waves.

Tsung Tsai believed in landscape, in connection with earth; the poetry of memory. He looked toward the mysterious horizon and casually traced a route west-by-northwest. "I don't care map. Map cannot tell my stories. I know where is. Exactly here," he said and tapped a spot. There was a mountain range at the place on the map where his finger had come to rest, where the Gobi and the Taklimakan conjoin—three maybe four hundred miles east of the epicenter of radical Islam, where the Winding Road runs into Afghanistan, Pakistan, Tajikistan, Uzbekistan, Kyrgyzstan, and Kazakhstan.

Owen Lattimore had covered this same country in 1926. He was told that somewhere in the Lang Shan—the Wolf Mountains— there is a group of three holy peaks. And that beneath the central, the highest peak—possibly Bei Lang Shan, Two Wolf Mountain— is a rock bearing the imprint of the face of a saint. In his journal he drew a map and wrote:

> I say imprint rather than carving, because this appears to be connected with an ancient legend of a saint sitting in meditation before a rock and impressing his image on it. The approach to the place is over a log laid across a chasm.

The map Lattimore drew shows that his route along the Winding Road, across the length of Mongolia to Chinese Turkistan, took him past Puh Jih, Tsung Tsai's Crow Pull Mountain monastery, and about a thousand kilometers west-northwest, beyond a place the explorer identified as the House of the False Lama. It was located, as Tsung Tsai said it would be, in the Wolf Mountains, below the north face of the highest peak.

"Look," I said, running my finger from here to there. "The map shows the lama house. More than one thousand Chinese miles from here."

Tsung Tsai was immediately interested. "Your map show Not Too Real Lama place?"

"Here." I pointed.

Tsung Tsai squinted at the map where my finger had come to rest, his grin making cracks in his dust-caked face. "So good map," he said. "But Two Wolf a little far I guess."

"A little."

We were out of time. We had set the first week in December as the last safe time to leave. The wind was moving south. Every day now there was more sand in the air. Deep winter was approaching. It grew colder every day. In the mountains, in some of the higher blue-shaded passes, there was ice. Gun-gun had never been in this desert before. He was lost. There was no road to follow but the cast-off bones of travelers drifted out of their graves.

"Perhaps it picks up ahead. Not too far. We can just try."

Tsung Tsai shook his head. "We cannot. Next time."

I knew. Still, it was like eating sand. I was sour and slipping into bitterness. I was thinking, the Chinese are lousy travelers, as their paranoiac passion for walls proves. Only totalitarians and bureaucrats love walls; they box and freeze the world. This place, the world's oldest, subtlest, most intelligent civilization, had been ruined by walls.

Advance always, as Rimbaud says.

"I hate going back," I said. "I've been there."

Tsung Tsai grunted. He brought his hand up and with thumb and forefinger plucked a vagrant hair from his chin. He examined it carefully before flicking it to the wind.

"Patience is also meditation," he said.

Back in Woodstock, after noodles Tsung Tsai made tea once again. "Chinese people use tea-leaf three times," he said. "First time tea come, they say it must taste bitter like life; second time become sweet like love; third time tea come soft like old age. Now tea come. Taste. See."

I sipped and smacked, nodding my head. "Bitter," I said.

Tsung Tsai was pleased. "I never lose wisdom. Always I see true." He chuckled, amused by his own monkish brilliance. "In this world, Georgie, you have special incarnation. Must be because you meet me."

"Must be," I agreed.

After three pots of tea (the last soft like old age) and a decision to leave next spring, I made a move to go.

"Stay little bit," Tsung Tsai said.

"Can't. I have to pick Siri up at the library."

"Wonderful. Wonderful your baby. Hello her for me. Give her kiss." He handed me a box wrapped in Chinese newspaper. "Moon cakes. Someone leave at my door so special. But I don't want eat. Give to your family. They can enjoy like for Chinese New Year. And tell them no worry."

The next morning at breakfast I made coffee and served my family the black sugar cakes that Tsung Tsai had given me to celebrate the Year of the Golden Dragon, 4636. "Very good luck time."

"We're going back. I'll want to leave in April," I told them between mouthfuls of *moon cake so special*. "Tsung Tsai says to tell you, 'No worry.'"

"You have to be back by my birthday," my daughter said. Seventeen, about to be eighteen, my little girl had become—at least when she was not a three-year-old, a baby otter by the name of Bright Eyes—a woman of centered intelligence; she of the elegant walk, her tawny tendril hair shading her shoulders and back.

"I promise. That gives me until September. I wouldn't miss your birthday for anything. Perhaps we can meet in Paris, celebrate there."

I was already hatching a plan to get to Paris by rail—from Jining on the Trans-Mongolian Railway to Ulan-Ude, Lake Baikal and Irkutsk in Siberia, and then west through the Urals on the Trans-Siberian to Moscow, chugging into Paris on the *Orient Express*.

"I'll bring you the bone of the lama who could walk on water."

My daughter rolled her eyes. "*Right*."

My wife said, "Get life insurance."

I threw the coins. OXXOXO. Whole. Broken. Broken. Whole. Broken. Whole.

The monk looked over his glasses and humphed. "I Ching say special opportunity soon come. Meantime you must be patience. Discipline. Speak careful and true. Chew your thoughts and ideas very well."

I don't put any stock in prophecy, but Tsung Tsai is a spellbinder and it was all good advice, even if clichéd. So I nodded and thought I should and would but didn't, and the opposite happened. *Shit happens and then you die.* In an infinite universe of infinite universes always expanding and bubbling over, everything that can happen will happen. *Yes!* Though the latest theory buzzing cosmologists proposes a universe that in all ten of its dimensions (nine of space and one of time) is finite rather than infinite. A hateful theory. It is pessimism pure and simple. Aesthetically and optimistically, I believe in infinity, infinite expansion. Give me all possibilities. More! For me, everything—*everything!*

By April 2002 it was obvious that plans for a return to the deserts of High Asia, the Gobi and Taklimakan, would be sidetracked, delayed another year, until at least the following spring. Indefinitely perhaps. First there was money—that is, not enough of it. Bankruptcy loomed. Then my marriage and psychology got shaky. I had a stoned, adrenalized fantasy, quickly dropped, of crossing the Gobi Desert and Tarim Basin on sandsailers or of racing in the Great Silk Road Rally, twenty thousand miles from London to Sydney.

The last straw was that Tsung Tsai was focused on writing. He was working on a collection of poems he called *Clouds Fly, Birds Talk*. "Many poems. I write really almost three hundred. Now I need fix and fix again. Yes. Oh very beautiful."

Also in the works was his most important summing up, Tsung Tsai's unified field theory: a treatise on consciousness. His theory of everything, the holy grail, the mind of god. Of whom? Who knows? You do? Who do? Voodoo.

Just what his theory proposed he didn't say. I asked, knowing ahead of time the answer. But I did know he had as good a chance as any. Better than most. For he's a poet, and every theory about ultimate things must be made in the suggestive form, in poetry, for like the Tao it can't be conveyed by words or silence. In the realm of creation, of matter and antimatter, of quarks and superstrings, of time, of gods, of consciousness, the direct form of writing, the indicative form of speech can say nothing but no, no; since what can be described and categorized belongs to the conventional realm— the realm of bookkeepers and lawyers. So if the question is whether to art or fart, the answer always is to fart. But if the question is whether to poem or to fact, the answer always is to poem.

"Too complicated for you. Only I can do it. Just need work little. Make research. Experiment. And now I can understand. Finish. It is completely Zen mind. Not like you, Georgie. You almost Zen."

There was more. I waited for it. But Tsung Tsai would say nothing more. There would be no further explanations. No answers. And though I didn't know what Tsung Tsai's consciousness theory was, I knew what it wasn't. It most certainly wasn't the pure biomechanistic view of Robert Koch, who with James Watson and Francis Crick had unraveled the secrets of DNA, of our genetic code—which as it turns out is not very different than that of the worm. Regardless, Koch now proposes that we—our joys, sorrows, memories, ambitions, identity, free will (in short, the whole ball of wax, all that makes us *we*)—are nothing more than the behavior of nerve cells, their electrical discharges and their associate chemicals. That there is no person, that there is no soul independent of body; no life after death. It is a theory that is almost Zen. But conventional and not a liberation from convention. We are the sum of our parts. Nothing more. The functions that for Koch explain all are for Tsung Tsai just fantasy: personal, idiosyncratic, and temporal, another illusion.

The scientist tries to explain everything that happens in one point of place; the poet tries to feel everything that happens in one point of time. Take your choice. But I'd put my money on Tsung Tsai. On the poets.

I took a breath, but I already knew. "So just when can you go?"

He thought for a moment. "I don't want go again. Too busy. A little sick. You know my lung problem. Too old."

"Wonderful," I said, relieved at this other divorce. Another responsibility lifted. Another freedom granted. Another door opening.

"Yes, very happy," he said.

Poor, dear old Tsung Tsai. It came over me as I sat there. I was alone. I wasn't thinking of Tsung Tsai or his welfare. No more questions as to when, how, and where. No more waiting. I could go as it pleased me. Where it pleased me. Just go. I was thinking only about this book I was writing; this book had become more important to me than him, than our friendship.

I don't know how long after, but breaking the silence, Tsung Tsai continued, apropos of nothing we were talking about, "Also Georgie, my snow poems. You remember we translate."

"Yes. Of course I remember. *A Thousand Pieces of Snow.*"

As both the thirteenth century and the Yüan dynasty (1260–1368) were ending, the poet Fung Hae Suh, who called himself Guaiguai Daoren, the Weird Monk, wrote his most famous work, *One Hundred Verses on Flowering Plums*, a meditation on the illusory nature of a tree that bears no fruit but flowers in late winter, dropping yellow petals dot-dot-dot on the snow.

More than three centuries later, near the end of the Ming dynasty (1368–1643), Zhou Lu Jing, a poet fond of metal and stone, of calligraphy and ancient texts, and who had adopted the name Midian Daoren, Hermit Crazy About Plum, wrote, perhaps in the garden he'd planted with plum and bamboo, 101 verse answers to Fung Hae Suh. Combined, they are "a thousand pieces of snow."[3]

"Exactly. *Pieces of snow.* Now I think. And it bother my mind. Make me crazy, very uncomfortable. This is a shadow in my head. You make too complicated." Tsung Tsai pulled on his ear. "Georgie, do you have mind to change a little?"

"Yes."

"Good. Then I teaching you. Just need do again, aii one by one. You must know this quality. Be like baby. Make simple. Simple but special. If you find out truth, you don't care complicated."

I was surprised. We had translated twenty-two of the poems in winter through spring of 1995. Our method of translation was improvisational. The style and line breaks were mine. There was no reason but intuition. I didn't speak Chinese and Tsung Tsai's English was even more eccentric then than now. We played in dictionaries. We pantomimed, running out into the meadow to point at cloud or tree, rock or flower, shadow or light. We yammered. We

---

[3] Information for biographical notes thanks to Edwin A. Cranston and Emanuel Pastreich, Department of East Asian Languages and Civilizations, Harvard University.

laughed. He yelled when I didn't understand. "But don't worry. No problem," he would say. "We can do easy. We speak air."

We hadn't talked about the poems since. I knew, however, that they were incredibly important to him. They were, I'd always felt, his visceral connection to the lost world of his past, to the old ways. These were the poems his father had read to him on the occasion of the first snow of winter, the poems that he had wanted to save from the book burnings of Mao's Cultural Revolution. They were family; they were redolent with nostalgia, broken dreams, innocence; they were old China.

"Simple? How? What do you mean?" I asked.

"Aii, Georgie, how many times I need tell you? You can't understand my mind. So you make mess. You make words run around paper. This moment don't do that. You must be learning what simple means. You *must,* for if in this life you don't do that, you can become like nothing. But easy for you. You just need have special mind. You must have reason. Even hungry ghost have reason. Very philosophy."

I hesitated. "Okay," I said, a bit too hesitant to satisfy the old man.

"Not okay," he shot back, angry. "Please understand."

"I'm trying."

"No more trying," he said, repeating his oft-repeated mantra. "Only mental. Only wisdom. Just doing."

I had no idea what he had in mind. Still, "I will," I promised. "I will. I'll begin tonight."

"I know this moment a little confusion. But I know your mind. You want to make right."

"I do."

He laced his fingers across his belly and rocked with satisfaction. "So good. Now my mind rest. So lucky. So happy. Yes, very happy," he added cheerfully.

And I did as I'd promised. I looked at the poems for weeks before doing anything, before seeing anything. Finally I changed two words and radically simplified the line breaks, the syntax. That was all, but it was enough.

I called him. "Tsung Tsai, it worked. You were right. Snow poems are, even on the page, just to look at, more beautiful."

"Okay. I think okay. Always I can see right." I could see him nodding his huge head with satisfaction as he said, "My eye like X-ray. See clear. See very deep."

Ancient Plum

1.

By the sky
oh how long ago
grew
ancient Gua-shan

celebrated flower
shared
before and after
Po-sung River

only today
I woke early
to plant
new trees

next generation
watch
all is the same
as before
—Fung Hae Suh

2.

Gorgeous
great and magnificent tree
no one knows
in what year?

fresh and
gray—
ancient
horizontal branch

the whole
an old dragon
twisted and curled
in its cave

blooming
flowers
like snow
cover Jiang-cheng
—Zhou Lu Jing

Old Plum

3.

Inchoate
disheveled
locked
in green moss

half-dead
half-alive
still it fashions
flowers

don't question
the season
it is not necessary
to speak of spring

and everybody says
hands
nurtured
this tree
—F.H.S.

4.

Aged
disheveled
weathered
seasoned

unadorned
your hanging branches
hug
the stone steps

the blue god
the old
the tender
are equal

and so in time
a few clusters—
flowers will flower
toward my study
—Z.L.J.

Sparse Plum

5.

I counted
on two or three
twigs
ice flowers

newly dressed
by the east wind
it grows
lovelier

clear twilight
shines
shallow shadows
approach

and I copy
one sentence
of Lin Pua's
poetry
—F.H.S.

6.

In the yard
a couple of
graceful
twigs

dot dot
flower petals
like stars
disperse

insomnia
midnight on
the gloomy
verandah

upon windowpanes
the moon
moves
shadows
—Z.L.J.

Orphan Plum

7.

Pure
nature
singular
dignity

serene
it blossoms
and falls
alone

alive
in ice
in frost
it blossoms

omniscient
blue eye
who sees
sees
—F.H.S.

8.

Erect
one branch
decorates
the east side

ancient
one branch
gravitates
toward snow

like high noon
its soul
radiates
beauty

breezy-breezy
shadows
sway
the shades
—Z.L.J.

Thin Plum

9.

Its skin peeled
by ice
its muscles scraped
by snow

purified
to
thinness
by nature

as distinct as
the peach
is from
the lychee

only past life
has different
bones
sir
—F.H.S.

10.

Fine-
boned
like green
bamboo

just one
or two
branches
a few calyxes

virgin spring yes
unlike the peach
and the lychee
has no rival

and like
a model
dresses
the earth
—Z.L.J.

Short Plum

11.

Twig
not even a few feet
can you
grow

because I fear
your virgin green
crossing
the neighbor's wall

but power
is not
difficult
to use

look:
in great Yu's palace
apricot beams like clouds
cover and embrace the earth
—F.H.S.

12.

Just
cut
new spring
shorter

the blossom
fears
disturbing
the high wall

listen:
at yang spring's return
I don't care
if the twig is long or short

but—oh that same
sweet-smelling
loveliness of any
fragrant flower
—Z.L.J.

Twisted Plum

13.

*Humpback
branch
you coil and return
adorned in twigs*

*fascinating
charmer
you bewitch
us all*

*even Pu
that hard-hearted
spirit
can't resist*

*yes even he
is seduced
by your radiance
your beauty*
—F.H.S.

14.

*Bent
coiled
twigs
like a peaceful dragon*

*living
all the years of your years
patient
through frost and ice*

*not only the successful
the accomplished sir
can come again and again
to adore*

*but also Gua-shan's
hermit
wandering monk
again and again*
—Z.L.J.

Mallard Plum

15.

Twin stems and twigs
join
two clusters—
cluster

as illumining light throws
and I am partial to
shadows
on the frigid lake

but then sorrow
blows
painting
a frightening horn

and in an instant
accidentally
broken shadow-
pieces fly
—F.H.S.

16.

In solitude
twin stems
and twigs tenderly
speak

moon-sent
layers of shadows
climb up
my green windows

I'm not worried
that snow and frost
attack
your tips

but only fear
primitive musicians
blowing
new sounds
—Z.L.J.

Thousand-Leafed Plum

17.

*Many-layered
petals
surrounded it seems by
marble-like sepals*

*good news
dharma
your secret secrets
I get*

*wait until
the water moon
the pure-clear moment
becomes*

*just as
Bodhisattva
instantly
became*
—F.H.S.

18.

*Thousands of marbled
and layered
petals cluster ah—
excellent corolla*

*but beyond compare
are the flowers
on Gua-shan's
trees*

*beautiful
beautiful
like Cui Fei
her ingenue smile*

*even the moon rising
hanging
close above your limbs
senses an exotic perfume*
—Z.L.J.

Moss Plum

19.

Teal-gray gauze
my angel aunt
masks
the Phoenix

mist—
mist
sweet fog wets
your unicorn

flutter-flutter
dancing
drops
your rainbow dress

but a jade skirt
you leave
protecting warmth
for night
　—F.H.S.

20.

Pure grace
and jade bone
but timid in night
cool

so you use that gray
that teal
that gauze to mask
to bind your branches

in deep night
whispering
beguiling
the moon

ah yes I guess
even the Phoenix
from the unicorn
can fall
　—Z.L.J.

Cold Plum

21.

In the mountain woods
freezing
cold
demolishes

underneath the forest
fond of your own
gloomy
fragrance

strange orphan
your solitary roots
patient
a pillar of strength

primal
heart
and guts
like metal
—F.H.S.

22.

Beginning last month
windblown
snow
in the air

in mountain woods fading
injured
insulted branches
almost bare

solitary orphan waiting
coveting
and sentimental
patient for ice

fond of New Year's night
flowering
wafting
pure perfume
—Z.L.J.

II
Hurricane Run; or, Wind Is the Purpose

Summer 2002

A few years back, in the Bahamas, near Georgetown, I met a man building a sailboat. The hull was so beautifully shaped, such a sensuous female curve, that I couldn't help but stroke her, bow to stern.

"Beautiful," I said.

"Wind is the purpose," he said.

Gentlemen never sail to weather.
                    —Anonymous English sailor

The sea is a horrible place.
                    —Robert Louis Stevenson

On the first Sunday of the following month, earlier than usual, the middle of May 2002 imitated late summer, with heat, humidity, and buzzwingers banging against window screens. The grapes set out on the kitchen table were green and wet. In a white saucer was the stub of a sugar-tipped Dominican cigarillo, a gray curling worm of ash, and four burnt matches. Also left out from last night's dinner were the dregs of a bottle of a pale yellow Grigio, a paring knife, my wife's brass dangle earrings and Spanish comb, her socks. What else was left was unessential. I had no desire other than to watch the sky grow light, seemingly painted vermilion, so red it was at dawn when the crows began their shout.

But by June when I woke in the morning and went to the window I was bored with trees. With the Hudson Valley. With family. Everything was too much the same. I knew how and where I would begin tomorrow, that when I made a left onto County Route 209 from Kripplebush Road the cows would be chewing cud to the left, the sagging barn and silos would be on my right, and I would wave to whoever was working near the barn. I was angry most of the time. Life was crowded with obligations, details, and I was hungry for distance. I was daydreaming about the immense sweep of the Mongolian upland deserts when Captain Bananas stopped by my toolshed-turned-writing-shack and asked me to help him deliver his boat, a fifty-eight-foot cement-hulled Samson ketch, the *Lady M,* to Grenada. He wanted to get it out of Key Largo, *the bull's-eye,* ahead of what he was sure would be a mean hurricane season.

I had never gone sailing, except in the silvery faint light of dreams, with salt and sweat in the air—dreams in which, anchored off Haiti, I would hear voodoo drums at night in the cane breaks. So, still tasting breakfast, espresso, and raspberry jam, I found my-self saying, "Yes, count me in," before he'd finished asking. Yes. *Yes!* Again the universe had delivered another romance, another escape, another story, this time an easy alternative to my who-knows-when trip to Mongolia. Things change and the stars move.

Run George, run. Go!

"It begins to get tricky in July, when we'll be sailing and the big storms start rumbling north." Bananas was seriously gleeful. "So we gotta get south fast to the equator, through the Crooked's to Cuba, Jamaica, Trinidad, and Grenada, the hurricane hole. Living is cheap. It's outlaw. We can go interior. I know the runnin's."

Bananas was a big Dutchman, six-one, 230, built bearlike, with massive shoulders and a neck so thick from rowing that it merged with his ears. He had slim, handsome legs with delicate ankles and was vain about them. He was perpetually tanned and had the Japanese symbol for the universe—the circle, square, and triangle—tattooed on his left biceps. On his right wrist two gold bracelets from the Sudan jangled. Around his neck hung a necklace of gold and coral beads. He looked like a hip, macho Rembrandt and had the eye, the child-mind of the artist—that is, always in awe.

Though in his early fifties and worn at the edges from burning, he was still strong as an ox, still a boy. And his high blood pressure didn't worry him, though it had killed his father young. "Close to my age. Had a heart attack on the way to visit his girlfriend." His pride and happiness at such a fate were hard to hide. "Outlaw stress" was how he explained it, cultivating an air of reason.

Seemed reasonable. After all, *outlaw* is derived from an Icelandic word that suggests sleeping outside, no better than an animal. Hence the fearful power of outlawry—the official declaration by which the accused, if convicted, was expelled from the legal system, and thereafter could be killed without redress.

Unquestionably a stress.

Bananas was good at everything but routine. A clownish stylist, he would wear on special occasions his captain's uniform—a wide silk blouse and pantaloons decorated with yellow stars, stripes, and polka dots. "My Incredible Red Banana Suit. Made in L.A.," he said, nodding as if that explained it all.

He carried a pair of white feather angel wings and a cutlass in a gray sateen duffel bag appliquéd with golden sequins in swirls. His sailboat, the *Lady M,* flew his pirate's flag, the skull and crossed bananas—one yellow fruit peeled back and bitten.

Unfortunately, his cannon had been confiscated by the Bahamian police. An accidental outlaw—too much fun is illegal—Banana-man was always hungry for more: books, food, art, booze, design, drugs, travel, bullshitting, sex. The order changes with time, but always more than anything else he loved the ladies. And his friends. He'd give you the shirt off his back in a snowstorm. I loved his honor, his loyalty. We smoked, drank, and storied together, knew and loved each other in the automatic way that happens only one or twice in a lifetime.

"I'm taking you to the sixties," Bananas said. "I'm taking you so far back in time you won't believe it. We're going where the wind blows; where the wind is always going our way."

Bananas was vibrating with excitement now, his head bobbing and jerking, his thinning hair—graying curls of faded red—whipping around his neck. His cheeks puffed out like Dizzy blowing his horn as he blew the wind.

"Phew-www. Odds are we'll see forty-foot seas. And always we gotta watch our backs, know what's happening off Africa. The weather is our number one priority check because we're in the bull's eye. So anytime the vibe says *wind,* we're gonna dive south to hide. Venezuela or maybe up the Rio Dulce to Livingston—I don't care where. I don't go into the bite; I don't *need* to go into the bite. I got no time for hurricanes, no time to go into the reef. I don't mess with wind and reefs; they tear you up."

"When do you want to sail?"

"July 5. But I leave for the Keys next week. I need a month to re- pair, to outfit the *Lady.*"

"I need some time to prepare too. I'll meet you in Key Largo. Mid-June, the latest."

"Great. Just *great.* You're gonna love doing the wind, short guy," he said.

"You're not serious," my wife said. "You're from *Chicago,* for chris- sakes. You've never sailed. You don't even like *swimming* all that much."

She was right. When I was nine I'd almost drowned; it was in Beverly Hills, in my rich uncle's pool. And since then, above all other possibilities, I've feared death by drowning—eyes fixed in terror, staring up at the rippling blue water-sky, dead but aware; trapped in a corpse, buried alive for the eternity it takes for the brain to die after the body has drowned. A biblical horror. But fear, like everything else, is fantasy, the weather of the inner world. Just something else to ignore.

Let not the water flood drown me,
let the deep not swallow me up
and shut her mouth upon me . . .

"Ned thinks he can sell the story to *Outside* or *Esquire*." I lied. She knew.

"Don't be silly." She was laughing. She still loved me. That she needed me gone, that our marriage was already over, was left unsaid, not yet admitted.

"Silly?"

"With excuses, darling. You're just feeling guilty about leaving us again and you can't take it. But you're going no matter what I say. So just go. Get out of here."

She was standing, her legs planted. She was barefoot and had nothing on underneath her pale green nightgown. The light from the lamp was enough that I could see most of her through the length of its silk. I watched her belly rise and slide. It was darker than ever outside and the bugs were noisy.

"I'll sell the story. The money's for you and Siri."

She stroked my hair back from my forehead and snickered. "You cut your hair," she said and flashed her consequential smile.

"You noticed?"

"Hard not to."

"As bad as that?"

She nodded. "It's a bit ragged. *Very* ragged." She paused. "Kind of cute, though. Boyish."

"Yeah," I groused. "An old boy. A very old boy. Nothing is as pitiful."

Nestling between my hip bones, she hoisted my T-shirt out of my jeans. Her voice got lower. "I love your lobes," she whispered. And for what I didn't know would be the last time, I felt her breath against my ear; neat white teeth, biting.

9

July 3. Key Largo: 25°1' north latitude / 80°30' west longitude.

The sun glaring through the windshield and the greasy smell of fried chicken wings was a fitting introduction to Florida. The Keys as seen from Highway 1 were uglier for having once been so beautiful. Homestead to Key West was an interrupted world of seashell strip malls, motels, and fast-food franchises that had me cheering for the hurricane, the Big One that would scrape the land clean again.

"She'll be ready in a week," Bananas said. "Motor's not running. So we gotta see Wilson first. Wilson's the motor man."

"What's the weather look like?"

"Hey boy, we're pushing the gauntlet for real now. Every day we wait, we're getting closer to the hurricanes."

Bananas had his batty stoned smile on. A big operatic baritone, he intoned, "Wonderfully fearful."

We detoured onto Card Sound Road, driving south through a long stretch of freaky glades. Bleached-out shrubs and poisoned Australian pines. Thickets of mangrove solid to the edge of the road. Sun-blitzed. The windows open for the wind. The air conditioner set to blow at our feet. The midafternoon sky faded to a dull silvery white. The water out toward Cuba was the blue of dreams. There was Black Water Sound to the right and Biscayne Bay to the left. Roseate spoonbills and alligators.

The fat yellow light was fading when we got to Curtis Marine. The wind was a gusty fifteen to twenty knots from the southwest, whipping the sea into a stiff chop. The air was poised for rain from the ocean. And there she was, the *Lady M;* thirty-five gross tons of marine cement of Dutch registry, she was built in 1980 in Tampa. Riding low in the water, she moved gracefully, but more like a weight lifter than a ballet dancer. I tossed my duffel into the cockpit and kicked off my sandals. The deck was hot underfoot. I sucked in the air and held it like smoke.

Bananas ducked below, sliding into the aft cabin. He reappeared, Poseidon rising, with a bottle of black Puerto Rican rum and three books: Royce's *Sailing Illustrated,* Reed's *Nautical Almanac,* and Chapman's *Piloting, Seamanship, and Small Boat Handling.* He handed me the books and took a long pull from the bottle, his throat jumping.

"There's not a sailor yet that can't learn from reading these books. You can never have too many answers."

I closed one eye.

"Hell," he said, shrugging, "just learn the bowline and the hitch and you'll be in heaven."

I turned to put the books down and stumbled over one of the tools crowding the cockpit, a Milwaukee cordless drill, weaving, almost falling.

Bananas laughed. "First thing we're gonna do is teach you how to walk."

I grabbed the bottle, drank a slug of his rum, and felt it burn. "I'm for heaven," I said.

"Let's go," he said.

The rest of the evening would prove foggy and exhausting. We stopped for dinner at Ballyhoo, a classic Keys joint where they were as serious about food as they were about drink. A husky old-fashioned blond with a dazzling smile, an ankle bracelet, varicose veins, and bloodshot eyes manned the bar. On the walls were pictures of tough guys posed with big fish, and fishing paraphernalia—a stuffed swordfish, nets, floats, reels, rods, a spear gun. We ordered blackened tuna—served up rare and fiery, with piles of sweet slaw, steak-fried potatoes, and sweating cold mugs of Bud Light—lining our guts before driving out to the *club,* in preparation for what promised to be a long night of excess.

Café Carib, "Where the Famous Movie *Key Largo* Was Filmed"—or so the sign read—was the roadside hangout of the hard-core outlaws: the full-time drinkers, dopers, and adrenaline junkies. No Cubans. The local conchs and Cubans don't hang. The place was spangled with red, white, and blue colored lights, blasted by hillbilly rock and roll, and filled with smoke. It smelled of course of piss, stale beer, fried fish, and flowers.

Like Henry Miller, and for the same reason, I have always fallen in with thieves and rogues and murderers. And have been comfortable with them. They are my brothers, for like them—like you, my friends—I'm guilty of every crime. And it is because of our communal crimes that all of us are so closely united. We have met the murderers and they are us.

The regulars had names like Louie the Neck, Lavish Tom, Tattoo Mike, Little Joe, Johnny Fix-'em, Kid Twist, Deadlegs Flynn, Plumber George, Humpty Jackson, Shanghai Pierce, Hot Stove Jimmy Quinn, Hinky-dink Dixon, John the Sweep, and Wilson the Motor Man. They were a rummy lot. Running into old age, precariously balanced; their paranoia was earned. They were all still making a play, and there was a *federale* behind every tree. The moral imperative was simple: survive, but don't rat out your pals—an imperative that outlaw Sam Bass lived and died by:

If a man knows anything he ought to die with it in him. Let me go. Let me go. The world is bobbing around.

"I ache all over," the drunk sitting on the stool next to me was saying, his voice a growl. "Had an engine die at takeoff. Ain't nothing you can do. I was 'bout high as that tower there." He pointed somewhere beyond the bartender's head, his eyes all pupil. "I was fixing to land in a cotton field when oh shit there was pickers and tank trucks working—thought, I'll kill 'em all and myself—so I fluttered her over a few times and went crashing in a corner. A total wreck but I'm still standing. Knocked all my teeth clean out." He showed me with a big gummy smile. "But any day above ground is a good day, and as a matter of fact the ladies do love it. Do-ooo." He laughed and laughed and laughed and smacked me on the back, squeaking, coughing, and spitting.

"Listen, buddy," he said, getting theatrically serious, "I can eat steak with my lips. And that's class. And it's the only thing that counts. Class. Without class, without style, a man's a bum; might as well be dead."

The television set, hung above the display of bar bottles, was silently on the Weather Channel–the isobars, the highs and lows, the patterns–the maps and satellite photos with time-lapse clouds scurrying about the globe.

"Butthead."

Dirty Neil was shouting in my ear. A slugger, his face was a mask of banal, piercing violence. A sociopath who in the winter of '03 would stick an automatic in his mouth and pull. His one solid contribution to civilization. Good riddance.

Blow away. Blow my brains out. I couldn't care less. A shot of adrenaline. *Don't make no fool moves.*

"What?"

"*Butthead.* Name of my boat, pal. She's steel. Built her myself."

"Great. How long did it take you?"

"Ten years, pal, but she ain't done yet."

"Pleased ta meetcha." I stuck out my hand.

Then it was Little Joe, mustachioed, five-three, 280, doing the talking. "I'm proud of everything I've ever done. I never did one thing wrong but break the law. Listen, my grandpa was a slave trader in Turkey, a gunrunner in Rio, and the robber of the Sonora and Navarro Railroad." He slapped the bar, spilling drinks. "Whaddaya drinking? Wanna hit? A bump?"

I had another rum. Another hit. A bump.

"I'm gonna fuck up your head," he said.

"Right," I said, worrying about my sinuses and the clatter of Buddha's rosary that my wrist *mala*'s sandalwood beads were making against the bar top, no matter how gently I set down my beer.

Go easy, I thought. Be easy. Be cool. And I do for the most part now, *go easy,* except for the occasional binge, still loving, needing that certain wild rush through altered reality and twisted perception. Just a little something to reorder the synapses. Zero out the register. See the world anew, recreated. A storyteller's nirvana. And one of the sentient apes' primary drives, survival functions—food, drugs, sex, shelter, art.

What I still like, in order of preference: espresso, cannabis, social alcohol (wine, cognac, vodka, whiskey), a cigar once in awhile. But back then there was the most alluring high, that seductive Lady Opium that for three decades now I've not seen or touched. The fact that it still puckers cheeks, that I can still taste it, feel it in my throat and lungs, feel it in my belly when I merely write or think the word—those three luxuriating syllables rolling off the tongue, tripping over lips, *ooh-pee-uum*—is a testament to its addictive powers. "Opium is the real story," wrote novelist Kunal Basu. "The others are mere distractions."

Yes. Yes. But addiction is so unbecoming, so out of control. A slavery.

She had bellied her way up to the bar. Tall as me, spiky hair dyed yellow and orange. Huge purple eyes. Her skin was tanned and wrinkled. Her lips were thin and mean. Blowsy in a tank top and old cutoffs. Good long legs. She smelled sour. She looked vacant and confused, her stare flat as a pancake. Suspicious.

"Whaddaya doin'?"

Nothing! I want to be like Li Po, who over a thousand years ago wrote:

> *three or four naps every day*
> *still don't exhaust all my free time*
> *I circle the jade bamboo once or twice*
> *and gaze at far mountains above the green pine*

"Doing?" I shrugged.

She shrugged. "Doing here?"

I shrugged again. "Research."

"Research? That's a good one." She snickered. "Just what you researching?"

"You. I'm a writer."

Her eyes narrowed and hardened with suspicion; her mouth twisted to a frown. She leaned toward me. Her breath was foul.

"You bullshitting me, right?"

I shook my head. "Nope."

Then she shook her head. "Can you make a living on it?"

"You sound like my mother."

"I'm twenty-six, and nobody's mother." She was forty-six if she was a day and spit when she laughed and puckered up. "You can kiss my ass."

I stared down the mouth of my glass and felt bad about saying, "Thank you but no thank you."

She brushed at her hair absentmindedly.

"Listen," she said, turning angry and teary, "nobody ever gave me a goddamn thing except my father, and he gave me every goddamn thing I wanted."

The mix of intoxicants was beginning to take effect. I felt vaguely ill. Sweat trickled down my legs. My thoughts curved deliciously to a woman I'd spied earlier in the day. I couldn't picture her face now, but she'd been a mink: muscular, tight-bellied—hard and dangerous. Her skirt had taken a hike. I saw again her underthighs and a patch of lollipop white panties. Milky skin, a long expanse of café crème. She'd been sitting on the deck of a boat called *Gone,* her feet propped up on a hatch cover, cotton balls between her toes, painting her nails red.

The next thing I got was jabbed, four stiff fingers in the ribs. "Rise and shine."

It was Bananas. He was wearing the official T-shirt of the sailing vessel *Lady M.* His logo, silk-screened on it, was stretched to curving by the girth of his chest.

Bizarre is what we are.

Unique is what we seek.

"I need to park it. You drive. I'm done." He popped a beer and handed over the car keys. His laugh cracked huge and his arms came down around my back in a formidable hug—foam dribbling down my back—and whispered close to my ear words of wisdom. "Big hurry . . . dangerous. Remember, bad shit can pop up anytime. Anywhere."

"Right."

I followed him out to the dark shadow cast by the big marquee, to the growl of traffic, the headlights and horns, the blasting discordant rush of jukeboxes, electric bands, and car stereos blending almost harmonically.

Bananas flopped and slept like a wheezy baby. I drove back to Curtis Marine through a quick cloudburst. The air thickened and the sky fell down. It lasted no more than a minute. Then mosquitoes boiled out of the mangroves and there were flashes of lightning from out at sea, where new clouds were starting to form.

First light. Stirred by so many water birds, I woke queasy and hungry and wanting coffee. The mosquitoes and no-see-ums had been bad. They like fresh northern skin. My feet and ankles were spotted with bites, a hundred or more, burning and itching. It was futile to resist. Insects rule. Nature's toughest niche. The survivors. Even as fliers, they were already up in the air in the dim shadows of the Silurian period, more than 400 million years ago, when plants were just edging up onto the land—170 million years before anything else, including flying dinosaurs.

Even with the fan aimed on me down the tunnel from the main cabin, my bunk was too sweat-soaked to loll. I pulled on a pair of shorts, a gift from my daughter, that had red penguins waddling on them. And then, after grabbing towel and kit, I smacked my head crawling out of the V-berth and my right shin climbing through the forward hatch.

After a night of rain, dawn was sudden and hot. The water utterly calm and flat. The sky huge and cloudless but smeared with haze. Not even breeze enough to stir the shrouds.

Shroud—the word itself sounded ominous, onomatopoetic. When used as a verb it means to cover, hide from sight; when a noun, it's a winding-sheet (the cloth used to wrap a corpse for burial) or, in boating, any of the set of ropes and lines stretching from masthead to the deck, perhaps entangling the drowned sailor—his winding-sheet, so to speak.

A cormorant perched on a near piling didn't move when I wobbled past it down the steep incline of the low-tide gangplank. There was a bleach bottle float trapped against the dock, bobbing with furry yellow seaweed and some dead thing bloated to unrecognizable decay. Next to the marina washroom, a garbage can bristled with palm leaves. I took a shower and examined my grizzled face and hair grown wild, impressed by the deep lines around my black slits for eyes that seemed as always a bit beat up, posed. How do they describe John or Clint? Craggy.

When I returned, there was a man in the cockpit sorting hardware. He looked up when he heard me. We were both already sweating in the sun.

"You must be the writer."

"Guilty."

He was a little younger than I, my height but bigger, much more powerfully built. His arms and legs were corded, but he'd gone a bit soft with age around the chest and gut. What was left of his hair was bristle-cut, same as his beard. The top of his head was burnt red and peeling. His eyes were pale gray and amused. I liked him instantly. Here, instinct said, was a genuine sweetheart, serious and honorable.

"Jim," he said and stuck out his hand. His right thumb had been pounded black and wide, flat as a flipper. His shake was straightforward, no testosterone bullshit in it.

Here was Captain Jim, powerboat captain, electrician, master craftsman, boatbuilder, and big brother. Protector of the weak. Lover of fragile women, the crazies. He would tell me that it was

August, that it was ninety-six in the shade the day he met his lady. She was wearing a fox scarf, head chasing tail, wrapped twice around her neck, a little bikini bra, a very mini miniskirt, and flip-flops. Her ankle was bandaged, and though as it turned out there was nothing wrong with her, she walked with a cane. Her eyes were red and watery. She was from Tennessee and on the lam from a husband who had regularly beat her.

He loved the damaged. Loved demented beauty. Beauty broken.

"And you're just another soft-hearted Dutchman," I said.

"Guilty," he said. His laugh was easy, uncomplicated. "I'd give a hundred bucks for a cup of coffee. You?"

"At least. What about B?"

"He's making the morning run to West Marine. Picking up hardware. He'll meet us at Annie's."

Breakfast at Tugboat Annie's was boiled fish, poached eggs, buttered grits, and shots of that legal speed, Cuban coffee—sweet and grainy black—to jangle our motivation. I saw the toenail painter again. She was our waitress. Toned brown thighs disappearing this time into (would you believe?) pink bicycle shorts under a white frilled apron. On her feet, strappy high-heeled sandals and oh yes those red toenails. She poured the water. Sandalwood notes fumed. She had blue-ice eyes. Her lips were unnaturally parted. She moved well. Cut the air. Her auburn hair floated behind her as she walked.

"Frenchy," said Jim.

"What?"

"The waitress. That's her name. The one you're staring at. Frenchy."

Jim was leaning an elbow on the table, his chin philosophically cupped in his palm. The lines in his face showed a smile. I thought it much too early in the day for nostalgia or desire or the blue-smoke music coming from the juke.

I make love to women
while I'm livin'.
I know this can't go on.

I looked from her to him. "You joking?"

"Nope. Makes you shiver, don't she?" He gestured his flat black thumb back over his shoulder at Frenchy. "That one will ruin your day. She'll tear the crotch right out of your knickers."

Today's revelation: efficiency—we needed it, needed to get up to speed. We were victims of the calendar. We had precious little time. The hurricane season was heating up, and the boat was still a construction site. Jim hadn't finished the wiring. Another few days. The engine was questionable and awaiting a few sober hours from Wilson, the motor man. The fuel tanks were full of rotten diesel and needed flushing. The doghouse covering the cockpit was a who-knows-when. The installation of the new jib, the roller-reefer that so pleased Bananas, was an *almost* no problem.

"She's a wicked Wanda. That jib's the most powerful sail we got; takes up to a third of the boat almost."

But the main needed mending and the mizzen had seen better days. The hydraulics for the helm were not yet installed. The compass and autopilot hadn't been tested or calibrated. The rigging was flabby and needed tuning. The dinghy was an often and poorly patched rag, salt, ozone, and ultraviolet having done their ruinous work. There was no aerial for the second- or was it thirdhand single sideband radio, the SG-2000. *Yeah it's good; the army used it in*

Eeee-rak. No EPIRB emergency beacon. We were not yet provisioned. The riggers, except for Jim, were stoned—tied to the bottle, the bone, the line. We were one sailor short.

It was a messy beginning.

I know less than nothing about boats or mechanics, and tools in my hands are weapons of destruction, so I'm mostly useless except as a gofer or bilge-boy.

Gunky, the barge-crane man, scrawny with a chewed-up face, was contemptuous. "You ain't much of a bright boy to run this shit pig into the Gulf Stream." He chuckled. "Fucking blowboaters. You bastards got no sense and no i-tin-er-ry. Niggers and piss." A stentorian snort exited his nose. "I'd go anywhere, you give me a-couple motors. But I ain't going nowhere on no blowboat." He gave me a what-kind-of-asshole-are-you look. "Why you going?"

The sky seemed unusually crowded with seabirds playing. "Because I've never been," I said.

"Shit. Better you assholes than me. I wouldn't sail with Bananas. No way." Then Gunky, pissed to the gills, mumbled barely audibly, "Stupid fuckers."

Bananas flushed red, the tendons in his neck tightened, and he leaned close to Gunky. "To hell with that. Now I understand how your face got chewed off. Get the fuck off my boat. I don't do negative. When you go to sea you're on your own. You either abort and turn back or go forward with what you got. I'm talking sailing. And everybody knows I sail."

Bananas was always sure, never uncertain, when it was about something really important, like an adventure or survival; blind optimism was one of the tenets of his faith.

Putting on the good cheer, Gunky raised his beer in a mock salute and chugged what was left in the bottle in one long swallow.

"Cocksuckers."

I raised my bottle in return. "Cocksuckers," I toasted. "Here's to us all." My beer was warm and flat. Gunky stuffed his empty into his pants pocket, turned, and lurched mule-headed across deck and down the gangplank without saying another word.

Skinny Pete, the cadaver-thin dockmaster, rattled the shrouds and looked confused as he tried to look important. He had a discouraged, depraved-vibing face with a stubble of yellowed gray beard. Stringy arms and bandy legs stuck out of a dirty, once-white T-shirt and tattered khaki shorts. He had a little lisp and his step was slow.

"All I got to thay is not on Friday. No, no man. Not on Friday. Never on Friday. Nobody leavth on a thailing trip on Friday."

Friday, named after Freya, the Norse goddess of love and beauty who rode onto a battlefield to claim the dead, has always been regarded by mariners, a superstitious lot, as a bad day to go to sea, to begin construction of a ship, or to launch a ship. In the early years of the nineteenth century the British navy, trying to dispel this belief, lay the keel of a new ship, the HMS *Friday,* on a Friday. She was launched on Friday and went to sea on Friday with a Captain named Friday. Neither the ship nor her crew was ever heard from again.

"This is great." Bananas turned and punched me in the shoulder.

"Just get us out of here. There's nothing here for me but trouble."

My feeling was, and I'm somewhat past illusion, that if we didn't soon sail or I soon get back to the calming influence of home—back to conversations, to travel with Tsung Tsai—I would sink into my private fires, toward the sociopath I was always fighting to escape.

"Really great." He punched me again. His eyes were bright with pleasure after blowing Gunky off. He grabbed me by the shoulders and shook me hard enough to fuzz my vision.

"Yeah, great, man. But slow down. Take it easy. Try not to kill me until after we sail."

Then for reasons unknown, and not unlike two goofy school-girls, we started laughing. Bananas got to laughing so big it took him a few minutes just to catch breath enough to speak.

"Hey boy, we'll be waiting for them drunken sad-asses down-island. The equator, boy."

Skinny peered dumbly at us, and I could see by the cloudy blue color of his eyes that he must be nearly blind. He was dour enough to be a wife beater. A bad drunk.

Bananas was moving urgently, obviously on the hunt, waving his arms in the general direction of half the horizon. "C'mon, we gotta go. Let's move it. I got no time to waste. I need to find Dusty. We gotta fly. Low and fast. Flat, man."

On the way out to Islamorada to find Dusty we stopped at a package store and picked up a bottle of Captain Morgan and a six-pack of Bud. With Bananas driving very fast but capably, it was a quick trip down Route 1. The only real thrill was crossing the bridge, where we passed a drunk who was barely holding his lane.

"Most dangerous highway in America," Bananas said, speed-shifting down into third.

We turned right down a driveway topped with pinky-white crushed coral and parked under the sign of the flashing mermaid. The Lor-e-lei was an open rectangular thatched tiki bar and restaurant built on stilts in anticipation of tropical storms. Dusty's boat, the *Duga,* was moored in the mangroves in a back-alley canal, an illegal dockage. We walked around back, behind a dance stage where a funk band was playing and a baby-beef with a ponytail was singing loudly and not very well.

We walked another half mile down a rutted two-track, rank with the iodine smell of tidal flats, palm fronds rattling over a canal choked by vegetation—a watery-green uproar of mangrove, bougainvillea, ferns, strangler vines, and oleander—along with various stranded garbage and swelling sea scum–drifting orange peels, plastic bottles, and scrap wood. Even the beached boats were ripe, spilling their overflow gaudily onto the mudflats, where quick brown lizards darted amid the tangle of algae-bearded shrouds, sea grape, and yellow extra-heavy-duty extension cords.

I love lizards. Time has slipped past these magnificent survivors. Almost eternal, they not only persist, they triumph. The first known biped was a lizard, a speedy long-legged creature that made the scene some eighty million years before the dinosaur. There is also a Jesus Christ lizard, a Central American animal able to run on water, much like some far more recent inheritors of the planet—a few holy men.

"Lizards," I said.

"Duga," Bananas said, pointing at a rusting hulk moored at the dead end of the canal where three sagging Cuban wicker chairs, sunk ankle-deep into the cool muck, were faced toward the South Atlantic long beyond the *Duga's* ragged rigging. The blades of her white-paddled windbugger drifted concentrically and moaned. On the opposite bank, in the shade of the last trees, an egret tiptoed its way toward the Gulf, which was just around the corner.

The way to the *Duga* was across a couple of two-by-twelves precariously balanced on cinder blocks. The palmetto bugs were out in force, their hard carapaces and juicy little bodies cracking and squishing underfoot.

Dusty Nettuno, gaunt and strung tight, was skipper of the *Duga* and the spitting image of Dustin Hoffman in *Papillon,* complete with rickety wire-mended frames supporting bottle-bottom lenses. His boat was a steel-hulled thirty-six-footer. A former coal-fired steamer, she was built in London in 1879. Dusty bought her thirty years ago, just after he got back from two tours as a medic in 'Nam. It took him more than a year to make a sailboat out of her. Soon as she was finished, he weighed anchor and disappeared for fifteen years. Then, in the mid-1980s, he surfaced again, now as navigator aboard the *Sea Shepherd,* a ship of Operation Greenpeace's eco-guerrilla fleet, making war on whalers. Ten years ago he was diagnosed with multiple sclerosis. He's been slowly losing it since.

"Can he do it?" I asked Bananas. "MS tends to make one a bit unsteady."

"No problem. He's a hard one. All we need do is load in enough ice to keep his medicine cold. He's gotta shoot up twice a day."

"Why not? I know I'd rather die running than pissing my diapers in hospice."

Bananas's right foot was vibrating, keeping time with his nerves and blood pressure. "I'm gonna do it Bahamian style," he said.

"How's that?"

"The old way. Row a dinghy out to blue water. Bring a bottle. Get drunk. Roll over. Very clean. Honorable."

In Raymond Firth's 1936 monograph, *We the Tikopia,* there's a reference to an ancient song in which the loss of a man at sea is called a "sweet burial." Such is the attitude of the first Polynesian sailors. Fear of storms, of drowning left them undeterred, accepting. Fired by a lust for adventure and discovery, they set out in canoe after canoe, ranging the sea.

Soon after humans first walked upright, we sailed. It's that primal. We hoisted sails before we saddled horses, navigated the open seas before we rode on wheels along roads.

"How soon y'all leaving?" was Dusty's only question.

"A week at most. By next Tuesday."

I sipped at my rum and watched him. He waved me off when I handed him the huge spliff Bananas had rolled. He was looking blankly over my shoulder and out toward the horizon.

"I guess I'll go."

I was dubious. We had finished the better part of the bottle we'd brought and I thought it was the rum talking. But not Bananas: that puckish optimist was dancing, his shadow bobbing and weaving along with him on the water.

"Anything special I can get you, Dusty? Just name it," he said.

The sun was dying out. Dusty said, "I like a tipple of sweet liquor at sunset."

"Not a problem. Name your poison. And don't worry about a thing, boy. If you check out we'll give you a fine sea burial with full ceremonies. We'll fire the cannon for you," Bananas said in a rush, conveniently ignoring, for the sake of story, that the cannon had long ago been confiscated by the Bahamian police.

Life is but a dream, tra-la.

Dusty nodded, staring out to sea. "Wish I could see the islands from here," he said.

We lost Dusty the next day. He'd spent the morning tuning the *Lady M*'s rig, softening the running backstays, easing up the tensions on the mast.

"I guess I won't be going," he said when he'd finished. Sweat popped off his forehead. "Can't do it anymore."

"That's cool," Bananas said, for once only gently pissed. Unusually magnanimous.

Dusty had surrendered to reality. To fear. To safety. But whatever the reasons, Bananas couldn't abide it. "Reality," he spat. Excuses and all the rest were just another rut. He'd rather have Dusty swimming with the fishes. I was ambivalent. Fear was everywhere. Security is a sham. No matter what we do, time will soon pass us by, leave us behind. But wouldn't it be a great story? Dusty's death. Heartbreaking to write. It was the absolute opportunism of the writer speaking now, everything—emotions included—was fodder, grist for the mill. Even my shame. Tsung Tsai had once showed me, tracing the lines with the tip of a chopstick, how the Chinese ideogram for writing looks like a tiny set of animal tracks. The perfect allusion. Just a trail. Poor Dusty lost at sea. *The Perfect Squall.*

"Can't do it, huh?" Bananas stood on the stern with eyes only for his *Lady M.* "Look at her. She ain't a boat; she's a ship." He was buzzed, rubbing his optimism like a cicada its horny feet. "If you can't, you can't. Not a problem. You can't?" A pause, to give Dusty a chance to redeem himself, to come to his senses. Bananas continued to stand there awhile, calmly staring up the mast, nodding his head gently. Dusty turned around finally and walked down the gangplank, at first hunched over, but then erect and striding after he hit the dock and the land allowed it.

"Okay. Okay, not a biggie," Bananas said dismissively.

He turned to me and winked, Dusty already forgotten, new plans brewing. "I'll get hold of Ken. His *Music* is anchored off Grenada. Internet café there. Picks up e-mail once a week. He'll sail. He's always ready. You'll love him. He's your people. South African Jew. Special forces frogman. Deserter. A Kiwi now. One of the world's best sailors. Round the world six times by thirty. Whitbread racer."

"What about time?"

"We're pushing it. We've got to get out. Soon as we can. We're close to the turning point."

"All right. That's the point I like."

"Gives us time to finish, to get her perfect. Kenny will come soon as he gets his family settled and his boat in a hole. We'll be outta here by week's end. But we're in a real hurry now. Maybe have to make a straight run through hurricane alley. There's a flotilla of Miami Cubans off to Havana on the eighteenth. We need to avoid those assholes. We can make it, though. No problem. Another week."

It took three.

It was full into hurricane season when the *Lady M* with her motley crew—Bananas, Jim, Ken, and me—finally cleared the dock on the afternoon of July 23, throwing off lines at 3:18 p.m., just in time to catch high tide in high swirling clouds, a golden tint, a radiance—like Buddha's birthday. All the boating clan saw us off. They were coming in, I noted, while we were going out: waving, wishing luck, and looking just a tad dubious.

Out past Molasses Reef and into blue water at 4:30. Bananas was rattling pots in the galley.

Jim was fishing. "A nice bloody dorado for dinner. Flopping-fresh sashimi. Now wouldn't *that* be a bonus."

Ken was still trying to get the single sideband to work, with no luck. He was disgusted. "Bananas, get rid of this damn thing before I throw it overboard. I'm sick of it. I can't even pick up David Jones."

David Jones was the Caribbean sailors' weather guru. He had broadcast for as long as most could remember, sending out his own forecasts twice a day, morning and evening (more in heavy weather emergencies) to all ships at sea. He was a former sailor, which is, by definition (in Ken's argot), a bitch.

"Davy Jones, huh? Perfect." I laughed.

Ken wasn't amused by or interested in the weather guy's name being the same as that of the spirit of the sea, the eighteenth-century sailor's tongue-in-cheek idiom for the bottom of the ocean—"Davy Jones's locker," where sunken ships and sailors go to their rest.

"He's just a fat, toothless old rummy. But he's the best in the business for blowboaters. Better than the coast guard."

I was watching the helm. There was nothing to it. Just had to be sure the autopilot didn't cut out. We were crabbing, bearing 70° to go 55°. With wind veering from the north-northeast, we were headed toward Great Isaac, making eight to eight and a half knots. Nowhere to go but south, fourteen hundred miles of ocean. We'd done fifteen nautical miles.

"We still got fifty miles of Gulf Stream ahead, about five hours worth of push."

"How's that compare again to land miles?"

"One's bigger, mate." Ken pumped his arm. "Like my dick."

"Imagine if this breeze kicks in," Jim shouted.

Always starving, about to faint from low blood sugar, Bananas was rubbing his stomach and serving up plantains and black beans mixed with onions, tomatoes, picadillo, and shredded lettuce. Tortillas. Matouk's pepper sauce, the only kind worth eating. Cokes all around. A shag of rum for dessert.

"Whoever complains about the food has to cook," Bananas said.

"This food tastes like shit. . . but it's the best shit I've ever eaten," I said.

Ken looked up from reading the single sideband instruction manual in an effort to make the radio work. "Hey, crack it down five degrees, Bananas; it's just too sharp an angle."

Darts of spray. Bucking like a bronco. War whoops.

Eight p.m. Yesterday was long ago. Seventy miles to the lighthouse at Isaac, less than ten hours at this speed. Eight to nine hours before first light. I watched daylight's red end burn out, the sky darkening; warm air, cold stars rocking. Ahead, to the south, were low green islands, black water, and a full burning moon.

Jim popped up out of the forward cabin in a silhouette of smoke and handed me a sweet cheroot, then lit it for me. I exhaled my own halo.

"Well, George," he said, reaching up to slap palms. "We're off the dot."

13

It was close to the end of night . . .

. . . in that tiny universe stuck between water and sky.

Ken woke me by pulling on my foot, and I was up and on deck to take last watch before my eyes were really open.

"Currents. The fucking zones. Laugh, you hoary bastard." Ken was talking into the darkness ahead. He stood spread-legged and rolled with the waves, his rectangular linebacker's body draped in an orchid flower sarong.

Ken was born in Cape Town, South Africa. Now, though, he was a New Zealand citizen. He looked to be in his early forties. His hair was thinning and curly, the color of straw. He had a red Fu Manchu mustache, a stubble of beard, and a tight smile. His lips were permanently cracked from sun and salt. Huge hands. Thick fingers. He moved about the boat with the easy grace of a big baboon and looked his role: the romantic bastard—right-wing warrior, racist, misanthrope, sailboat captain—unshakable in a crisis.

His father, Mordechai Brodsky, was a Belgian Jew, atheist, and brewmaster from Antwerp. In 1939 he eluded the Nazis and made for America on a ship that was torpedoed and sank. After three days in a lifeboat he was picked up by a mail ship going to South Africa. He stayed, fell in love with a Polish girl, a pious Jew from Danzig, married her, opened a brewery, and got wealthy. Together they had six children, five girls and a boy.

Kenneth was the youngest. Nothing in his soul was suited for the life of a brew burgher in the strangled suburbia of white South Africa. He became, in turn, a special forces killer, fighting the Cubans in Angola ("We kicked butt: took ears"), a deserter, then a nomad, a sailboat samurai—and in all these roles a racist, a bit of a fascist, but a good man to have at your back. Fanatically loyal and seemingly fearless.

"Step aside, shallow-ripple sailors. I'm not afraid of any man. I've seen so much shit, nothing can scare me."

In a frantic two-year stretch, he'd designed and built a steel boat, a thirty-eight-footer, on a friend's farm three hundred miles from the sea. He named her *Music,* for that was what weather and water were for him. He followed the wind. It was all he knew or truly loved, though he had a lusty Irish wife and two children, a boy and a girl. They'd been living for nine years on the boat. "Megan's ten," he told me. "She's got a filthy Irish mouth." He laughed. "Same as her bloody mother." Dylan *the villain,* his six-year-old son, was born mid-Atlantic and had sailed some fourteen thousand miles before his first birthday. He had yet to sleep a night on land.

"Sailing is a beautiful thing, mate. It's freedom. You don't pay taxes and you shit in the water," he said, grunting his pleasure. "Yaayh. Some people climb mountains; I go to sea. It's my passion, George. I love sailing boats to their max. So sure I'm a bloody asshole. Fucking look at me. I left my wife and kids and lost money to take a shitbox out on the ocean." He threw a vicious right cross at the air. "Welcome to blowboating, mate. Seventy percent is shit. But the 30 percent that's exhilarating makes the 70 percent shit worth it."

"Not bad," I said. "Same with writing, except the odds are longer."

"I don't get it. That mind of yours just keeps clicking on. How do you write?"

"I dunno. Just listen to the beat, I guess, follow the words as they play; go where they and the story take me. How do you sail a storm?"

"Depends on the storm. But it's always a shit fight to the end. It's not what happens that matters; it's how you deal with it. All I can tell you is that I *will* deal with it."

"It's the same with writing. You're a philosopher."

"Fuck philosophy. I bash on."

"I'll stick to the desert. At the very least, I can get out and walk. I'm always looking for a way out."

"Americans, jeeesuss" he exploded. "Dumb-ass paper-pushers. You all just want to write books. Weaklings."

"That's why I'm a writer. I've no choice. Incompetent. Nothing else I can do. And I'm a liar too—but an honest liar. The truth, or what I can understand of it, always errs more or less. So I'm chasing after something different."

"Right," he said, grabbing, groping his crotch, and giving me a lecher's grin. "Like strange pussy."

I quoted (without saying so) the French writer Guy de Maupassant—"The best part of love is walking up the stairs"—and grabbed at myself in turn.

Ken whistled and hooted. He slapped his leg. "We're men after all," he said. "We're the superior race, the runners, always chasing after stuff. Women are just around to keep us responsible, sort life out for us. They're the serious ones."

"But smarter," I said.

"Shit yes. But they don't have as much fun."

"Maybe. But they have more joy. They're more connected. Compassionate."

"Yeah, mate, but could you, *would* you, trade places? That's the test."

"Not a chance. But that's a function of hormones, testosterone poisoning. A paucity of imagination."

"What a wanker."

"You don't know the half of it."

Once, in Ensenada, I fell in love with a whore. I'd gone down to Mexico with Bruce B., a struggling producer/director, an old friend from my summer theater days. I was in L.A. for a quick ten-day visit.

"Let's go down to Mexico and dance with those girls in red dresses," Bruce said.

Elena was her name. A-*lay*-nah. She pronounced it like Humbert did Lo-*li*-ta, three trips down the tongue. She was an Indio. She had the bones. And a widow in black. In *luto*. A slim-fitting black linen suit. A mini. She was delicate with small breasts. They were apples. Her upper lip was fleshy, with beads of sweat, but perfect with lipstick, and she had babies to support. I was drinking and watching the mating dance at Anthony's Bar and Disco when she tugged my grizzled beard.

Her face was so close. "Bew-ti-fool," she said. "*Tu.*"

We spent that one evening whispering together. She had so much hair. There was no warning that the warmth of her skin, so tender at the nape, would carry the fragrance of magenta flowers.

To disco music that was bad and fast we slow-danced. Caught in the sway of her hips, I moved with her, my hand always cupping her ass. I was never prepared. The acute pleasures of new love, of yearning, were my mainline jones. "You're my Lady Opium," I said just before she closed the door. After all, the old gods fucked often and joyously, hilariously. And yes, it would be, at least in fantasy, always wonderful in the morning to see daylight, to get out of bed and drink coffee too much, read too much and write too much, and love her much too much. Of course she didn't love me; I was just another pushover gringo john. She doesn't remember me and will never know I remember her and was thinking again how wonderful it would be to stare one more time openmouthed into those dark animal eyes.

I was shivering when she left. We never fucked; it was love. I'm an idealist, a proud, card-carrying male egoist, a monster of self-involvement, hoping only that love with all its confusions and potential destructiveness can repair madness, weakness, aloneness. So I don't—I've never paid for sex. Still, she went home to her babies with all my cash, three hundred–odd bucks, and I drove south down Baja along the Golfo de California. Nothing as good for love as a long hard trip through the night.

a night without end.
I can't sleep,
so when after moonrise,
from somewhere someone calls,
gratefully I answer,
yes.

"You got me," I said. "A wanker and a lover. I make love even to mama."

"What kind of bullshit you talking now, mate?"

"You know, lying alone in a meadow or on a beach, the sun hot on your back, humping the giving earth. Mama." I waggled my hips obscenely.

He laughed. "Does the ocean count?"

"You bet. Especially these warm tropic waters."

He laughed again. "The deck is yours. I got her set on autopilot. Make sure she stays there. Nothing to do. Just keep a lookout for water spouts. This wind is a finicky sister." He looked to the tell-tales, the bright ribbons hung aloft to show apparent direction and how the wind was working. "How's the stomach?" he asked.

The first hint of seasickness that hit me shortly after we set sail had shocked and neurotically embarrassed me. Now, by day three everything in the boat was dank and crusty with salt, and everything stank. The portholes leaked badly in rough weather, a sheen of water seeping down the dark varnished mahogany of the cabin and V-berth, soaking our bunks. Each drop of seawater teeming with invisible marine monsters: zooplankton and phytoplankton. Nonmotile because they're too small, too weak to swim against the current, they exist by drifting, their movement (like ours) dependent on tide, current, and wind, that floating state. (The other floaters, the seaweeds such as the sargassum that clogs the Sargasso Sea, are not considered plankton but pleuston.) And these—the algae, diatoms, bacteria, protozoans, jellyfish, worms, crustaceans, mollusks, coelenterates, eggs, and larvae that all life on earth depends on for survival—were dying and rotting below deck. Combine that with the heady perfumes of onions, garlic, the kerosene and motor oil spilled, the chemicals in the head, the shit in the pipes; our rank human grease, the reek of fetid tissue thickened with the heat.

Dinner had been a stew of chopped raw onions, refried beans, and canned chicken slop. Pepper sauce. Tortillas. I was nonstop queasy but didn't want to let them know just how dilapidated I felt, crazed by claustrophobia and nausea. I woke the next morning at the kiss of dawn with bricks on my chest from a brief, horrifying dream of drowning, alone in the dark. I tried to breathe deeply but couldn't. My skin was crawling off my body. The deck spun; the walls wiggled; there was a ringing.

I felt three days as an eternity, the sea as a prison—a vast foreignness, wild and mysterious and unfathomably dangerous. What I wanted was a crisp autumn night in a dry bed, feather pillows and a comforter, rumpled sheets fresh with *she*-smells.

"Not too bad." I yawned and scratched. "But I wouldn't mind if port were just around the corner."

"At least you're not puking. Mary gets it so bad I have to stuff suppositories up her ass."

Mary, his wife, had just turned forty. In snapshots she looked the bomb: red hair, freckles, heated smile; plump and undulant.

"You're so sweet, a darling man," I said.

He cocked his head, squinted, and gave me the once-over. "Forget it, mate; you're not me type." He went aft to check the lines holding Mary's birthday surprise, a red sea kayak, to the railing opposite to where six jerry cans of gas and Bananas's two rusting beach bikes were tied. Then, after one last look around, he went below to sleep. And I was alone with the amber running lights, twin blurs in the dark.

14

After an hour, a steady breeze, eight- to ten-foot swells, a hint of land, a yet distant storm. Crash and bash, the *Lady* going woof-woof, creaking and moaning incessantly, metal and wood fretting the cement hull. The shrouds whistling; the billowed sheets. Sailing lovely. Speed in the sevens as stars faded and vanished, the wake teeming with the din of phosphorescence.

A low sky tipped the main. It was close to daybreak and the air was smoke and melting into dream when I heard the radio call. *Mayday! Mayday! Mayday!* It crackled and vanished instantly into static and unreality. Close, I thought. Must be close. Our Intrepid Marine VHF, essentially a fancy walkie-talkie good only for in-port gab, had a broadcast range of fifteen to twenty miles at best, rarely over the horizon.

I grabbed the mic, nerves cocked. There was another rush of static. Entropy. No more sounds like words. "Uhhh . . . calling un-known vessel. This is the *Lady M*. Do you copy? Over."

I waited a few minutes for an answer and repeated, "Unknown vessel in distress, this is the *Lady M*. Do you copy? Over."

And again, "Vessel in distress, do you copy? Do you copy? Over."

White noise was the reply. Must have been a dream. Just a dream, I thought, but it was impossible not to feel the chill and hear the call: the summons to action, to arms. And there was nothing I could do, nothing to be done. I was as mute and as lost as that mayday. *Mayday! Mayday!*

The sea, like the desert in its silence, gives voice to the unconscious, which, as even Neanderthal man understood, is the voice of god. That cry for help must have been my unconscious speaking, the voice of impotence in the face of loss—for against the flood, the endless ocean of death, each death, mine included, is like a drop of water evaporating. Less.

I switched channels, working the radio with no luck. I studied the ocean, searching 360 degrees to the horizon with the binoculars. But only waving swells and some insubstantial wind clouds showed. Nothing more. Never the buzz of insects in warm air was proof that this, like the deepest desert, was not the human world. Over the reef the water turned glass, and beneath its turquoise translucence white sand and coral fanned, dropping off to cold deep-water blues ahead.

On deck a tiny flying fish, spread wings like a dragonfly, fried in the August heat lifting off the cement hull. My tongue was hairy and tasted coppery. I unscrewed the cap from the gallon jug of springwater we kept in the cockpit and, after pouring some over my head, drank a quart. It was still somewhat cool from the night and a little salty. The sun rolled up onto the horizon and the day exploded into heat, the crests of waves catching fire and sparks. The *Lady M* looked the pretty pirate ship in the sunshine; her ice-white decks and patched sails, her red and blue shrouds; pale turquoise and pinky-salmon trim. Bananas had painted her, to the nagging disapproval of the yachties, with house paint—water-based latex, no less. "Ain't she sweet?" he'd said with pride. "She's an island lady, man. Cheeky."

In the few minutes of solitude that I had left before they all woke, I got out my book and was soon in second-century Rome again. I was reading *Memoirs of Hadrian,* by Marguerite Yourcenar. It was fine but somehow lacked the moisture that poetry requires. In it, Hadrian, the great Roman emperor, soliloquies as he lies dying, having reached that point, that moment of freedom, where life for every man is accepted defeat:

Every bliss achieved is a masterpiece and it puzzles me that these joys, so precarious at best, so rarely perfect in the course of human life should be regarded with such mistrust by the so-called wise, who denounce the dangers in sensuous delight, instead of fearing its absence or its loss; in tyrannizing over their senses they pass time which would be better occupied in putting their souls to rights.

The crew ate for breakfast what my stomach shrank and heaved at even the thought of, my throat pinching vomitus back—heaping plates of fried eggs, onions, and plantains with sweet bread, a side of oily sardines in tomato sauce, and rum-dosed coffee. I sipped warm Coke and nibbled the corners off a saltine.

That afternoon, at 25°51' north, 77°53' west, thirty miles off Stirrup Cay, it was hotter than yesterday, and the wind was dying. The water turned so blue that it was purple, furrowed in the late light. Dazzling.

"Perfect example of pressure killing wind," Ken said. "Shuuush and it's gone. But it'll be back, giving us more than we want."

At twilight, under power, we cleared the passage Bananas called Hole in the Wall, passing between (somewhere beyond the horizon) the Berry Islands to port and the Abacos to starboard. The night came on with another variety of darkness, not so black. A crescent waxing moon broke a cloud line. We had fifty gallons of fuel left. The engine ticked off heat.

We were on what looked to me like a collision course with, some few hundred yards to our northeast, a rust-ugly island freighter lit up like a Christmas tree.

"*Wellinius. Wellinius,* this is the sailing vessel *Lady M.* Do you copy? Over."

"We copy, *Lady M.* Man, you a *sail*boat? Over."

"Yes. Over."

"There be weather, man. What the hell you doin' out here?"

"Sailing, *Wellinius.* Can you give us a weather update? Over."

Nothing but noise.

"*Wellinius. Wellinius,* do you copy?"

Nothing more.

"They're on autopilot. They're drinking. They're fucking their old ladies. They're not looking. They're bomb-heads. They don't give a shit." He was impatient for a fight. "Cut the engine. Crack the sheets. Crank it! Bananas, tack! Ten degrees down. Enough. This thing is a pig. She won't even take a tack."

Bananas was mad about his boat. "But she sails," he said.

"She sails like shit." Ken shot him another *you asshole* stare.

I checked the Magellan GPS, which could lay a course to any point on earth, changing it automatically as necessary due to chaos—the fluidity of wind, tide, and drift; it displayed latitude and longitude to the second decimal place of a geographical minute, along with the distance traveled and the distance yet to go, the speed, and the estimated time of arrival to the nearest second.

"White man's magic," Ken called it. "Makes every asshole alive think he's a sailor." He was unable to look at any situation without seeing the possibilities for imminent disaster. But he was a survivor, trusting only his gut and his fearless self-sufficiency. He could deal with it all. Alone. "When you go to sea," he would say, "you're on your own."

"We're making three and a half knots now. Same as burning oil," I told him. With no run or glide, against what little wind there was, we were beating, tack upon tack. Making almost no progress.

Ken reclined against the bulkhead, an aqua flotation pillow at his back, tuning the autopilot with his big toe. He rolled his eyes skyward. A little shake of his head. "Right, mate, and we're going north when we need south." He leaned forward, cupped his hand around my ear, and hissed, "Pray for trades."

"Aii . . . wanna take you on a slow boat to China," I tried crooning, but my voice cracked and broke.

We all laughed except for Bananas, who said, "It would've been nice to know the weather, if anything is coming at us."

"Another dead issue. It's too late; we're committed," Ken said. "Roll the headsail up a tad."

For Ken, Grenada—or for that matter, any destination he's charted for—becomes the imperative; he cannot deviate. Hard as iron. He's a stickler for duty. Everything—shit weather, a slipping clutch, low on fuel, a hopeless radio, lousy rigging, worried wives and girlfriends—be damned. Bash on.

Things kept going wrong with the boat.

On the afternoon of the fourth day we lost the main. We heard a few pecks of rain on the canvas roof of the doghouse. The ocean humped with wind-feathered whitecaps and had a sheen like oiled pewter. Thunder-boomers were running across the sun, a fabulous barrage of lightning fizzling the edges of silver clouds. A few minutes later, a little weather—wind gusting at twenty to thirty knots—sucked us in. Sheets of green water broke over the bow, as the sail tore at the seams.

"If this keeps up, we'll be sitting on eights and nines all the way," Ken said—and with a crack like that of bone snapping, the three-quarter-inch stainless-steel bracket holding the starboard winch fractured. Twenty pounds of stainless exploded past my head, shredding shrouds and canvas and taking out four feet of railing and safety stanchions. An inch or so to the left and my head would have been smashed; I'd have been dead before I knew it. A boat under sail is a firing squad of cocked ten-ton slingshots—whipping shrouds and snapping, decapitating steel.

Bananas's first response was to lay an arm protectively around my shoulders, using his big body as a shield against whatever was coming next.

"Fuck!" Ken screamed. "Drop it. Drop it. Bananas, *move.* Nothing on this boat is seaworthy. We're getting slaughtered. Eighteen miles in the right direction in the last twenty-four." He smacked the helm repeatedly with the heel of his hand. "Oh, you piece of shit."

The wind slammed us around for half an hour or so before stopping abruptly. The light got impossible. The sky to port, in full sunlight, was a stunning blue, shot through by vertical rays of orange; to starboard, a double rainbow hung by an incandescent beam. It was like nothing on earth and kept me from noticing what the others already knew. The dinghy we'd tied to the bow was torn up, a mere splash of yellow. Deflated. Useless.

"Welcome to blowboating with people who don't know shit from clay. You bullshit riggers! You bunch of bloody rummies! What was I thinking, swinging my dick with you fucking land-based people? Just idiocy," Ken shouted. He was happy to be angry. He liked nothing better than enemies.

Bananas folded his arms across his chest, waited for the tirade to end, and said, "Four days, we've gone a few miles, blown some shit off the deck, used a bit of diesel. We're okay."

"Bananas, I hate you more every day," Ken snapped. "Asshole!"

"I'd rather be an asshole and enjoy my life. I come from *duh*."

"*Duh?*"

"Yeah. Who-*duh*-fuck-knows."

"Well, that *duh* will kill you."

"No matter. *Living* will kill me."

The next day our jerry-rigged repairs failed, and ten tons of sheer load-force let go. The shrapnel stanchions and whipping lines tore up another piece of deck and a couple more feet of railing.

Twenty-four/seven the wind gave us nothing. The clutch was slipping, and we were making less than three knots in the wrong direction with the engine cranked. Some three thousand miles to the east, a big hot-air mass blowing out of the Sahara slammed into the cold Atlantic wall, and a bundle of disarranged weather exploded. A week later the first weather alert we wouldn't receive was broadcast.

Alberto, the first named storm of the Atlantic hurricane season, was running west. We were skirting the edges of it, working the wind shifts. Grabbing anything we could, crabbing, sailing east and north, looking for the trades that would blow us west and south.

We were coming up on Silver Banks, seventeen miles to the northwest. Jim was climbing up from below, talking. I could hear him before I could see him.

"Many a treasure ship was taken by pirates near to here. They don't call it Silver Banks because of its color." And then, without segue, he said, "We got a bit of a problem. One tank's dry. The other's got ten, maybe twenty gallons left."

"We'll go for another four-five hours and then tack, see what kind of lift we get," Ken said. Turning, he began shouting out to the horizon, "C'mon squally! C'mon! Lift! Give me lift." He was grinning when he turned toward me. "We're sailing from now on, mate. We got just enough to recharge the batteries and motor up to the fuel dock. Nothing for emergency."

Heat and air and water and dusk and dawn crowded together. We passed through the Mona Passage and spent a miserable night fighting the beating waves and currents of August. Running off the banks and over those deep canyons, the sea became confused, the water lumpy. That night the sky was huge and full of other planets, but by dawn there was enough haze in the air so that the sun rose a pale disk.

There was a little wind.

Next afternoon the little wind got big fast.

Wind is air in motion; its root is to wander. In the Oxford English Dictionary, its definition takes up nine and a half two-column small print pages. In Arabic the wind is called *ruh*, meaning breath and spirit. The breath of the universe, the Chinese say, is called the wind. In Hebrew, the word is *ruach,* which reverberates to include the concepts of divinity, creation. In Greek it's *pneuma* and in Latin *animus,* both of which are redolent not just of air, but of the very stuff of soul, of life itself; of Gaia herself, alive and breathing. No wind. No life. Emptiness.

There are winds and then there are the big winds, the monsters. In the North Atlantic they are called hurricane, after the Mayan storm god, *hunraken.* They're called *huracan* by the Taino in Antilles, *hyoracan* by the Galibi in Guiana, and *aracan* or *huiranvucan* by the Caribs. They're a *hurleblast* in old Caribbean and *jimmycane* in Jamaican patois. In the Indian Ocean it is a cyclone, from the Greek *kyklon* (or coiled snake); in the China Sea, a typhoon, from *ty fung* (or great wind); in the Philippines a *baguoi*; in Japan *reppu*; in

Australia, a *willy-willy*; and in the Arabian Gulf it is an *asifa-t* (or whirlwind).

But by whatever name, this is the mightiest of all windstorms. A full-fledged hurricane is a huge, self-sustaining heat engine a hundred times larger than a thunderstorm, a thousand times more powerful than a tornado. An average storm can precipitate about 20,000,000,000 tons of water a day, the energy equivalent of a half million A-bombs. In 1737 a cyclone at Calcutta destroyed 20,000 boats and drowned 200,000. In 1970 an unnamed cyclone hit the coast of Bangladesh, killing perhaps 300,000. The highest wind ever officially recorded during a hurricane was a gust of 185 miles an hour from the 1938 "Long Island Express," which swept up the eastern United States, though observers of Camille, a hurricane that ravaged the Gulf of Mexico in 1969, claim evidence for wind gusts of up to 215 miles an hour.

At sea such winds can generate waves more than sixty-five feet high, and meteorologists suggest that waves of eighty feet or more are probably not uncommon. L. Draper, in a 1961 article titled "Freak Ocean Waves" published in the journal *Weather,* reported that during a 1933 typhoon the USS *Ramapo,* on patrol in the North Pacific, encountered a wave of more than 110 feet from trough to crest.

The average life of an Atlantic hurricane is about nine days. In that time it will travel two thousand miles or more while sending out waves that travel ahead of the storm at speeds of more than thirty miles per hour. These heavy swells have an ominously slow beat pounding on distant shores, three to four a minute compared to the average seven to ten. Boom. Boom. Boom. Like the war drums of an approaching army, warning, *Beware;* an ominous orchestral soundtrack, the voice of doom.

Hurricanes are hatched in the Cape Verde Basin, ironically, in the doldrums, ten degrees or more north of the equator, off the coasts of Senegal, Guinea, Sierra Leone. All are disturbances that begin as just a bit of low pressure over a hot spot on the late summer tropical ocean, just a small vortex of heat over water with some hot, humid air rising, spiraling upward, cooling, condensing—a long, twisting trough of chaotic air. Clouds form, rain falls, and energy is released, warming the air, strengthening the updraft; more moisture-laden air rushes in, the spiral spins faster—a centrifugal effect, a partial vacuum now also draws air from the upper atmosphere down into the core, into the heat mass in the growing heart of darkness.

And now it begins to undulate, moving toplike, slowly at first, westward with the sun; but as it spins, clockwise in the southern hemisphere, anticlockwise in the north, it slides away from the equator, deflecting in a long parabolic curve back to the east, crossing the fifteen-twenty fracture zone, the Barracuda Ridge, continually feeding, continually gaining speed and power. When its wind speeds reach force twelve, 72 miles an hour, the system is upgraded by the NOAA, the National Oceanic and Atmospheric Administration, to hurricane status and given a name. By the time it hits the Puerto Rico Trench, it either keeps curving, running into the Caribbean, or skids north up the middle of the ocean, where the cold ocean cools its ardor, reducing it to a fey Atlantic depression. Alberto took that course, but spawned, as he turned his back on us, a squall, a vagrant bit of ugliness.

"Major shit." Ken's eyes were bright with the rush of adrenaline. "It's out there now. I can feel it. Let the headsail out about two feet. We gotta start sailing. It's going to get bloody kinky."

The day had started with heaps of white cotton-candy, fair-weather cumulus scudding. There were shifting mirages—islands, palm trees bending to offshore breezes, breaching whales, black backs glistening. It had rained a little in the night and the air felt freshened, but by ten the wind began to get chopped up and shifty.

There was a clump of sea grapes from who knows where hanging from an anchor chain. As the morning passed, the ocean turned more lumpy, with heavy invisible swells, great Atlantic rollers. Then finally, with the genoa (the big triangular jib up front) full-out and with the torn main tied down, we began sailing pretty—making eight to ten knots, butting through the August seas, not exactly in the right direction, but on a reasonable tack, with the stereo blasting out the reggae of Rasta-man Peter Tosh, just a-wailing: "Walking in the Future."

About one, we began to see lofty wispy cirrus, looking like the sun's eyelashes, with whipped silver, icy-looking spumes trailing off to the west, dropping below the horizon. Thunder boomers in full sunlight, a curious green light, and a dark tumescent cloudbank piled high on the eastern horizon. From the same direction, long swells rolling in long, even intervals rolled up to meet a fuzzy sky and sun.

About two, the wind turned southeasterly, quickening as it veered, and with it came a shower ghosting across the water, hissing on the hot deck as it sometimes hisses across a meadow, blowing crests and troughs in the waves of tall, late summer weeds and grasses.

"Jim, what's the barometer doing?" Ken asked.

"Free fall."

The air tensed, and smooth sheets of altostratus formed, thin enough to let the sun shine through, as if through green glass. And now visible in the almost evilly hot sky, a strung-out smear of ugly beauty, spirals of hungry air, a great black-domed cloud mass loomed, and lightning spinners advanced in a phalanx, like death on the run. I felt strangled in the steamy vaporous air, the flood of poisonous heat. In seconds rain—huge drops—soaked us.

"Look at that. Sonofabitch!" Ken was louder than usual. His face was luminous. "This is my passion, George. I love sailing boats to their max."

"Major fucking weather. Major fucker," someone shouted, maybe me.

Thin tendrils like octopus legs twisting outward accelerated swiftly over the water, changing the aqua surface to foam, spume, and black-green doom. A universe emptied of hope.

"Hold on, boys." Bananas was grinning. What was left of his hair was plastered to his skull in dripping snakes.

Then the squall line, a heavy black wall, a voracious air-sucking cumulonimbus, dropped and the sun failed. Wind in bursts. Cascades of foaming breakers like whipped cream beating over the bow. Darts of horizontal rain. Wave-top spray in sheets. Stays, shrouds, and backstays flapping. The tone of the rigging rising to a shriek.

Out of habit I wiped my glasses, and in an attempt to keep them dry pulled a long-billed fishing cap low over my eyebrows. It had Bananas's e-mail address, irbananas@hotmail.com, and a question—*How's my driving?*—embroidered on the crown. It blew away. I looked up just in time to watch the windbugger blow apart, the blades and odd mechanical bits following the cap.

With her low-slung lines and thirty-five tons of cement beneath her deck, the *Lady M* climbed the creaming slopes of waves, slipped through the roaring torrents, sank back in the troughs, riding it out. Not too bad—we'll make it, I thought, until I heard Ken's warning shout, "Hold on. Here she comes, she's almost on us."

We had come to the edge of the world. There was no sky. No difference between ocean and air. No horizon. There was nothing but frothing walls of waves that swept toward us—jagged and thrust-up slate mountains of ocean— an unbroken, impenetrable wall of rain. Time stopped. It was forever. Heeling over to the gunnels—pitching, rolling, yawing, heaving, surging, rollercoastering. Ken madly worked the helm to keep her into the wind. Jim and I held on, trying to keep the forward hatch closed, the sea out.

Fingers of lightning clawed close around us, and where they struck, the ocean was torn apart. There was an explosion of molecules shattering, of burning air and boiling water—an explosion that turned the sea to a white, flaring nova of blinding incandescence, so dazzling it erased what was left of sensation, erased even the horizontal spears of stinging rain and hurtling water. The sound was overwhelming, a deafening shriek filled with more horror than anything I could remember except the time I saw a pack of coyotes disembowel a fawn in the Willow Valley. Then, as now, I shivered so my teeth chattered.

How deep is a fathom? Six feet, same as a grave.

Ken, again the samurai, noticed none of it. Not the sound or the color. Not the fear. He knew only the exhilaration of being in the zone, awake, where everything is one point of space and time; knew only the movement of the boat under his feet, the helm, the direction of the wind, the feel of the water. Mindless intuitive perfection. *Don't think. Just do.* It's that fierce moment of face-to-face confrontation. Zen practice number one: spit out the truth or die.

The engine, a Perkins 85, cried like a baby, and the mizzen came apart. Bananas rushed up on deck without a lifeline, fighting the wind to save the sail. He still looked to be having fun when he disappeared into a wave high as a house.

"Bananas is gone." Jim shouted. "I can't see him. I think that wave took him. Fuck! *Fuck!* Bananas, you there? Beeeeeeee!"

"Stupid sonofabitch." Ken shouted, impervious to all but the water and the screaming wind.

I was pumping with adrenaline and suddenly so intoxicated with the idea that we were all about to die that I inexplicably started to laugh. Fear is never the appropriate response. There's no reason to collapse with grief before the icy terra incognita of death. But I do; I always do. I wasn't wired for stoicism, the supreme

courage of indifference. Still, I never wanted to be the stupid bastard who didn't have sense enough to enjoy his own death, the last
thing after all I would ever do. I still have no real sense of mortality;
I've yet to shed that particular naïveté of youth. I say I do, but I
don't truly believe it, don't believe in the end of my consciousness. I
will continue. Everyone dies but me. I will go on and on. To taste it
once is to taste it forever—life and death. Love also. A leap in the
dark with no possibility of returning to what was before.

Goodbye, Bananas, I was thinking as he fell back into the cockpit, looking extraordinarily elated and light as a feather. His feet
were dancing and his eyes were big and getting brighter and
brighter. He was marked, everywhere the rain had hit him, with
red dots, like a baby with the measles. He was beautiful with life,
on top of the world with no roof. And it was contagious—oh
yes!—and again I experienced the weird delight, the spaciousness
of freedom from worry; the voluptuous sensation of being on the
verge of discovery, on the verge of the future; the sensation of loving everybody, of loving the world.

"Fucking asshole. . . fucking asshole. . . you fucking *asshole!*"
Jim's voice rose with the storm to a shriek as we locked into a hug.

After that it was a ride. All of it fun, another kind of dream, no
waiting for the resurrection—just the overwhelming, unavoid-
able, unstoppable *now*—as necessary as wind. Heavy weather,
love, passionate intensity—only the over-the-top counts as life; all
the rest is ash.

It was a baby as storms go, most likely a category 1 on the Saffir-
Simpson Hurricane Scale, as compared to storms in tougher cate-
gories: the stone-cold killers, the category 5 hurricanes with winds
that can top 150 miles per hour and on average cause two hundred–plus times the damage of a category 1 storm. Now all that
was left of it was a little swell, and to the west a black line ruled as

if by a straight edge across the sea, and the memory of terror among the tangle of our gear. The sky was unbelievably blue, a deep shade running toward purple; the air, washed clean and sweet with salt and ozone, carried the hope of a westerly. The new, soft ocean—cobalt, sapphire, turquoise—lipped the hull as trails of sea-weed followed in our wake.

What happened was the same old story. Ten days overdue, with some luck and thirty gallons of fuel from the coast guard ship *Northland,* we made Puerto Rico, San Juan harbor, looking ourselves a lot like the *Lady M:* beat, disreputable, older than ever.

"*Sudah!*" said Jim on our arrival.

"*Sudah?*"

"It's an Indonesian word, George. Means 'enough.' 'That's all, the end.'"

"*Sudah!*" I repeated with feeling, eternally grateful to be off the water.

First thing I did was call my wife. The telephone booth was rocking. Sea legs.

"Sweetheart."

"Thank god," she said.

"I'm fine. I love you."

"Not a minute too soon. I just took a couple of Valium . . . was about to call the coast guard. A few days ago, I think it was, there was a news bulletin on NPR, something about a storm in the Atlantic. It was five a.m. I was half-asleep but sat bolt upright, because I knew you were there. I knew it would find you. 'That fucking asshole!' I said."

"How's my daughter?"

"Cooler than I am. What happened?"

"We had a few problems."

"I'm sure you did." She sniffed. I could see her nose scrunch. "You're full of shit," she said. She must have smiled, for a little of that teasing lilt had crept into her voice. "Now just come home. *Now*. But just for a while. This changes nothing. I still love you with all my heart. I don't think I can live with you. I think you need to go."

I swallowed hard but was silent. There was no use begging. I was drowning. "I won't be long. Another week or two."

"*Or two*. No doubt," she said.

After I talked to my daughter, who was angry and less willing to forgive, I called the old man at Master Lo Tu's place in the Bronx, thinking he too would be worried.

"Hello, Tsung Tsai, how are you? It's George. I've come back. I'll be home soon," I said in a rush.

He grunted, cleared his throat, spit into what sounded like a tin can. In the pause that followed, I could hear his wheeze.

He asked, "Georgie, you have be somewhere?"

III
Lost in Paris

Autumn 2002 to Summer 2003

The heart is pleased by one thing after another.
            —Archilochus, Greek warrior and poet

We are of one flesh, but separated like stars.
            —Henry Miller, Tropic of Capricorn

16

I went to see Tsung Tsai when I returned from the Caribbean the first week of September 2002. It was still four months before I would leave my family and—just after the New Year—*run George, run* for Paris. He'd called early on a blustery autumn morning to tell me he would be at his cabin in Woodstock the next afternoon.

The conversation was peculiar from the start.

"Georgie, you must come quickly. Tomorrow in afternoon. I be there only little time. Few hours. I need find some special paper, then go away. Korea monks pick me."

"Where are you going?"

"I don't like say."

"How long will you be gone?"

"Maybe long time. Who can know?"

"I'll be there about two," I said.

"Good time. Bring bagel," he said. "I make tea."

The rutted road up to his house was more rutted that September. Nothing else had changed except that the wood pile we'd cut and stacked a few years back was weathered grayer, sagging a bit with dry rot.

That had been a good day. There'd been no talk. Only rice and tea and work: *you must be work*. There'd been the simple perfection of growth rings, of stump and ax and swing, of grunt, of wedge and mall and crack, of exhaustion, of sweat and thirst. As much as anything, I'd loved splitting, with him, that cord of firewood, newly hauled and bucked. The weather that day had been balmy; bright, sharp-angled sun, the air warm, dry, sweet.

Now, though, I knew only one thing was certain: Tsung Tsai wasn't going back to Mongolia. He had finished with that now. He was on to other things. But I asked anyway.

"I thought you needed to burn your teacher. That it was your karma. That not to do so was bad for your life," I teased.

He didn't take the bait. He shrugged and said, "I change. I have no time for you now, Georgie. Too old, me!" He slapped his chest. "I need work. Oh, very much now I need do research on numbers and emptiness."

Tsung Tsai sat on a folding metal card chair, his legs crossed under him half-lotus, almost imperceptibly rocking. He closed his eyes, and still he rocked. He'd gone somewhere I couldn't get to, so I waited for him to come back. Above his head a piece of soot from the woodstove was falling in slow-slow motion. It was mesmerizing, like watching one of those time-lapse nature photography films where a seed sprouts, grows, matures, opens into a flower, and wilts in about five seconds.

Suddenly his eyes popped open. "Yes-yes-true. I tell you, Georgie, this kind research, only monk can do. Must be me. And now I need talk to Korea. They have knowledge."

"About what? What kind of knowledge?"

Tsung Tsai squinted. "Special kind," he said. "Very few people can understand."

"Can you explain it to me?"

He shook his head. "Now doesn't work. Maybe later. Now is too hard for you. Tsung Tsai closed his eyes and again went silent. He leaned elbows on the table and cupped both his hands, fingers interlaced, atop his head and rocked faster. After what seemed an interminable silence, he said, "Also you need be careful. Watch for hungry ghosts who look like people, exactly same as people, but not real people." He marched his fingers double-time across the table. "They walk-walk-walk and talk-talk-talk, but never know life. So you must be careful listen. Then you must be looking. Easy for you. No problem. You are good looker. Just look. But take nail steps because path hangs over emptiness. Where is broken you need on toes to jump. Very concentrated. Even if fall is ten thousand feet, try not to shake." He leaned back in his chair, crossed his arms over his chest and sighed, deeply satisfied that he had given me "best advice," another unimpeachable road map to follow.

I scratched and remembered reading somewhere about a disease of the Mongolian steppe that causes unappeasable itching of the testicles. I nodded.

He uncrossed his arms and held them out toward me, hands opened in seeming supplication. "Georgie, I'm sorry but I need say that you are too tied by beauty, sometimes like flower."

Too tied by beauty, sometimes like flower.

"Can you understand?"

I'm always concerned about not understanding, about missing the important. "I'm not sure," I said.

What I got back was annihilation from all directions. Tsung Tsai—*wham*—slapped the table with the flat of his hand. "Not sure means you can't understand. This make me very uncomfortable. How can you find out anything? This moment sensitive. This moment shadow in my mind." He shook his head and clucked. "You can't understand. I teach you *many* times. Very philosophy."

The wind yodeled. The setting sun through the window was blinding. I was wandering, following his thoughts as best I could.

At times it was like listening to a language I'd never heard before, but almost understood, its sentences resonating, echoing in my head like Mozart, Dexter Gordon's ballads, and the poetry of the T'ang masters. Teasing and coaxing.

Too tied to beauty, sometimes like flower.

"Sometimes you cannot hear. Sometimes big mouth. Sometimes mad-dog mind. Now maybe just confusion. In future maybe no." Tsung Tsai pulled on his ear. The sun dropped behind the tree line opposite the meadow, splintering branches. The sky was a gorgeous deep cerulean pool.

"If you find out truth, you don't care, don't need answers." He continued working that ear. "But in this life, if you don't do that, you like nothing. So go be travel. Work. Write book like soul. Tell the people only what you know is true."

"I'm sure that's the idea. I'm just not sure I know what is true. All my memories are maybe only stories or dreams. Sometimes true feels like someplace I've never been."

My wife had said, "I've never met anyone less concerned with the facts, with the truth."

"That's the truth," I said.

But then the truth is boring because it's not really the truth or it's only the truth in a very limited way. Memory doesn't know fact from fiction. Facts are opaque, muddy waters. There's only interpretation. Everything passing through mind is fiction. All memory a process, an act of imagination—the past a riff, an ever-changing improvisation, always altering, always enhancing. And if you're a writer, facts are just the formless clay, something you need to dominate, twist to the needs of the story at hand. To surround a subject fully requires synthesis, a collage—essay, novelistic narrative, autobiography, history, flights of imagination, poetry.

Memory pretends because just as inflation can grow a whole universe from an ounce of primordial stuff, an ounce of vacuum, so can the imagination create from a smidgen of information a new world. It is, for god and us, the ultimate free lunch. Creative non-fiction.

When W. B. Yeats was told by his friend, the poet and painter George Russell, that his memoir had hardly a single fact accurate, Yeats answered, "I do not want accuracy. I only want a picturesque sentence."

Way to go, William.

"Everyone is right," a famous French writer wrote. "Things become true as soon as someone believes in them." I passed that thought on to Tsung Tsai.

"Zen idea same. Must bend," Tsung Tsai said, with an approving smile and nod. The good-natured finger he wagged in my face was crooked. His knuckles and finger joints, I noticed for the first time, were swollen, distorted by arthritis. He seemed suddenly aged. "Now you must begin. But if you write only my little story," he was both shaking and wagging, "not enough. Please, Georgie. You must make bigger."

Tsung Tsai sat by the window, silhouetted by the last blue light of the day. It was already dark in his kitchen, so I couldn't see his eyes. We sat in silence. He closed his eyes and went away. I wrote what I wanted to say in my notebook:

All writing is plagiarized and forged, made up of bits and pieces of other work. Some of me. Some of them. The subconscious collage. A little of this. A little of that. I'm trying for a style that is as effortless as speech, as whimsical as dreams. Something like the Sung dynasty aesthetic, when the supreme goal was to become a sage and the highest form of literary art was the sui-pi or pi-chi—literally, the pen jottings; a kind of notebook containing hundreds and thousands of short pieces and fragments ranging from scholarship and poetry, to songs of love and yearning, to laments, to trivia and foolery of every sort. Just talk. A bullshit jam. One man telling another of the happenings in his mind. A kind of telepathic story, direct without any intermediaries or impairments. The rules are simple: learn everything, read everything, and above all be flexible—that is, thieve.

Soon as I finished writing, he opened his eyes and began again. "Zen idea same. Must bend. Like noodle. Also forget everything I say. Talk is only mental. Remember only wisdom. Pity the people. Navigate the world with kindness. Then you can write new book. Then you can be okay. Maybe okay. Very danger. And don't take knife. Cruel. Very cruel. That is bad religion. Bad roots. Poison roots."

I'd never grown used to Tsung Tsai's apparent psychic powers, which came without warning out of left field and seemed so ordinary to him but were so contradictory to my version of reality. Those powers so much belonged to that bleating nitwit New Age realm of sensibility that they always pricked my certainty to the point of irritation, though I promised now, without question or sarcasm, not to take the knife I'd never told him I had and he had no way of knowing about.

When we said goodbye that evening the night was full of little sounds. It was just after sunset and, as was his habit, Tsung Tsai walked with me out to the sweet '67 Pontiac my good friend Jeff M. had lent me. Tsung Tsai waved as I drove off. I had my own moment of premonition, so terrifyingly real that I shivered and was happy to remember there were four fingers of some smooth Audry cognac left in the bottle in the bookcase. The thought had crossed my mind that I would never see him again. This man I loved. My spiritual father. It was pure selfishness. I had arrived at his door a barbarian and was still hoping to leave as a human being. But at this moment Tsung Tsai was tired of me and I of him. It was time to move on again. Find another teacher. Come back to Tsung Tsai another time. Or never. Murphy had it right. Everything that can go wrong will go wrong.

I braked to a stop in a shower of gravel, rolled down the window. He was gone. I shouted into the darkness. "Tsung Tsai, I'll miss you."

"Me too, Georgie," he shouted back.

I'd gotten the knife with the advice of Sean C., a California guitar-playing poet and warrior. Son of a special forces colonel, Sean looks to be made, like the knives he loves, of tempered steel. He's been a movie stuntman, a bouncer, a bodyguard. He teaches Kenpo-Jujitsu along with his own specialty, Basic Blade, the knife arts.

"I've studied several blade styles," he told me, "but I got my most important lessons on street corners, in dark alleys, in nightclubs, and from some wise old soldiers."

In the living room of his Topanga Canyon house, he taught me, in under an hour, one killing move: the reverse hammer grip and swing thrust. "The point of your blade should impact somewhere between your attacker's inner thigh and, depending on his height, his lower abdomen."

There were a few other words of advice. "Be treacherous. Never give an assailant any kind of chance. I can't stress this enough. A blade fight can be, *should* be, over in a second, leaving someone maimed or dead. Don't be the dead one! If you want to fight fair, go be a boxer. Good luck. Be careful. Run if you can."

The knife, a folding Emerson CQB7, was developed for use by the military, particularly the special forces. It was a beautiful thing, terrifying in its black-bladed singular perfection. It had been made with one purpose in mind: to maim or kill. I held it lovingly and practiced until the move Sean had taught me became sinuous and thoughtless, second nature. I don't know why I loved touching this masterpiece of clean steel and even less why I so diligently practiced the killing thrust. For defense, my court of last resort, I told myself. For the place that Sun Tzu, the ancient Chinese sage of war, called the dying ground:

> *When you will survive if you fight quickly*
> *or perish if you do not,*
> *this is called the dying ground.*

Still, I don't know if I could, in the no-mind live-or-die moment— and at lightning speed—strike. Make the cut. The kill. Probably not.

Survival, as Picasso saw it, was the highest human imperative. What it is to be human is to be strong and survive; the rest is sentimental rubbish. But of course he was an ego-maddened prick, a savage, who rumor has it had no pubic hair.

Survival is Darwinism, pure and simple. Biology and destiny. Atavistic theater. There are winners and losers, the scream and the silence.

> *Under the lights*
> *it's a hundred and one*
> *in the shade for the fight*
> *between two up-and-comers,*
> *the boxer and the puncher.*
> *Potentials both,*
> *but the loser goes nowhere,*

slow and painful—
no-future-no-big-bucks.
So the blood is up
and Badass fires out dancing,
shooting jabs,
hard and fast,
a steady diet,
bap-bap-bap and . . .
And . . . Rojas throws the big right,
too slow.
The Badass express had left the station,
and so Rojas left,
in the seventh.
It's sad but that's the kick;
atavistic theater,
delicious biology,
winners
and losers.

Zen it was, a kind of Zen. The perfection of Zen after all is to live life spontaneously, without illusion. The world is form, not substance. Matter does not exist; atoms and human beings are not things; they are patterns, like ripples in water—persistent patterns—and our brains are imagination machines that create an inner world to look at the outer. The Zen master Yen Hui told Confucius that he had acquired the art of sitting and forgetting. When asked what he meant, he said, "To discard my body, abandon intelligence and matter and so become impervious to perception." By this method he became, he said, "one with the all."

By the time I got back home a new sliver crescent of moon was up, and the stars were visible. The last fragments of cloud had scattered. After dinner, and after I'd written up my notes and stared into space, the anxiety I felt leaving the old man lifted, and I lifted; lifting, lifting, lifting in every corner a leg to the dance. Part excitement, part terror; I understood once again that every moment, every sticky moment was a blessing and a nightmare.

Even so, if I should die tonight my obituary would be short:

> Crane laughed a lot, read a bunch of fine books, and survived longer than anyone, including himself, would have guessed or bet on, but he couldn't hide the free-floating pissed-offness that he should have gotten over at nineteen, when it's at least understandable for one to stew in one's own dark hormonal juices, when one thinks one understands it all. Crane held a few odd jobs, worked at poetry, wrote one critically successful travel memoir, had numerous lovers, married three times, had one glorious daughter, loved dogs, was a bad husband, father, and provider; he was a burden to his friends, a failed Buddhist; he left a second book unfinished.

But it was just a cold, a stuffed nose—the bullshit of the claustrophobic drama queen. I'd live.

I'd best live. I'm a work in progress.

Heeding Tsung Tsai's warning, I'd given the knife to Bananas for Christmas, just before I left for Paris. And so here I am in France, now knifeless, closing in on senior citizenship, bankrupt and on the run. My agent has refused to advance me even a paltry five thousand against my brightly shining future. Who could blame him? Reality is somewhere I've never been. I've always been the biggest damn moron in the world about money that I was certain would show up in time to save the day. Sometimes it didn't.

I had no phone. No permanent address but e-mail. My credit

was shot. The book I had contracted for with Harper Collins was slipping away from their November deadline. My wife and daughter were on another continent, and sliding slowly farther and farther away from me on my persistent undercurrent of homesickness, of longing for a life that now existed only in kaleidoscopic snatches—memories and dreams, succulent fragments and hashish vapors. I missed and was angry at myself for losing my wife. Sometimes I saw her face, eyes wide open, taking as much as possible in, when we were making love.

a woman haunts
until you find another
that haunts
a life . . .
a woman haunts
even if you find another
that haunts,
that haunts . . .

Everything I still owned—twenty boxes of mostly books, along with odd treasures picked up over the years—was in storage as I was always moving. I'd gone primal. The nauseating press of responsibility had lifted, and beneath the guilt, the whole percussive sadness of things, hummed a bar of pure joy that is freedom. The song of a hopeless sociopath if one goes by the new rules; a spiritual pilgrim, like some Chinese ancient, if one follows the old ways.

There was flux, the always occurring accidents of the moment, and my fortune cookie fortune:

You are a traveler at heart.
There will be many journeys.
Lucky numbers: 1, 14, 17, 24, 25, 32.

And so I would travel as if I were some Zen monk—albeit a broken one. The Chinese ideogram for *monk* translates as "wandering boy;" the monk's job is to bring enlightenment, compassion to the world. Nice work if you can get it, but more than I could hope for; I was a bad bet, not just for permanence but for saintliness. But then again, as the man sez: one never know, do one?

Everything I needed for the next leg of my escape was packed in two small duffels, along with a backpack for my tools—laptop, GPS, camera, microcassette, batteries, charger, notebook, pens, and the various maps I always carried when traveling, an odd and ever-changing collection, my current dream lines. For this trip I had chosen to take, almost at random, a chart of the North Atlantic Ocean showing the West Indies, with magnetic variation curves, depths and heights in meters, and doubtful data reported but indicated by encircling dotted lines, from Blue Water Books and Charts in Fort Lauderdale (published by the Defense Mapping Agency Hydrographic/Topographic Center in Bethesda); a map of China and one of northern China published by Nelles Verlag of München; a travel map of Mongolia from ITMB Publishing in Vancouver, Canada; an indexed map of China and Mongolia published by Cartographia of Germany; CIA-compiled maps of Mongolia and China (numbers 503358 and 802528 respectively); a sketched map showing Mongolian trade routes, compiled and drawn by Owen Lattimore in 1926 with a notation showing the location of the House of the False Lama; a map of the Mongolian Empire, Central Asia, circa CE 1330, showing principal trade routes; a map of Persia circa CE 1370 after the fall of the II-Khans; a map of the principal voyages of discovery to America, 1492 to 1611, with unexplored territory shown in white; Napoleon's campaign in Egypt, 1798; Europe in 1812, showing the Empire of the French States (that is, those either under the control of or allied with

Napoleon) and the independent states (that is, Portugal, the United Kingdom of Great Britain and Ireland, the Kingdom of Sweden, the Empire of Russia, the Ottoman Empire, the Protectorate of Lucca, the Kingdom of Sardinia, the Kingdom of Sicily, and the Ionian Islands); Europe after the Congress of Vienna, showing the boundary of the Germanic Confederation, 1815; a map of Paris; and the new pocket *Paris Classique par Arrondissement* with the *Plan Métro et RER, l'indispensable.*

Another map, pasted into my notebook, showed how, starting more than two millennia ago, East met West. At Xi'an, China's ancient capital, the caravan routes of the Silk Road—a vast conduit for cultures, languages, customs, and faiths—coursed across the deserts and mountains of High Asia and Persia, wending through Anxi, Turpan, Hotan, Kashi, Samarqand, Bukhara, Mary, Rey, Hamadan, Baghdad, Antioch, Tyre. It was also from Xi'an that travelers could make their way to Canton and other ports on the South China Sea, following maritime routes along the coast of China and Thailand into the Bay of Bengal and north up India's east coast to Calcutta and south to Mauritius, Barygaza, and Barbarican (Banbhore) before making the westward crossing of the Arabian Sea to Muscat, Sur, Kané, Aden, and Muza in Arabia, there to meet up with traders plying the East African trade lanes from Mombassa and Mogadishu. From there it was a west-by-northwest run up the Red Sea to Berenice and a short run, three hundred miles up the great Nile, to the fabled port city Alexandria, the Mediterranean Sea, the crossing to Tyre and Antioch, and the crossing past Turkey and Greece to Imperial Rome.

I always love running my index finger across the ancient routes of the traders and great wanderers, imagining the dream life of the monks, nomads, and outlaws who for thousands of years cross-pollinated the world's diverse cultures. I marvel every time that the

Turpan Depression—the northern wastes of the terrifying Takla-makan Desert in China's Inner Mongolia—and Rome in Italy both sit at approximately the same latitude.

I'd also packed a slender 1969 paperback, picked up one summer at the library book fair in Stone Ridge, New York. Titled *The Chinese Written Character as a Medium for Poetry,* it was an essay edited by Ezra Pound from the unfinished manuscript of poet and American Orientalist, Ernest Fenollosa (1853–1908), first published in the journal *Instigations* in London in 1920 and reissued by City Lights Books. It is also a map of sorts, offering the theory that the meaning of a word, the thing or concept it represents, is carried by imagery; that words are essentially pictures; that as the Chinese character is ideogrammic, so too, by extension, is the essential nature of language itself, imagistic and thus poetic, speaking at once with the vividness of painting and the mobility of sound, presenting the inherent drama that comes not from juggling mental encounters but from watching things work out their own fate. Dream lines again.

In my wallet I carried, along with a batch of defunct credit cards—so that I might, in the watchful eyes of the authorities, at least *look* solvent—a Guaranty Loan Office business card that advertised: DIAMONDS, WATCHES, JEWELRY, PISTOLS, GUNS, MUSICAL INSTRUMENTS, OLD GOLD, AND LUGGAGE BOUGHT AND SOLD. UNREDEEMED PLEDGES FOR SALE AT HALF PRICE. ALL BUSINESS STRICTLY CONFIDENTIAL. (OVER). And on the *over* was a poem titled "Pawnbrokers":

> *God bless pawnbrokers!*
> *They are quiet men.*
> *You may go once—*
> *You may go again—*
> *They do not question*
> *As a brother might;*

They never say
What they think is right;
They never hint
All you ought to know;
Lay your treasure down,
Take your cash and go,
Fold your ticket up
In a secret place
With your shaken pride
And your shy disgrace,
Take the burly world
By the throat again—
God bless pawnbrokers,
They are quiet men.

They are bodhisattvas. More or less.

Not long before I left for Paris to wait out the Mongolian winter
and my broken heart, I ran into the charismatic Tibetan Buddhist
scholar, lecturer, writer, and famous father Robert Thurman at a
friend's sixtieth birthday party—her last, AIDS was killing her.

"How you doing?" Another one-eyed buddha, he stuck out a
huge hand to shake mine. "Still trying to find Shambhala?" There
was humor and more than a touch of sarcasm coloring the question.

"Yes, of course." I laughed. "Aren't we all? I leave next month,"
I said with a certainty that was pure fiction.

"Good luck, then."

"Thanks, I need all I can get," I said as he went to hold court in
the living room and I turned back to the kitchen where the still-
crazy-after-all-these-years, pushed by wine and weed, traded
monologues.

In 1901, a frozen mammoth's cock was discovered by a party of hunters on the Berezovka River in Siberia. The organ was erect, nearly three feet long, and (having been flattened in the icy tundra) eight inches in diameter. The beast's testicles, equally frozen, were tucked inside the overlying carcass. The meat was dark and marbled, like perfectly aged beef. The men ate the testicles, broiling them over their campfire. They were still sweet after being frozen for something like 44,000 years.

The above, my current party fave, I'd stolen from an old friend, that fine but unheralded poet R.B., who wants only to find in life a bit of recognition, but whose social gifts aren't strong enough, obsessive enough, to overcome an uninterested world, to overcome failure and fear of failure. He phones from time to time, always after midnight, to regale me with some bit of marvelous minutia culled from the flotsam and jetsam just washed ashore his consciousness.

Fantástico.

"Hello," I said.

The last time he called he started straight in. "David Ignatow [the great American poet who died just a few years ago] in his notebook admitted that, like Gide, he continued masturbating through his fifties."

"Ditto," I said.

"Despair," he said, "it's like a flame. You're drawn to it. You feel your wings burning. And still you fly closer."

I said, "Yes."

Two months before Paris, on a raw late October afternoon in up-
state New York, the last of the summer's one-winged catalpa spears
were spinning down on the slight breeze *tinging* the wind chime.
The radio was on, reminding that even time, which is god, has its
seasons:

> *fall back*
> *remember to turn back*
> *those clocks*
> *remember*
> *fall back tonight*
> *one hour*
> *the radio kept reminding*
> *that afternoon;*
> *an afternoon when*
> *while walking the meadow*
> *with my dog Bird*
> *he froze into a point*
> *when a cricket wailed*

in the leaf mulch,
in the sweet syrupy decay
of turning back.

The meadow was murmur, curve, and bare bluestone bone. By the middle of November it had turned oddly almost warm. Lost in a perfect sky, in the celebration underfoot of crisp burnt umber, sepia, and ocher, I turned and walked into a tree. That same day I broke my nose wrestling with the dog, and while examining my scratched face and again swollen schnozola in the mirror noticed my eyebrows; my eyebrows, my friends, were going gray. Going, going, going . . .

That day, which had begun in Indian summer, turned soupy gray and freezing again, with rain and then snow blowing around my head. With the days piling, weighing, I wanted only against the cold and pain of our separation to hole up, to stroke between thumb and first finger the arc of my lips or my beard at the chin and remember times when we were young.

An almost-winter flux, ominous and beautiful, scudding clouds; that night was thick with hungry ghosts. My wife and I, with the season, mused on change; about not only our broken marriage, but our losses in general and those of friends, of family—the failure of art and careers, the debts, the debilitating illnesses, the insanities, divorces, suicides, and other deaths.

"Mother had no friends—nowhere to go for comfort, no one to talk to. She'd married badly. And so she drank," my wife said, brushing her hair by the fire.

Through the skylight, the nights of memories passed. There were the stars. Implacable stars. Twinkle-twinkle.

Cold as Mongolia, from where, almost eight centuries ago, at about this time, after fattening and resting his horses in summer pastures, Genghis Khan and his armies—led by General Subotai, the greatest of his *four hounds*—attacked northern China. Coordinating as precisely as chess moves the movements of tens of thousands of men, across mountain ranges and in unknown territory, they began to systematically grind down the world's most populous, oldest, and most sophisticated civilization. The strengths of the Mongol army were speed, maneuverability, firepower, discipline, and an officer corps chosen for ability and not birth or favor. Not for centuries would there be an army as efficient at the gruesome business of leveling other people's countries. Cities fell and were destroyed; 30 percent of China's population was killed. For a time the invincible khan considered depopulating the whole of the north, plowing its cities under and converting it into one huge pasture for his horses. He was deterred from his goal only when an adviser dryly noted that the living pay more taxes than the dead.

On the morning of the last day of 2002, as time ran out on yet another year in the dolorous history of our species, I felt more than ever that there has always been little hope. But then the holiday season—Thanksgiving, Christmas, another birthday, New Year's Eve; December like bad breath, redolent of nostalgia and broken dreams, decay—has always rendered me melancholic, sappy.

A hard-boiled egg for breakfast? The smallest decisions were most difficult. There was snow, frozen air, and four long months before the equinox, that spring song. There was fear, the taste of adrenaline like copper on the tongue. There was intoxication: my obsessive passion wanted to be pregnant, said a baby is the universe. I can't disagree. Can't deny that female eminence, rooted in blood and earth, prevails over reason. I decided on espresso.

Let babies fall where they will.

At ten in the morning, after three cups, sopping up the last drops with a slice of cinnamon raisin, I also decided to get it over with (the year, that is)—outwit the old, in with the new—and lit in turn a pipe, a cigar, then popped the champagne and alone with the Kiribatians began celebrating the new year, 2003.

Kiribati, Oceania, which includes the area formerly known as the Gilbert Islands, is a string of thirty-three coral atolls (125°N, 172°E) in the Pacific Ocean, straddling the equator; the capital, Tarawa, is about halfway between Hawaii and Australia. The Gilbert Islands were granted self-rule by the United Kingdom in 1976, with complete independence and nationhood (as Kiribati) coming in 1979, when the United States relinquished, in a treaty of friendship, all claims to the sparsely inhabited Phoenix and Line island groups.

Then, on January 1, 1995, the people of Kiribati proclaimed that all of their country lies in the same time zone as its Gilbert Islands group (GMT +12)—even though the Phoenix Islands and the Line Islands are across the International Date Line—so ensuring that all Kiribatians would have the pleasures of being the first inhabited place on earth to ring in the new. An evolved people. Kissy. Kissy. Happy. Happy. So here's to you, my loves: *L'chaim. Again to life.*

Spinning back, bottle in hand, to my Kripplebush, New York, studio, I retrieved my new-book-ideas journal out from under a miscellaneous pile of uncorrected manuscript pages, unopened bills, unanswered mail, cutouts, and scraps. The notebook is thick, almost every page layered with scribbling and collage, a mélange of words and colors; the world tasted as accident rather than plan. The notebook that always made sense even when I didn't fell open to pages 106 and 107, where I'd pasted, folio style, two disparate news flashes straight from the wires of AP. Over and across both I'd scrawled, diagonally with a thick red marker, quoting D. H.

Lawrence, "Unless from us the future takes place, we are death only."

Macapá, Brazil, December 6
Renowned New Zealand Yachtsman Killed in Amazon
Sir Peter Blake, one of the world's leading yachtsmen, was shot and killed late Wednesday night when a gang of masked robbers boarded his vessel as it lay anchored in a harbor near the mouth of the Amazon River.

According to the local authorities, Sir Peter's yacht, the *Seamaster*, a 130-foot aluminum ketch-rigged research vessel, was attacked by a gang known as the Water Rats.

"It was a holdup, he resisted. They shot him twice," said Rosilene Serra, a police official in Macapá, a city of 250,000 people that is the capital of the state of Amapá, on the north bank of the Amazon.

Ulaanbaatar, Mongolia, September 14
Mongolia Accuses Archeologists
The location of Genghis Khan's grave is one of archaeology's enduring mysteries. According to legend, to keep it secret, his huge burial party killed everyone who saw them en route; the servants and soldiers at the funeral were also killed.

In the summer of 2002 digging at what is thought to be his tomb, a site called Oglogchiin Kherem—located 200 miles northeast of the Mongolian capital of Ulaanbaatar in Hentii province, the great Khan's homeland—revealed a series of flagstones covering long trenches. Horse teeth, animal bones and human skulls were found, but no grave was sighted.

"We hope to go back next year, but for now the future of the expedition is unknown," said University of Chicago historian John Woods.

The work was halted by order of Mongolian authorities after former Prime Minister Dashiin Byambasuren accused the team of driving cars over sacred soil and erecting tents near the historic walls.

"They have defiled the remains of the dead," the Associated Press reported, quoting Byambasuren. "I repeat, our ancestor's golden tomb has been disturbed and the purity of our burial places tainted for a few dollars. This place should remain pure for the souls of the dead."

Beneath this last paragraph, scribbled now in green marker (if nothing else I'm colorful) was this note: "Before Philippe Auguste left on his crusade in the year 1200 he built a wall to protect Paris. It was nine meters high and three meters wide at the base. A piece of it still stands in the Marais, in St. Paul. Another undertaking that needs to be nominated for a place of honor in the Universal Book of Human Vanities and Futilities."

This notebook, along with a couple of empties waiting for chance, was packed in my duffel bag when, on the morning of January 4, 2003, after the biggest nor'easter in a decade had blown through, leaving three feet of drifting snow, I would leave my family for Mongolia by way of Paris and Prague. It was a self-imposed exile. The whole family, Bird-dog included, piled into the trusty Outback and plowing through the drift blocking the driveway, followed the county plow down Oakley Road past the Oakley Farm and Sawmill. Once we made that right onto Krumville Road, we all knew we were home free for the run to the railway station on the Hudson River at Rhinecliff. Only the dog was happy.

•   •   •

Above the street noise of Paris, on rue Bonaparte, a horrible horn screamed and my thoughts strayed apropos the pawnbrokers: I wondered if alliteration is as natural to thought as rhyme.

To round out the moment, war was coming on full-tilt boogie. Like winter is a-comin' on. Lawd sing goddamn. The stupid drums were beating. All one heard was the dum-dum-dumming of cultures clashing, of American righteousness—thunder, darkness like a pincer closing to the attack. That infinite shit factory, the shitty carnivorous chaos called human history, teetered on the edge of an even more nightmarish future. Hope was a rare commodity. I was sometimes angry, sometimes frightened that my Zen wouldn't hold, though at the same time I'd never felt so strongly that I loved living. Life rises, and I still lusted after it so intensely that more and more I'd become insomniac, hating the terrible reality of unconsciousness. I wanted instead to forget ugliness in the dream that is life, wanted to be lost in dream not in sleep, allied, at least in matters of sleep, with Vladimir Nabokov, who wrote in *Speak Memory:*

All my life I have been a poor go-to-sleeper. Sleep is the most moronic fraternity in the world, with the heaviest dues and the crudest rituals. It is a mental torture I find debasing. No matter how great my weariness, the wrench of parting with consciousness is unspeakably repulsive to me.

Last night I peed on Pont Neuf, the oldest bridge in Paris, beneath the stern and watchful gaze of Henry IV's statue. Standing in the puddle I made, I looked up the Seine toward the Eiffel Tower. The Louvre was on my right, Notre Dame behind. Easy was cheering me on and guarding my back. After an extended cold spell, the evening was clear and mild. Reflections sparkled, spinning and undulating in the wake of a tour boat. A young couple embraced at center bridge, winding into each other. And a half bottle of a good

red, from Wine and Bubbles on rue Français in the first arrondissement, near Les Halles where North African musicians rapped on
the plaza fronting Saint Eustache, was nesting round the base of
my spine; also there was a chocolate bar of hashish, newly purchased from Joseph S., a brilliant, gentle, but sad-eyed expat poet,
zippered into the inside pocket of my old leather jacket.

It's January 2003, four months after I'd returned from hurricane
season in the Caribbean. I was still fighting the devils of debt and
work. Love and family. Monogamy. Desire versus detachment.
And losing on every front.

"You're miserable," my wife had said. "Often angry. Family life
doesn't suit you. And I can't take it any longer. You need to go.
Just go."

So now I seemed to be living the life of the chronic vagabond,
and I could see no end to it. Like a hermit crab moving from vacant
shell to vacant shell—this time a friend's Paris studio apartment. It
suited me perfectly—no alarm clock, no responsibilities, no plans
for tomorrow, completely dependent on the benevolence of others
and the luck of the draw. Perfect. It *was* perfect, I was trying to
convince myself. Just perfect. The highest priority was never again
to hear the telephone ring, to not be at the beck and call of any fool
who can afford the price of a call.

I had dropped out of time. Fallen through the rabbit hole. It
couldn't be 2003. It was more like the sixties, even to the fact that
another war was fast unfolding; the sweet, nauseating smell of
blood electrified the media; another chapter in the history of tears,
another crusade, the billion-footed mob blindly stirring, the sick-
ness that has no end.

A bank of fine mist drifted low over the Seine and under the
bridge.

•　　•　　•

This wasn't the first time that I had dynamited my life—three marriages and one long love affair blown away, two novels and god only knows how many poems abandoned. Not the first time that I had to glue everything back together, start again. It probably wouldn't be the last. There was never a last, until the last. I seem to be that kind of fool. Nonstop.

Noise troubled my dreams and I didn't sleep well. I woke in fits and starts. Failure was the working object of my self-analysis, as in *I am a failure*. All I had to do was look in the mirror to know how yesterday went.

What is the color of unhappiness? Pale.

In that reflection was grief for a marriage, a family life irretrievably lost, and the shadows that follow, those irrational fluctuations of consciousness that can at any moment give rise to heartache, paralyzing melancholia. Divorce like death. Loss. Loss. I was in mourning.

The next thing I knew I'd lost six months. I hadn't worked on the new book for almost the same amount of time. And though I was in Paris now, I was still planning to drop out of the West as best I could, by traveling to Mongolia, one of the planet's few remaining empty places—*here be dragons*—where there is an extraordinary poverty of life. But it would have to wait. I thought to hole up in Paris, as I once did in San Francisco—crash-pad nirvana. Save money, scheme; live on bread, cheese, espresso, wine, and words, all cheap highs. Wait for the SARS epidemic and my pain to burn out. Escape. The pleasure of going far foreign, that atavistic mental comfort, that soothing, that settling sense that divorce from one's time and culture brings; the distractions of survival and tasting the unknown, the new, the different. Change.

The theory was simplicity itself: when a relationship, when love shatters, put a continent at least—an ocean is better, half the globe is best—between you and what was. Run from complications, from that love, from the ruin of all that was and still is; run to where verbs are attached to no person, no number, no mood, no tense; to where all is process, process, process only; to where dreams are flat white in the distance beyond. There's a sweet, vaguely scary feeling in disappearance. A blank slate.

"Now you've done it, mate. Your wife has fallen out of love with you. Your daughter hates you," was what my friend English had said, rounding out, even more than usual for emphasis, those fat vowels.

"Pray for this year to go fast," he added. "This is not your year. But you're alive. It could be worse."

Why had I lived my life this way? Why indeed. Because it's made me happy. Because I get bored. And then surly. Because I've lusted after new lives, dramatic changes with no waiting, the intensity that an intentional fused stick of dynamite up the ass brings. Because I'm a fool.

I came back to what were the sweetest moments in life and missed what I had taken for granted and ached for what I had lost. Prophecy, hallucination, memory, vision, whatever you call consciousness, it makes no difference: all are ambiguous, subjective realities, nothing but an imaginative record. Nostalgia.

And perhaps nothing ever will be as lovely, as perfect, as the memory of our finding each other, of being young and in love that one summer. Ah, romance, the classic Hollywood cliché. It was August 1979, Lexington, New York, the northern Catskills: that first kiss, our lips opening together, in front of the League of Theatre Artists' improvised and tongue-in-cheek-named Blue Moon Café. It was nothing more than a recycled, ramshackle log-pole and slab-pine stable smelling of beer, hormones, and hay; just a trace of manure. It sat between the Barn Theater and the old Lexington Hotel, and it was there that cast and crew and audience would gather, postperformance, to play *La Dolce Vita*—to drink hard, to dance, to sing, to argue art (proving the accuracy of the English critic Ian Hamilton's dictum that "very few friendships can survive your saying: 'I like you but I don't like your poems.' Much better to say: 'I don't like you but I like your poems.' Yes, that would be ok"), to occasionally fight, and most importantly, to pair for the night. It was there that, at just that moment, conveniently, my current and soon to be former videographer wife, was to raucous applause, heaving hips on top of the bar with her teen amour. While we, my darling, were leaning against the hood of a patron's Buick Roadmaster, a maroon '55 classic, glittering under a single bare blue bulb, moths fluttering around. After three months of drama and flirt, of electric tidal pull, that night we walked up the mountain together, gravel crunching underfoot, looking for a soft place to fall down amid the cicadas' racket. We were born to be lovers. It was fate. We were sure.

Then there was that car trip we took at the end of that League of Theatre Artists' second summer season, leaving immediately after the last performance of *A Streetcar Named Desire:* September in Provincetown, the empty beaches, the little room we rented, the four-poster bed that sagged, the faded flowered wallpaper. And now we will not, it seems, accompany each other, as we had thought—as I, at least, was sure—into old age. But we have a daughter and she is beautiful. And we have our memories and some of them are also beautiful. It was perfect, and twenty-five years later remains so. That first kiss. The walk. The fuck on the grass. The falling in love. That was the time, the place, the moment. It was heaven. It was home.

Home? Where is it?

I picked up a hitchhiker once—it was the end of the sixties—on Highway 1, near Big Sur, California, on Lime Kiln Creek. He was obviously a traveler, long on the road. Our conversation still haunts me, now more than ever, because after all these years I understand where he was at and find myself in similar circumstances.

"Where are you going?" I'd asked after he threw his pack in back and settled in for the ride.

"Home."

"Where's that?"

"Don't know."

"You don't know?"

"I know what it looks like but don't know how to get there. Just drop me off anywhere. Where you're going. Anywhere is fine."

And now I was in hiding. I hadn't kept in touch with friends. Called none of my Paris contacts. I owed John Loudon, my editor, an explanation of what I was up to and how the work was coming. The advance I'd taken on the new book had been spent. I was bankrupt. I had made nothing like as much as people thought on my last book and had spent more.

My daughter was silent. Angry that I'd left her for what she called "a penis quest." She wrote one e-mail: "I'm bored with poetry. Tired of literature. I want more. You at least owe me that." She hadn't written since. *Most of the time, my girl, I'd rather nuzzle you or run with you through the woods to the first meadow—you remember, to the first meadow, along the muddy path to the stream—where once, while we sat chewing grass stalks, to our delight, delicately on your knee, as the sun set, a purple hazed dragonfly with three pairs of wings fluttered.*

My wife wrote mostly loving and generous but sometimes angry e-mails, detailing everything from my most recent failings as provider, friend, husband, and father, to some of my historical ethical and moral failures. It was then, as I read her letters, that I confessed for the first time the horror that was the me of some four decades ago. And remembered, if only briefly, Anna V., the midwestern farm girl turned escort-service queen I lived with for a year in 1967, in San Francisco, when I was immortal; young enough, stupid enough to think the world was mine instead of the opposite; when I'd left my first wife after I looked across the table and saw not the young raven-haired beauty I'd married but the catatonic, wizened old lady she would become.

I returned late one evening to the Haight-Ashbury apartment we shared, to find this goodbye note from Anna. She'd left, gone home to her family in Michigan:

The sickest example of our madness is you, the poet, sitting on the bed watching your lover, the whore, put on makeup and go (in a limo) to a party in Marin to make the overdue rent, so that you would not have to dirty your hands and precious art with work. I was sometimes nauseous with fear but wouldn't admit it and kept waiting for you to say, "Don't do this," but you didn't. You never did. And you can say I'm the guilty party because it was my decision, that I was a whore before you met me, working the high rollers, but as you know (and I know you do because you never spoke of it), it could have, at any moment, ended badly except for luck, or my talent for persuasion, or god or something. I should have walked out and caught the next plane home—to anywhere else—but we got stoned and had sex. No apologies! Yes, as I write this, I could bang your head against the wall. How do you explain it to yourself? I'd really like to know. You never explained it to me. But now I don't care anymore. Goodbye.

Anna: I don't. I want to be able to write something beyond the sweet, beyond the comforting, beyond passion itself—something that will heal, will explain. I can't. I'll never be able to explain it to you, to myself. I can't imagine what I was thinking or not thinking. I was too stoned to think. Too young. Too narcissistic. Too selfish to care. Too damaged. All of that and more is the truth. You lived completely for love in a way I could not, could never, but that perhaps is simply the essential difference between boys and women.

Little Annie Sunshine Bear, with your full generous smile; I remember now your puffed lips, fat like secret candies, and the radio playing:

lollipop, lollipop,
oh loll-lollipop,
oh!

It's another babble of guilt that won't go away, though I've tried to forget, or at least not to dwell. I've tried to forgive myself, but the guilty mind is its own torturer.

"The forgiveness of sin is perpetual, and righteousness first is not required," Saul Bellow wrote in *Henderson the Rain King,* and I've held on to that ideal. I've held on.

I was never the man I tried to be—or, more accurately, *pretended* to be. And there's nothing I can do to excuse the me that was, or make it better, except to say that bastard boy is dead. Goodbye. I'm sorry. So sorry. Sorry.

"I wasn't a very good husband," wrote the polar explorer Robert Scott in his final letter, an apology to his wife, Kathleen, "but I hope I shall be a good memory."

I've always been happy only in flux—always dissatisfied, always going or coming back from somewhere—some poem, some book, some jazz, some idea, some exaggeration, some lie, some late-night jam session, some woman, some ocean, some island, some desert, some mountain, some monastery, some ancient ruin; some new thing steaming my brain like a toy locomotive. An in-and-out reporter, there then gone. A long, bloody nomadized history.

Normally the sexual passion that passes for love is quickly exhausted. I've been lucky and have been dazzled, graced, and drawn under the spell of a love driven by a compulsion that overwhelms the soul, that consumes; a love that is impossible and implacable, quixotic and pathetic. The glory and tragedy of great passion, its wonder and its sorrow, last forever; the relationship may not. And there is nothing that can replace it. Nothing. Ideas are a lousy substitute. Wine and mindless sex also. What is left is longing for something that is always irretrievable, existing now only in brief snatches, memories, and dreams. So I write; there's nothing else to do. And since literature, as Kenneth Patchen perfectly intuits, is what one writes when one thinks one should be saying something, and writing begins when one would rather be doing anything else but has just done it, well then, maybe I'm a writer now. Or maybe I just like to hear myself talk.

Truth is that I'm always looking for a reason to celebrate. Any reason will do. I'm easy. Today I toasted the weather turning and the thought that, from just a little stream, beavers working one-two years can make a pond.

19

The room in Paris that I worked and slept in, a spacious twenty feet by twenty feet, was once the bedroom of the apartment of a Madame Malabar de Cueva, a nineteenth-century courtesan. It was located in the sixth arrondissement, on rue Bonaparte, close to rue Visconti, where Balzac, in 1826, opened his first *imprimerie*. In this same arrondisement, or so I've been told, (where every block boasts a dead artist or philosopher), at number five rue somewhere, Manet lived and died. In this room, styled à la Louis XIV, there were seven chairs, two of them stuffed green velvet, a footstool, three three-legged round black marble–topped tables, a rather large four-drawer mahogany bureau, also topped in black marble, four gilt-framed mirrors (two the size of a small bathroom), four lamps and an overhead pear-shaped crystal chandelier, three plants in various stages of distress, a broken fireplace with yet more black marble, a worn oriental that gave off faintly the scent of frangipani. The floor was wide-planked oak, golden with age, with varnish and oil. I had a child's yellow school desk to write at and a bed upholstered in magenta velvet and haphazardly decorated with two throw pillows needlepointed with tropical leaves.

There were five small oil paintings. Four were typical nineteenth-century landscapes; the fifth was of an unknown royal dandy, Goya-dark and mysterious. There were six etchings. In one, *The Nightmare,* a squalid fiend grinned and groped the breasts of a swooned fair maid in the evening fog. Two were of dancers in clinging diaphanous gowns. There was a naked goddess with long flowing tresses whipping across her loins; she was riding spread-legged on the broad back of a centaur—half man, half horse—her hands pulling at his mane. In another, *Nonchalance,* two nude harem girls cavorted, one sprawling ecstatic on a tiger's skin while the other, wearing a brocade hat and silver amulet, played the lute. Lastly there was a Japanese woodblock of a bodhisattva cloaked in red robes; he looked through illusion.

The walls were white with the moldings painted in alternating stripes of aqua and pale orange. Ah yes, there was also a brass pig and two orange porcelain Greek Revival vases with flowers painted round them.

The bookcase opposite the window was filled with cracked leather-bound books, all but two published in the nineteenth century. These latter twentieth-century acquisitions, perhaps inspired by the life of the notorious Madame, were *Histoire de ma vie,* by Jacques Casanova de Senegal (10 vols., pub. 1966) and an *Anthologie des lectures érotiques,* by Boris Vian à Xaviera Hollander (a boxed set bound in red suede, 4 vols., pub. 1981).

It was cozy and exotic, this first stop on my self-imposed exile, my odyssey. I felt calmer if not saner now that I was isolated and loose in the world. My real name is Kovalchik, the Little Black-smith, and of course not Crane, not some pilgrim Puritan; and not Cohen, not a Kohaine of the priestly caste—no, not a high priest, not one of the princes of the twelve tribes, the only ones empow-ered to sanctify the words of god. No, it turns out I'm a peasant, a born anarchist. A Russian Jew with a bit of Mongol mixed in, one of the homeless ones, a wanderer by the passage of blood that may also be the source of my endless longing and melancholy for which there is no cure. No psychological or chemical intervention will help. Some things it seems aren't meant to heal.

Five a.m. Sunday morning. February 2. I was woken out of a delicate sleep by a laugh. Five floors down in the streets a woman was laughing. I walked to the window and, looking out over the singular slate roofs and chimneys of Paris, heard a child's high-pitched cry in the dark, "*Mon père.*"

The sun wouldn't rise for more than three hours, five before the bells of St. Germain des Prés would begin to ring, and yet the sky was pink. I remembered Malraux's dictum, "Art and death are all I hope to rediscover here." To that dynamic duo I would add love and loss. My heart beat hard in my chest with the sound of wings. I got out of bed and to calm myself ate, standing at the sink, a box of Egyptian strawberries dipped in acacia honey.

When finally I fell back asleep, my dreams were a *wish* of wind, blue skies, and sailing with Dusty Nettuno on the *Duga* on the trail of Sir Francis Drake. I learned, months after the fact, the news catching up with me here in Paris, that Dusty had died sometime in the last half of 2002. Exactly when didn't—doesn't—matter, though there is death's time clock, the biology of death, starting with rigor mortis (postmortem stiffening), algor mortis (cooling), lividity (turning blue), and decomposition (rot and smell). They'd found him, a week after the fact, aboard his beloved sailing vessel, *Duga*. He'd already begun to stink. Complications from MS was the verdict, but not the cause. Dusty had weather in his blood. And so he died from melancholia, an urgent nostalgia for the sea he would never sail again.

The last time I saw Dusty was at his office in the Keys, a shaded table at the bar Lor-e-lei in Islamorada, Florida, the day before we set sail for Grenada. He was diminished with a nervous twitch.

"Sir John Hawkins, Queen Elizabeth's slave trader, died at sea in November 1595, a few months before Drake," he said, handing me a copy of the log entry of the HMS *Revenge* for the morning of January 28, 1596, which noted the death and burial at sea of Sir Francis Drake:

> The lande heare presentid therewith the firme [?] or running of Parte of the neck and from Nombre de Dios or I meane from the weste Cape of Nombre de Dios caulid [called] Basti-mentes until you com to the westwarde, onto the Islandes of Laies Rinas. *Viejas diseribmge* [the passage describes/shows/de-tails] the rocks and islands between these two places also the entrance into the good harburs calid [called] Puerto Bello, note how the coraunte [current] setith heare to the N.E. The variation of the compass 2 pomtes [points] to the weste and all what someuex [summary?] I have heare in this place noted it planelie with our Englishe compass as it hathe the wid [?] with respecte of variation. This morning when the diseription [description] notid or taken of this lande, beinge the 28 of Jan-uarie 1595, beinge wedens daie [Wednesday] in the morning S. Frauncis Dracke died of the bludie flix [the bloody flux, dysentery] in sighte of the Island de Buena Ventura, som 6 leauges [leagues] at see [sea] whom now restith with The LORDE.

A crudely drawn map titled *Terra Firma* accompanied the log entry. It showed the shoreline of the Island de Buena Ventura, its coves and bays, and its mountainous topography, and it noted the ship's compass settings and her course on that fateful morning.

Drake was sealed, according to Dusty, in a lead box along with his suit of golden armor and his jewel-encrusted sword.

"Worth a fortune," he said, waving Sir Francis's sword above his head.

Dusty wanted my help in raising money, organizing a small expedition—on blowboats of course—to search for Drake's remains. It was close to a sure thing, he said; for Dusty himself, that ace old-school sailor and navigator by the stars, by dead reckoning and the sextant, had made the secret calculations from information he'd found hidden in the map rooms of the Louvre and the British Museum, taking into account movements over four centuries of currents, winds, and tides.

I believed him. No one else did. And so yesterday afternoon, after work, after 511 words, I made my way to the Louvre to confirm Dusty's research. I wanted to see the Drake map and the log of HMS *Revenge*.

I was meandering through the north arch entrance, the archway where windows on either side overlook the salon of classical sculpture, and where one sees, like the light at the end of the tunnel, Pei's glass pyramids—the courtyard and palace reflecting a kaleidoscope of fractured imagery. It was there and then that I saw a man running and knew instantly from his face, the-guilt-the-terror-the-horror, knew before he screamed that he had lost his son. He was screaming, "Antonio! Antonio!" and slapping his head with both hands as he ran.

I ran after, but by the time I reached the courtyard he was gone. All was normal. Tourists. Postcard hawkers. Picture takers. No general alarm. All normal except for another of those terrible human echoes, that awful, lonely prayer for help, redemption, salvation.

Antonio!

Nothing more but this: there was in the Louvre's vast collection, as far I could discover, nothing on Drake. And no map room. No maps.

"*Certainement non. Non. Jamais,*" said the woman at the information desk. "*Absolument non.*"

So was it just another story, another fantasy, by yet another intoxicated dreamer? Another flotation device? Another life raft that failed?

"I still believe him," I told a friend.

"Of course you do," she said.

Truth is the murkiest, the most illusory of all human constructs. Fact number one: truth and lies both, equally, contradict themselves eventually. Nothing is as it seems. The one thing that all storytellers have in common is a wildly subjective approach to truth. No story is ever told the same way twice. Truth disappears with history. The only difference between fiction and nonfiction is that with fiction one changes the names.

"He knew," I repeated. "He knew."

I wanted to leave him with belief, an epitaph.

Dusty Nettuno.
Combat Medic. Blowboater. Navigator.
1947–2002
Discoverer of Sir Francis Drake's secrets.
Lost in the infinite eternities of time,
the voice of God is impenetrable.
Rest in peace.

If I'm tempted by goose eggs and wild-goose chases and their chasers, it's because there's no other path to pursue if one believes, as I do, that chaos is the natural state of the universe, that any kind of order must be regarded with suspicion.

And nothing is more anarchic, more random, more wildly improbable than life itself, life that is restless and unhappy in stasis. Its normal state is nomadic—evolution, survival demands it; and so the mind also wanders, straying from point to point in search of discovery. And the great thing about language—the voice of the mind, its anarchic ally—is that it prevents us from sticking to the matter at hand. It creates, invents, improvises. Language, like a virus, is creator and destroyer, transmitter of the old, carrier of the new, always evolving, mutating, leaving both death and new life in its wake. The suggestive power of words implies more than reality can provide. *Voilà!* The wonder of language. The magnificence of our spirit.

First came the word, and the word was god. The *word* was *god*. I don't believe in a god that created man but in a humanity that created god. A god created in our own best image, the best of our collective souls; a god that is no less powerful or omnipotent, no less miraculous for having been invented and accepted by us, his creators. The mystery has been called many things: magic and witchery, mysticism, the arts, religion, Buddha and the hungry ghosts; god and the devil; it's the search, the arrow shot from nothingness to nothingness; the *badimo,* that certain deviance that allows a man to slip through order's cracks and escape.

In psychology texts this perspective might be described as a personality disorder and referred to as—let's call it—the Ganzfield syndrome: one so afflicted is "a person who knows unlimited scope, knows no barriers or boundaries between themselves and reality; a person whose perception is unlimited, perceiving no barriers between themselves and what they want."

Those happy, those lucky, those enlightened few. Dudley Do-Right, for one, that guru of word-boppers, that master of counterpoint improvisation. "Begin where you are," he advised. "Write backwards and forwards; it's the jam session that never ends, it's the book of life forever; it's process, that's what it is."

20

Last night I'd made my way by metro to Église de la Madeleine for a performance of Mozart's *Requiem,* though sadly the sheer perfection of Mozart's music was lost in the less than mediocrity of the performance.

Afterward, the madame of the ticket booth was desolated to tell me that the metro system was *"très en retard,* taken down, *Monsieur,* by *une démonstration sociale. Oui-oui,* the wait will be long."

The day had dawned dun. It had fogged, rained, and at dawn snowed. Now the rain had ice in it and was blowing horizontal. The forecast for tomorrow was more of the same. I had neither hat nor umbrella, and it would be, with some exceptional directional luck, a forty-minute walk back to the sixth arrondissement. I decided to wait out the *retard* in a café, where under an awning and warmed by spectral overhead heat lamps, I drank cognac and espresso, two doubles, and read a paperback purchased at that fine used-book shop, the San Francisco Book Company, at 17 rue Monsieur le Prince. My find was Pablo Neruda's *Memoirs,* published by Penguin in their Twentieth Century Classics series. (Just three years into the twenty-first century and the imprint sounds vaguely quaint, gathering that rosy patina of the past, a product of what always seems like loftier, more eloquent literary times.)

Sitting next to me was an old man, in his eighties perhaps, his look lost in the distance, in the past. He was broad-shouldered and impeccably dressed—suit, vest, tie, a ring with a crest—his profile sharp as a fox. He had an aura of aristocracy, or at the very least carried himself in that manner, with exquisite grace and dignity, though half of his bushy white cavalier's moustache had been comically shaved off clean. He had a gin with lemon in front of him.

And later that evening, when the metro was again up and running, I watched a man fall in love on a crowded train. In passing, his eyes met hers, by chance, like a toss of coins or sticks—passion's I Ching. And it was love at first sight: delicious, obsessive love; a love in a time of cholera love; doubtless perfect love, a love for which one would gladly climb shaky bricks to the moon. Unmistakable. That glorious lust, the senseless sense that is grace.

With a great flourish of skirt, she turned her back on him when he began to speak and shook her head. She was a beauty. Tall. Elegant. Fifties. Pale lips and skin; fragile, lovely wrists; her hands. Dark eyes and dark smudged liner. Mahogany was the color of her silver-shot hair, looped into a loose bun, with wisps. Parisian haughty. And dressed: butter leather boots and layers of soft, draping beige wool, a scarf of pale orange. Cheekbones that had just begun to soften.

Her wannabe lover was a sour-smelling drunk with a face like a potato, but he had a satyr's grace and a radiant smile even though he was missing an inch and a half of front teeth, both upper and lower. The sweetness and irresistible vitality of his love was spellbinding. I heard him speak to her, radiant with the joy of someone who has found the solution to life. His hands achingly caressed the air her body displaced. He opened his heart, and his voice was virile and resonant in turn, a fiesta of flavors. He spoke of the food they would taste, of the wine they would swirl on their tongues, of the garden in the country where they would live; the blossoming trees, the nightingale's song; of how he would kiss her naked feet and of how he would wake her at sunrise by fluttering his eyelids against her sleeping belly.

With his arms spread wide like Jesus on the cross, he was pushed off the train at Châtelet and disappeared forever into the milling crowds, still cajoling the love of his life, now altered by the miracle that converts a hapless drunk into a poet.

First came the word *let. Let there be love. Let there be fingers. Fingertips.* The word falling over the tongue—*fin-ger-tips*—is lovely as the sensation, as touch trailing over skin. Quantum passion, selfless love, that precious grace, that chunk of the wild, the beautiful, the terrible, the insane that is ours, our humanity. And, like a metaphor—that way to measure things of similar resonance and volume but vastly different shape—it is at once exultation and despair.

Please excuse the slight digression here, but I can't resist: in the realm of the perfect, though accidental, metaphor—in this case, a cautionary tale, illustrating the danger inherent in writing, where the penalty for the common, the ordinary, the mediocre (that is, for *corn*) is mortality—comes this story.

Cairo, Egypt (AP)

Poet Disappears

The SS *Poet,* a converted troop ship carrying a load of corn for Egypt, disappeared in clear weather off the coast of Africa. Not a trace or sign of the *Poet* has ever been found.

It was half past two when I got back to rue Bonaparte. I was too aroused to sleep but intermittently; I ached and ached for lost loves, touched by memories like a hand. *So sad it is. So quick it is. So quick.* If there had been music, I would have danced.

My eyes were wide before the morning turned, when the shadows were still blue as I watched the orange contrails of the commercial jets out of and into Orly and Charles de Gaulle stretch and dissipate. Bistro Pré aux Clercs opened at seven a.m. and I dressed quickly, wanting two espressos, the first to be downed standing at the bar in one searing gulp, the second (and perhaps a third) to be savored slowly, at a table by the window, with a *tartine* (a lovely word that sounds both slithery and female), a baguette sliced lengthwise and slathered with sweet butter. And what about a tall glass of fresh-squeezed blood orange juice topped off with splash of Perrier and a spoon to stir with? Yes, it's health food. The French breakfast of champions.

In 1970 I was living in southern Spain, about forty kilometers south of Málaga, in Mijas, one of the "white villages" tucked into the mountains above the Andalusian coast. At that time in that town, the bakers fired their brick ovens with almond shells, and on mornings when the southeasterlies blew up the mountain off the Mediterranean, I came awake to the smell of baking bread and toasted almonds.

That June, though, it wasn't a breeze I felt, but a sirocco—a hot, evil blast of bone-dry air off the Sahara that's said to drive men mad. It had been blowing now nonstop for two weeks. In Mijas, which looked south and east, a straight shot across the Strait of Gibraltar to Morocco, the locals called this wind the *leveche*. For North Africans, it's a *nafhat* or an *aajej*. It's the wind that the fellahin would ride out into the desert to attack with knives.

In the shutter-closed shade of Bar Estefan, Jake Price and I were working our way through a bottle of Pedro Domecq sherry. Jake—

painter, writer, linguist, light heavyweight boxer, and World War II hero—sported a black eye patch. He was released from prison at eighteen when he enlisted, a badass to war, after serving five years of a fifteen-year sentence for extortion. At thirteen, a poor kid from Arkansas, he'd tried to extort five hundred bucks from a rich man by threatening to kidnap his son. Got a battlefield commission, made first louie, awarded the Silver Star when he was wounded and lost the eye in France—but not before taking out a couple of Nazi Panzers and a machine gun emplacement.

"Would have bled to death but for the cold, lying in a ditch buried in snow," he told me.

Jake's main love, his first wife, had died young. "She could shit and wipe her ass in the street and still look a queen," he said, drumming the tabletop to a Latin beat. "She would dance at the drop of the drum's first beat and boogie to the last."

All the men were hunched sullenly over their drinks; women were nowhere to be seen. What conversation there was, was brief and in whispers. Dust blowing through cracks was caught dancing in laser shards of sunlight coming from the same direction. While mumbling and muttering about his work, the blue hues he had been working in for the past ten years or so, Jake doodled in the dust, pushing it with his index finger into shapes and patterns on the tabletop.

What he loves most is women. "Because life goes by the numbers," he said, "and there isn't anything as good as pussy is: there isn't anything worth having as much." He talked about how, when as a kid he sold Bibles door to door during the Depression, an Italian lady used him to father her baby. "She just wanted a blue-eyed son." And so he has thirteen children by seven wives; the last he delivered himself in a tepee in Montana. He lived there for a while in a cabin that had, above the door, a faded sign that read PINE CONE, on the grounds of what was formerly a camp for insane children.

Baaaabeees! That was his battle cry. "I'd rather help birth a baby than fight," he said, and why he advises: "Smile at the gun that is waved at you, and wave back."

And without missing a beat he told how one of his wives, a Norwegian countess, six-two or -three, an astounding beauty—a big cat—shortly before she killed herself had put on red high heels and nothing else and begged him to cut her long thick hair—slowly, down to the scalp. She wanted, she told him, to be made ugly and to be his slave. He said she had also started sucking her thumb.

"She said it was because I hated her," he said, rubbing out the dust-doodles with the back of a hand that was blue-stained and splattered with white gesso. "I didn't know what to do. You know I loved her. I'll always love her."

He'd last talked to her just a week before she leaped from the Tangiers ferry.

"She was thin as a cadaver . . . trembled constantly. You could smell her sour sweat and breath. Her eyes were empty phone booths ringing."

She had begun asking everyone she met, her voice reedy, high like a record speeded up, "Do you have a suicide plan? Everybody needs a suicide plan."

Another full-time resident of Mijas was Randolph S. ("Don't call me Randy"), a short story writer who loved Spain, bullfighting, and Hemingway with equal passion. He was from Ashtabula, Ohio, and his father, Duane, still lived in the 3030 Brown Drive house where Randolph was born. His wife's name was Jane; she was a level-headed, big-hearted, big-breasted, broad-hipped Iowa girl who one afternoon swam naked with me in a Moorish pool that overlooked the Pillars of Hercules, undressing shyly next to a pot of bamboo so overgrown that it had tilted over.

After dinner we showered. She washed my hair. The water was cold. Then we drank the last of the wine and ate a cool, fleshy-wet fig that, like the night sky, was unquestionably purple.

They were all about the age I am now when I met them in the early seventies. But I've since lost track of them, so they're still and always for me what they were then, though now if alive they're in their nineties.

A decade later, Sigrid and I were living in Manhattan, squatting in a squalid Spring Street storefront railcar apartment. It was forty, maybe fifty feet long, but so narrow that when we sat on the couch we could rest our feet on the wall opposite. Every now and then a rat would crawl out of the bathtub drain. The roaches were dinosaurs. We were too poor to eat anything but take-out Cuban-Chinese.

We shared the place with Joseph L., a pervert, a masochist who loved boys. "I can manifest my neurotical emotions, emancipate an epicureal instinct, and elaborate my homosexual tendencies. You don't understand. How could you? You weren't a faggot-homo wimp for the first thirteen years of your life and a bisexual degenerate for the rest."

He was also a genius, an acid-quaffing improvisational player, and a visionary geek, inventor of electronic instruments; besides that a classical bassoonist, conductor, Julliard lecturer, philosopher. "You want to be a musician? Then *listen*. Listen to everything. Just listen. Listen to the subway, the lions, the tigers, the people, the grass. And yes, my friend, there's a lot that goes on between C and C-sharp— maybe not on the piano, but in life. Then he'd play a short riff on his electric wand. Fingers flying. The sound was of random neurons firing. "That was it!" he would shout. "It! That comes from being so curious about the past that I can't wait to see what happened next."

Sigrid spent her days at auditions or working the actor's craft. "I'm tired of sounding pretty and looking pretty and throwing my skirts around and kicking my legs," she said one morning, examining herself one last time before leaving for some audition or another. Wearing a black cashmere slink, she checked out her hands, held out at arm's length. "At least the length of my nails is perfect—long enough to leave scars, but not ostentatious."

"Go get 'em, sweetheart," I said, snapping my wrist. "Your sexual elegance is doubtless a classic, both visually and philosophically."

"Later." She waved and, puckering her full-red character lips, blew me a kiss.

In those days my writing room, on Eighty-sixth and Broadway in a down-and-out SRO, was a six-by-nine closet furnished with a chest, a cot, and a table; on the lamp shade, the one with cigarette holes burnt into it, St. George perpetually slew the dragon; the single window opened onto a brick wall. The radio was always on: 89.9. Jazz from Jersey. A Newark station. For erotic art there were high-heeled dancing shoes, toeless with feathery straps—black, silver, and red—hung on the wall. A black silk robe, designed by Fernando Somebody, hung from a hook behind the door, waiting. It was there that I had hoped to hatch, if not a poem, at least a good clean sentence, which like toughness, a balmy night, the wild violet, or the moth was delicate prey.

One of the first questions I remember Tsung Tsai asking after we first met—after we'd established that we both wrote poetry—was, "Have you written any good ones?" And by *good* I now understand that he meant great, brilliant, enlightening; literature immortal as the poetry of Tu Fu or Li Po. *Then* my easy answer was, "One, maybe two." I've since reevaluated and found that answer flatulent. Later, in Paris, late into the lonely nights I read what was left of the poems I'd written over the years—a few hundred left from out of the unknown thousands of attempts. Trying to find those miraculous *two,* I came to another, less flattering conclusion. It's a bit sad, particularly when all I ever wanted to be was an all-around literary genius and cultural demigod.

Back in Manhattan, though, some days were spent perusing the personals, the classifieds in the *New York Review of Books* or the *Times Literary Supplement,* and dreamily evaluating the prospects:

Literary woman and daughter, fifteen, wish to invite a bright, knowledgeable, discerning young man to be their guest once or twice a month when they see a film or play and to discuss and evaluate it with them later during dinner. If truly suitable, please write.

Intriguing.

SWF with large unsheltered income needs your depreciation, write-offs in exchange for partnership in my sometimes glamorous, often cozy, always delicious life.

Perfect.

But most days I just prowled the Bowery, looking for characters, listening for language, for freshness; for deviations that enrich, that give power and purity and depth to poetry because they come from experience rather than books. The streets became my teacher. Derelicts, winos, and rummies—long-suffering losers—engrossed me. They all had stories. They were all looking for something. Hope. History. Fame. They were me, the *who* I feared I would become, all too soon.

There was Jimmy Walker, former boxer, face like an old softball with cauliflower ears. Nothing like Brando's Terry Malloy. "I was never a contender, just a tough tough fight for the new kids, the up-and-comers that hadda get by Jimmy first," he said, pawing at what was left of his nose, bouncing up on his toes and throwing jabs.

He said, "Jimmy Walker, it was wrote, ain't no fancy-Dan, sharpshooter, or dancer: he's a bull. I *was* a bull. Forget stones, I had rocks for hands, and was, when younger, better looking. But I've been ripped. In the Bowery; in the ring—I got ripped sonofabitch in the fourth. The Kid really hit me: he throws a right; I block it; he throws a hook and smack on the button catches me. I coulda been dancing on Broadway for all I knew when sonofabitch I heard it break and so went nuts. I went to the kidneys. The kidneys. The kidneys. In the kidneys I got him good and got him good to the head. I tore his ears apart. He was out. Out-out-out, not getting up, no way in the world. I'm a killer sure.

"Yeah, a killer with the heart of a lamb. How's the Kid? I'm crying. And back in the dressing room when he's still out—praying. I was still at his side praying when he woke. To hell with it, I thought; and so said, You deserved it, Kid, you're a dirty fighter; you gave me the elbow so I gave you the head-butt and the beating that finished it. Finished you because you're not hard enough. Remember that, Kid, and remember soft boys are grave-meat booked to go. So be smart, be easy, be loose. The loose don't care. I got the fight to prove it."

And Mister Movie Picture, as he was known on the street, who had this to say: "It was during the depression, civilization had reached a certain, a decadent point, and I pulled the trigger. I pulled the trigger like other guys blew their noses. Those years were bleak and vicious; all luck came with the bark on. I was working with the Chicago mob as a driver and a soldier for Terrible Touhy and Cagney, the murder incorporated guys. We asked simple questions and took care of those little business problems. You don't need a glossary to get the picture. And I didn't give a damn. I was, in fact, in heaven. Fear is so deeply seducing that when I got shot it didn't bother me. It was just part of the game. As I remember it, 'I'm forever blowing bubbles pretty bubbles in the air' was playing on the juke when they let me have it. 'They got me,' I sure moaned. But as it turned out I wasn't killed, but you know that; you probably saw the movie."

"It's about love. It's always love. Only that. There ain't nothing else," William Walter Storm would say. Tex Bill Storm "once was a cowboy." He rode a scooter instead of a horse now, and instead of rope, saddlebag, and roll carried squeegees, rags, and buckets, herding downtown windows instead of cows. His face, weather-beaten and rutted as a dirt road, was perpetually shadowed by a brown sweat-stained Stetson sporting a braided leather band. He wore jeans that sagged around his bowlegged knees, a big silver rodeo buckle, a matted sheepskin vest over red plaid flannel shirt; there was a red bandanna tied around his neck; his boots were mostly gaffer's tape. Tucked inside the sweatband of that Stetson was a letter he'd written to the love of his life, a woman he'd met in New Mexico some fifty years earlier. He loved her still with the same obsessive passion as he loved her then. He would send that letter to her if only he knew her address, if only he could remember her name. He was sure that someday, someway, somehow he would find her and she would read these words:

dearest sweetheart, I sure do miss you and sure do get lone-some out here on the range. i wish i had your picture to re-member by and am enclosing one of me for you to keep and wish i could touch you. i'm going up to hollywood to play in western pictures. this is not trying to be a big shot talker but i've done that kind of work before. i'm the real cowboy and get letters from roy and dale and tex and several others asking why i don't come back and act. i'll be a star again and some-one will be proud they know me.

your admirer, w. w. storm, jr., tex bill storm, bronco bill and sundance kid, cousin of gene autry.

The picture he enclosed was of a young black cowboy on horse-back, wearing a sheepskin vest over a red plaid flannel shirt. There's a red bandanna around his neck. The horse is rearing back and the cowboy is waving his Stetson at the camera. It was signed, in a careful hand: W. W. Storm.

I handed the letter back to Bill. That day, as I remember it, was spectacular, painfully so: temperature about seventy-five, sky skin-deep, sun in and out, piling clouds on their way to Ohio: lovely, in-nocent, nebulous hallucinations.

"Beautiful," I said.

Paris, as February waned, got warmer. Past east-facing windows from the slate-roof dormer drizzle drip-drip-dripped. I was count-ing the bodies, taking names, remembering the dead, the missing in action. Now they're only names in an address book that is rapidly filling with the crossed-out: lost friends, lovers, parents, wives. It was a list of memories; a list of fears and hopes; a list of loves and losses; a list of laughs and tragedies; a list of successes and failures: a list of last times. I've always been fascinated by last times—the last healthy breath, the last rattle of breath; the cry, the laugh, the scream, the sight; the last goodbye. When was that last moment of doubtless perfect love, the passion that is grace? I hope, my darling, because I love you, it was the night before the door closed for the last time.

21

Saturday, March 15, 2003. Worldwide antiwar demonstrations, a turnout of 750,000 in London and Paris. And we all got goose bumps from our own goody-good feelings of ethical and intellectual superiority. But it is and was essentially useless. They got the power. Who do? They do.

That same day, on a news network, I heard a talking head—some public relations Marine Corps colonel—say of the Iraqis, "They are not fighting by the international rules of war. They seriously violate the rules."

What? Can you believe these assholes? Wrong but always certain. In their Orwellian logic there is no redemption. Only lies. You can't go against nature. The only rule of war is, All's fair. There's no choice. Surrender. Live or die. Destroy, maim, murder; by any means be the victor, not the vanquished.

To assuage sadness over the predictable and inevitable stupidity and violence of the human race, I splurged. On March 18, the evening of a full moon rising at sunset and the eve of the new century's first American war, I splurged. I smoked a corncob of hashish and at the shellfish stand on rue de Buci bought and ate a dozen oysters and three sea urchins, washing them down with a Coke-sized bottle of Piper-Heidsieck champagne that I drank through a straw. Then, while walking the streets, I scarfed a juice-dripping mango for dessert. Wiping my hands on my jeans and my beard on the tail of my red plaid flannel shirt, I stared at the house at number 7 rue des Grands-Augustins, where Balzac set the action of his novel *Le chef-d'oeuvre inconnu* and where Picasso lived from 1936 to 1955 and in 1938 painted *Guernica,* his great and anguished bellow against war—now a United Nations backdrop, in front of which the hypocritical mouth nonstop piety.

Then I got carried back in time, associative memory kicking in as it sometimes does, to Málaga. It was June of 1971, about eleven o'clock on a Sunday morning: I was watching the after-church *paseo* from a café on the square where the house—marked by a plaque—that Picasso was born in still stands, when I saw, looking like one of his blue-period paintings, a middle-aged couple, she in *luto* with black lace mantilla and he in formal wear with spats and a straw bowler. Using a purple velvet leash they were walking a tiny drooling dwarf dressed in fancy tapestry short pants and a white frilly shirt.

Stopping at the Café Palette for a nightcap, three shots of espresso mellowed with the same of cognac, I heard two nattily attired old-school tweeds, retired British military for certain, sipping whiskey and talking their latest war. Baghdad again.

"What will we do when we get to Baghdad?" queried one, a pipe stuck between his teeth.

The other paused to stroke his chin, considering before passing on his best military assessment. "Sticky," he said.

Now the pipe nodded his agreement, inhaling deeply and exhaling a sigh of smoke-clouded nostalgia. "Charles, do you remember when you resigned your commission? You were such a stalwart friend then."

Champaign/Urbana, home to the University of Illinois, October 27, 1962. The weather was perfect. The forecast for the next day was more of the same. The night had that certain chill and the shade had bite and rattle, but though it was almost November the sun still splashed warmth and the cicada's song still itched and itched. That morning there was a dreamy, listless fog over fields of cornstalk stubs that burned off by ten, endless blue skies. The surreal orange light was both oblique and brilliant, casting long, edgy shadows, and even the early turning sugar maples held leaves that were still, at this late date, almost full red. But then autumn leaves, like memories, are colored imagination.

It was another time of insanity, the Cold War; the lifeless mass of humanity had been conned and boiled into nuclear crescendo. The Cuban missile crisis was reaching toward finality. I had a night job feeding fruit flies in the subbasement of the biology lab. It was quiet there and deep underground. The air was alive with generations of escapee flies, circling my head as if I were overripe fruit, and moist with steam and smell, a cloying mixture of alcohol, ferment, and mold, bitter-sweetened by the odor of the molasses I used in the fly-chow. This I cooked up in a dented aluminum double boiler precariously balanced on a cobbled-together stove made from flask stands and a couple of Bunsen burners.

The radio was always on. The news was breathless. The Russians were steaming south toward the American blockade. The B-52s were in the air, flying toward that mythical point of no return. The missiles were cocked. Loaded and locked. Fingers were on the Armageddon buttons. Nobody had yet blinked. It was just past midnight; under the light of a desk lamp tiny insects struggled and

died. Heaven was silent. There was no hope, but I was not yet
without it.

The fruit flies and I would be the only survivors.

But as it turned out the fruit flies didn't make it. In my apocalyptic perambulations I screwed up the bottle-sterilization and feeding
schedule. Many generations were wiped out in the holocaust of
starvation and mold that followed. Experiments were ruined; I was
fired but the world was saved: the Russians had turned back.

Alone in my Paris room, lit by the radio dial and, low in the sky,
the glow of more than half a waxing moon, the streetlights, and the
after-hum of a *manifestation* I had joined earlier that evening
against what *Le Monde* was most accurately calling *la guerre améri-
caine,* I woke from a dream of the girl who had marched next to
me. Her hair was pink and jelled into a rooster comb; she had a
stud through her lower lip and a ring through an eyebrow. Claim-
ing she was an anarchist, she waved the flag of the defunct Soviet
Union. She had a hole in her pants, right side, midway between
the curving edge of her pelvis and the apex of her thighs—a hole
approximately the size of my little finger. I woke the next morning
with my hands squeezed between my legs; woke to a wet crotch
and a musk of sweat, to vague luxurious angst, the usual fears—the
blither of old age, the blather of dying—woke to the sweet-sweet-
sweet animal heat of life.

March 30, Sunday morning mass at Notre Dame, where I was
tempted to partake of the holy Eucharist, partake of the body and
the blood of Jesus Christ, but resisted. A rose is a rose is a rose is a
Catholic is a Catholic is a Catholic is a Jew is a Jew is a Jew is a

Buddhist is a Buddhist is a Buddhist is a rose is a rose. Amen. *Amitofu.*

April Fools' Day, 2003. It was time to move on. Next stop Prague, where I was scheduled to meet with my Czech publishers and do a reading at the Globe. I didn't, and didn't call either. I wandered aimlessly in a fog. I drank. I looked for antiquarian maps, went to jazz clubs, bought two copies of my newly published and translated book at the Franz Kafka Bookstore, met a woman from Africa, and after ten days left. *Next stop. Next stop.* Next stop doesn't matter. Satisfy your craft in the moment and move on. *Move on. Move on.*

On the flight from Prague to New York—not yet Ulaanbaatar (as it turned out, I wouldn't leave for my season in Mongolia until September)—I was tapped on the shoulder by a big-bearded bear of a man wearing a skullcap and prayer shawl. He was wrapped in *tefillin,* the phylacteries (boxlike appurtenances) worn by Jewish adult males at weekday morning services. The *tefillin* have leather thongs attached; one box is strapped on the head, the other on the left arm, near the heart. They contain biblical passages declaring the unity of god and the duty to love god and be mindful of him with all one's heart and mind.

"Are you Jewish?" he asked.

"No. I mean yes. I was *born* Jewish. But no, I'm not a Jew now. I don't practice. Never did. I'm a Zen Buddhist." And an idolater, I thought but didn't say.

He was only slightly taken aback, hesitating for just a moment before continuing. "We need a *minyan,* a quorum. Will you join us?"

"I can't. I don't believe."

"Doesn't matter. We need a Jewish body, another man. To pray. To have a service. Do you understand? Please."

The *please* did it. I couldn't refuse. "Okay. Sure. Just tell me what to do."

He handed me a skullcap and I followed him to the back of the plane, where eight other men waited for me, the tenth, the missing link, to make the *minyan*. And so they began, standing feet together and rocking in place, their conversation with god—a conversation that morning and night it is their obligation to perform. It is their affirmation of Judaism, their declaration of faith in one god. They recited the *shema,* the all-purpose blessing, chanted in the morning and evening (as a bedtime prayer) and as part of the deathbed confessional. "*Shema Yisrael Adonai eloheinu Adonai ehad,*" they began, the rhythm of their words rising and falling. *Hear O Israel, the Lord is our God; the Lord is One.*

I knew enough to say amen—which I've just discovered means "agreed"—when they kissed the fringes of their *talliths* and chanted in unison *Emet,* "Truth."

Standing there beside them, the odd man out, I tried to feel something, some elemental connection to my past, my heritage. Some tie to the collective unconscious, some universal Jewish archetype. But their chant, their prayer struck no chords. I felt nothing but unease, a vague embarrassment that in truth was no different than what I always felt at organized religious services—Christian, Buddhist, Jewish, any and all, it doesn't matter. I'm an equal-opportunity holy anarchist. If you meet the Buddha, kill him. *God needs to be met in private. Alone and without intervention, without dogma.*

There is another version of that same event, another memory, an alternative reality, one as real, as possible as the other. I don't know: both are, as far as I know, true. I do know that it is my way to muse on and prod at, to mess around with all versions of reality.

"We are miserable enough in this life without the absurdity of speculating upon another," Lord Byron reasoned. He was wrong. I prefer a corollary. We would be miserable in this life only if we held to the absurd conviction that there is but one reality, without speculating on others.

I know that belief ardently held on to becomes conviction, indistinguishable from fact. So now, did the scene on the plane happen as I first described it, complete with philosophical speculation and a bookish aesthete's discomfort with religion and prayer? Or was it really the scene described below, the weakling's way, the coward's way—the ashamed self-loathing Jew's denial of his heritage? You decide.

"Are you Jewish?" the man tapping my shoulder asked.

"No," I said and turned away, ignoring him, bothered, wondering how he knew, irritated that he knew. How *did* he know? In the hours I've spent—it's vanity and amusement—examining my face in mirrors, I've often thought I looked rather rabbinical, though a bit cynical and seedy, a beat rabbi. What was it? Just a shot in the dark, or was it the nose? The curly hair? The beard? Was it that I was reading a book? That it was poetry? Or just a sixth sense? Some cosmic tribal connection? Dog knows dog?

He stood there staring. He knew I was a liar. I didn't care. He mumbled something, then walked away, shaking his head. I glared at his back, ready to stare down his pitying surreptitious backward glance. He never looked back.

I'd planned to stop in New York for a quick visit. It turned long. Delirium. Time and travel plans muddied. SARS. Travel bans. Bankruptcy. A bout of poetry, then a love affair interrupted travel, balance, and work on the new book.

After the rainiest June on record, summer began with a heat wave and more lies. I was all excuses now. All inertia. On August 6 there was a flash-flood warning.

ALBANY NY 3:40 PM EDT WED AUG 6 2003:

THE NATIONAL WEATHER SERVICE HAS ISSUED A FLASH-FLOOD WARNING FOR CENTRAL ULSTER COUNTY IN EASTERN NEW YORK UNTIL 7:45 PM EDT. AT 3:33 PM EDT WEATHER SERVICE DOPPLER RADAR INDICATED VERY HEAVY RAIN FROM A NEARLY STATIONARY THUNDERSTORM. LOCATIONS IN THE WARNING INCLUDE BOICEVILLE, OLIVEBRIDGE, PEEKAMOOSE, WEST HURLEY, WEST SHOKAN, AND WOODSTOCK. DO NOT DRIVE YOUR VEHICLE INTO AREAS WHERE WATER COVERS THE ROADWAY; THE DEPTH MAY BE TOO GREAT TO CROSS SAFELY. VEHICLES CAUGHT IN RISING WATER SHOULD BE ABANDONED QUICKLY. MOVE TO HIGHER GROUND.

Move to higher ground seemed to be the imperative. I felt a restless itch to leave, an obsessive hurry, the only right, the only ethical thing was to go, time was rushing away, wasting, go no matter where, as long as it be somewhere else. Still I lingered. Drifting. A wait long enough to stir anticipation. Then panic. Escape, yes. Finally.

But it wasn't until September 23 that I would leave for Mongolia.

IV
A Season on the Steppe

Autumn 2003

I prefer poetry to nervous wealth.
          —Jack Kerouac

None of the characters in this book—and that includes the
narrator—is identical with any living person.
          —Ivan Klima, Love and Garbage

Through the fiction of memory I can see the Gobi—the brilliant light, the hard-blasted rock and shattered winter grass, the hallucinatory horizon. A slab of lofty country—Mongolia's arithmetic tells it—most of the steppe sits more than a mile above sea level. And the clear air lenses, telescoping details of mountains still a two-day drive away.

The days would be dry and incandescent; the nights, windy, cold, and exquisitely ridden with stars. And it is huge. Mongolia is twice as big as Texas but has a population of 2.3 million, with perhaps three-quarters of that number (estimates vary) living in the capital, Ulaanbaatar. It is one of the most sparsely populated nations on earth—one person per square kilometer. Always has been. The idea of "Mongol *hordes*" is a joke. There were never many Mongols, and so they were mostly assimilated—in Persia they became Muslims, in China they became Chinese, etcetera. Only in Mongolia did they maintain their identity. They were the Asian version of the Vikings. The Vikings had ships; the Mongols, horses. Both went where they wished, took what they wanted.

Mongolia is Middle Earth, the place on the planet farthest from any ocean. Immoderate. It has a sharply continental climate—long, dry winters and brief, mild, and relatively wet summers. Months ahead of the calendar, an overnight autumn, and then winter sets in, a winter against which, as always, all other winters will be measured. Snowier, windier, colder than any in memory.

When Arctic air masses dominate, midwinter temperatures average -4°F to -35°F. In the Uvs Lake basin in northwestern Mongolia, one of the coldest places in Asia, the lowest temperature ever recorded was -72°F. Ulaanbaatar is the coldest capital city in the world. By contrast, summer temperatures in the Gobi can climb as high as 104°F. Annual precipitation ranges from twenty-four inches in the Khentii, Altai, and Khovsgol mountains to less than four inches in the Gobi. In some parts of the desert, no precipitation may fall for several years in a row. A preserving dryness. Everything parched, pale-powdered browns.

The arid and unpopulated southeast, the central Gobi, where I hoped to wander, is the heart of the country. Located south and southwest of Ulaanbaatar, between the Khangai, Khan Khokhii, and Altai mountains, it is an apocalyptic country with an improbably tumbled topography. Here the steppe is greatly eroded and intersected by a labyrinth of ancient outwash plains: ravines, gullies, basins, and salt pans. Archaic rock massifs, congeries of ridges; the dry twinnings of terribly wasted ranges, gaunt fragments of montane skeletons rising five to six hundred feet above the plateau.

In the southwest, on the upland borders of the Gobi and Taklamakan, which foot the southern mountain ranges (the In-shan and the Nan-shan), the sand is constantly on the move. It is a country crowded with dunes, in some places one superimposed upon another, varying in height from thirty up to three hundred feet. On the windward side, the slope of a dune will be long and gentle, while the leeward side is steep, and in outline, concave. Freeze-framed waves, blowing sand feathering across their crests.

Though most of the eastern Gobi rises from 4,500 to 5,350 feet, the floor of the depression rises to between 2,900 and 3,200 feet. Here small lakes frequently appear and just as frequently disappear. The water in them is almost always salt or brackish. There is, until the bordering mountains are reached, an utter absence of trees and shrubs. A vast, dry, belligerent landscape.

It is largely uninhabited, except for the most recalcitrant of Mongolia's nomadic herders. Instead of an ocean, they have a sea of grass stretching from rising to setting sun. They live by the increase of their herds and build no permanent settlements; when the grass is eaten, they move to where there is more. They do not long for the ocean or the crops that come from tilling the earth, for they have never known them.

But they have the sky, open wide with prey-birds sailing, and a steppe littered with bones. And of all the things, there is nothing more congratulatory, more celebratory, than a weathered old skull. We have been here. Survived long enough to leave clues. Tracks. Marks on the earth. Faintly. Our remains. We have lived, they whisper. Welcome home.

It was the end of September when I left for Mongolia, all pretense of discovering lost temples having evaporated, intending who knows what: to find god, to look into the face of my insecurities, to wander—to be aimless, anarchic—to be thoroughly and dissonantly human. To find something. To find out.

I'd been staying in the house of my dear Elaine, a sweetheart, a bond broker gone bad, an ex–Wall Streeter who'd gotten lost to art and literature. Her house, near the top of California Quarry Road, perched as it was high on the southern face of Overlook Mountain, had a world-class, 180-degree unimpeded view stretching east to west from the Hudson River to the western Catskills, and across the Shawangunk Mountains to the Ramapo foothills—seventy-five miles to the southern horizon.

Nonetheless, tired of place and of waiting—I'd been home, in one place for four months, which was seemingly my limit—the afternoon before leaving Woodstock I spent some mindless minutes pouring water over a concrete garden statue of Buddha, watching as it evaporated under a warmish fall sun. It was a childish game; I was looking for omens. Invariably and aptly, when all that remained of the water was a few spots—a smudge, like a prosthetic red-rubber schnoz around the tip of Buddha's nose, and the even darker puddles of wet in his eyes, from which trails like tears fell— Buddha took on the look of one of America's cheesiest mass-market clichés: the black-velvet painting, the sad clown. It was very satisfying. Here was absolute confirmation of my character, proof of my fondest theory. Out of chaos had come the word; Buddha nature was *bonbu*. Buddha was a jerk, a fool, the most inept but truest of enlightenment's pretenders.

Flying from Kennedy to Inchon, where Korean Air had a twice-weekly flight to Ulaanbaatar, my seatmate was a dapper young Korean. His hair was slicked back smooth over a gaunt-faced skull. He was long, thin, and electric, his right leg bouncing continually to some internal quick-time beat, the rhythms of his nerves on edge. He was resplendent in black, the trousers creased to a knife-edge, a shirt with epaulets also perfectly pressed. A thin tooled-leather belt with an ornate silver buckle circled his waist. He propped one gray snakeskin cowboy boot, the quiet one, on the footrest and stuck out his hand.

"Call me Joe."

Without any plan, I decided to disappear, to fabricate. "Call me Jones," I said and shook his hand.

After a bare minimum of introductory biography, this part true, I said I was a traveler; he said, "I do business, import/export." I had lived in San Francisco from 1964 to 1969, in what was then the world's largest teenage ghetto, the Haight-Ashbury. He was living there now.

His smile was wry. "We are similar." Joe pointed at my wrist *mala*. "Buddhist?"

I have always been unsure how to describe myself. An exile from a lost tribe, I'm not comfortable admitting anything. Deny everything. Particularly anything even vaguely associated with the New Age herds.

I hesitated. "A bad Buddhist . . . a broken Buddhist."

He grunted as he nodded and gestured out through the window, out into space, perhaps into the void. "Do you meditate?"

I don't meditate; don't concentrate on breath or anything else for that matter, even Bodhisattva's damn blank wall. Words. Words work. And lips nibbling her neck warm at the nape. Jus' gimme dat old soft shoe, for nothing else will do. Da-dah. Da-dah. Da-dada-da-dah-da-dah.

"Not the sitting kind," I said.

"What kind?"

"The doing kind."

A familiar nod of the head. The chuckling back of a huge guffaw. "You like sex?"

I could feel a familiar grin crack. "Love," I said.

He patted my knee. "Better-better. Much better," he said, squirming, grinding his hips into his seat. "Any pussy, any woman . . . one night of sex is better-better than a million-million years of meditation."

Déjà vu. Where had I head that before? Filling my cup of noth-ingness . . . yes, absolutely transfigured by the overwhelming power of desire.

Together we laughed and slapped palms. "You're right," I said. "We're similar."

He nodded vigorously. "We have same worship."

That night, in Seoul, over dinner, I told him stories both real and imagined, and after piles of octopus, grilled live and twisting in the heat, and multiple bottles of rice wine along with a couple of pills of unknown derivation, he treated me to a massage at his private club, an evening of sensual play. It was a good beginning.

The next morning at 28,000 feet, I toasted my good beginning with four aspirin and a bottle of water, scribbling in commemora-tion a half-remembered half-improvised verse in the style of Ikkyu Sojunhere (1394–1491), the Zen monk who called himself Crazy Cloud, Japan's iconoclastic, irreverent, antiestablishment Zen mas-ter who celebrated freedom, wild ways, and the joys of eros— spread-your-legs sex.

After a Meal of Fresh Octopus with Joe

Lots of arms sacrificed,
and all for me
seasoned
with twists and condiments,
the various hot sauces,
the heat,
the heat;
all the passions,
the delusions,
I love them so.
Sorry Buddha,

this is but another law
I must break.

The masseuse I met through Joe was the embodiment of sensuality, unmitigated. Her lips, a shade darker than her rice-paper skin like pale honey, were full—the color of fall leaves, fading umber. Her bones were sharp and lovely; her hair, like a shampoo model's, fell in glistening waves. She didn't so much *move* as *glide*. There was a barely noticeable crosshatched scar beneath her left eye. It was heartbreaking. Her name wasn't Guinevere, but it sounded close enough, both in style and in resonance.

She took my hand lightly and with fingertips led the way. She undressed me. She oiled and worked my body, kneading, knuckling, slapping. All the while, her caressing voice poured out a gentle stream of phrases, none of which I could understand, but they were uniformly honeyed and filled with such affection that she might as well have been cradling my head in her lap, her hands running through my hair. Raw, direct, authentic; the now that is all there is to nirvana.

So please stop your babbling about soul and god and Buddha; all are without meaning, nothing but empty concepts; unborn and undying. Listen. Some seekers shut themselves up and meditate in solitude, some love wine, the joys of sex, and words; both are fine, both work, both are Zen; but some, the professional gurus, the fame and fortune monks, are hypocrites. They are the real enemies of understanding. Ikkyu wrote:

Yes, dharma seekers
and professional gurus all,
you who are so sure,
so perfect,
such perfect hypocrites.

A sex-loving bhikkhu
you object?
Koans and convoluted answers
that's all you've got.
Listen,
a massage girl in pale yellow silk
is worth more than all of you.

Mongols have an attitude similar to Ikkyu's about eros and sex. Free and easy. They are a people who celebrate the female elements: mother earth, the first god. One can hear it in their stories. The Borjigids (Yisugei, the father of Genghis Khan, was a Kiyat-Borjigid) are a race that traces the family tree back to Bodunchar, the illegitimate son of Alan-ko'a, the ancestress of the Mongol people. In *The Secret History of the Mongols*—written in 1240 CE by an unknown author—Alan-ko'a describes her son's conception with a bravado born of experience, the surety of female sexual superiority:

Night after night a golden glittering man snuck through the skylight of my *ger*.[1] He stroked my stomach, my pubis mound and below. He sank into my lap and his light penetrated my womb, but when he left, he crawled away like a yellow dog.

It was an old story. Gaia. Fertility. The first gods were female. The ancient Cretans, for example, would always rather pray to a woman, and their priests castrated themselves in service to the goddess.

---

[1] *ger* (n.): the Mongolian word for the Russian yurt or yurta, (of Turkish origin, literally dwelling, home). A circular tent of felt matting compacted over a kerege, a framework of lattice and wood poles, a ger can be erected or dismantled, packed and made ready to travel, within an hour.

• • •

I was on my way to Ulaanbaatar flogging the fiction that I needed Mongolia to satisfy the terms of a contract I'd signed for a book. The advance was already spent and I was about to miss my deadline. My agent was twitchy. My editor was getting itchy, threatening:

> George:
> The complete final ms. is now more than a month overdue. I need a report on when I should be able to receive it. Right away. I hope that this book won't have to be canceled for non-delivery and that a modest extension can be approved. But I need word now.
> Thanks,
> J.L.

My first thought was to lament in prayer, as Job did: "Oh, that my words were already written, that they were printed in a book." But then what would I do? I would have nothing to do.

"Don't think. Do," was the old man's advice, his most precise wisdom. "Go. Just do."

I did and do. Give myself to the wind. I'm one bodacious hell of a Zen-ist. A constant failure, the perfect seeker. So I had a litany of reasons. Good ones. Even some true ones—*completely* true. Some philosophical ones. Zen ones. In Zen as in all philosophical or religious systems, there's an answer for every question. A rebuttal to every criticism. So, depending on the beneficent universe which provides for poets and other deranged types, I answered:

> John:
> I write slow. My marriage broke up. I went bankrupt. Then

there was the SARS epidemic, an unappeasable itching of the testicles—I fell in and out of love, and you know how that goes. Also I had a near-death experience. High-altitude pulmonary edema. Crumpled lungs. But that, and all else, is illusion. Books. Publishing even. Writing something to leave behind is yet another kind of dream: when I awake I know there will be no one to read it.

Take care,
G.C.

P.S. I'll deliver the final ms. in spring.

I was pleased. "The most important thing is sincerity," as George Burns, that particularly idiosyncratic American philosopher, pointed out. "If you can fake that you've got it made." Only the stories survive. The legends endure. They are us, our humanity, how we make sense: gods and heroes, fools and cowards, saints and sinners, philosophers and clowns—Homer to Hemmingway. The rest fades away.

Entebbe, Uganda, 25 January 1954 (IHT)
Gregarious Birds Attack Hemingway

Ernest Hemingway arrived here by automobile tonight after a weekend which included two air crashes and a night spent around a campfire in the jungle.

"I feel wonderful," Mr. Hemingway said. He was clutching a bunch of bananas and a bottle of gin as he and his wife painfully climbed from their car. His shirt was torn, his arm was swollen and there was, oozing blood, a big plaster patch on his head.

Mr. Hemingway said the crash was caused when the plane dived to avoid ibises.

•   •   •

When we flew out of the long shadows of southern China clouds and into the light, it was dazzling, like being born again. That morning there was a splendid frost; uncut diamonds made the steppe glitter—the great beige land stretching away, it seemed, to an infinity in which nothing human had moved for time out of mind.

This is your captain speaking: local time is 9:42 a.m. in Ulaanbaatar. The temperature is 40°F and clear.

Winter was near when ten minutes later we crossed the Ordos Plateau and the Yellow River. Like an old photograph, brown and white: a hundred shades of sepia, these high stony uplands marked by fine hairlike tracks fanning out like tributaries from the mouth of an ancient Martian riverbed, pouring into long gone oceans. Closer to the capital there were isolated stands of maybe eight trees; closer still, a series of walls enclosing empty sections of steppe.

"Those trees we just passed over. All of 'em are birches," my burly seatmate said. His accent was pure southern. "Georgia," he told me before I could ask. He was Clanton C. Black, Jr.; his business card read, *Distinguished Research Professor,* Biochemistry and Molecular Biology, the University of Georgia.

"It doesn't look like much, but there are three thousand species of plants that we know about in Mongolia. As many as seven hundred may be medicinal. We've no idea. Discoveries are waiting."

Clanton C. Black, Jr., also reminded me, with more than a hint of satisfaction and conviction, which phylum—at least in the realm of biological success—was evolution's star. "Yes, one species of man, three hundred thousand species of plants," he said.

Professor Black had a straggly gray beard and a face too long exposed to wind and sun; he wore thick-soled hiking boots, corduroys, a red flannel shirt, and a Harris tweed sport jacket. He was an old Mongolian hand, he said. "Been coming here for more than ten years—since '92, after the Russians cut bait."

"Those walls you see down there are government work. Nomads don't like things that regular. They like the free life; settling down is a disgrace, life in large encampments a punishment. They're real gracious, easygoing—easy until you try to confine them. They don't like being organized. They don't leave much behind."

The above was written in my notebook on the page opposite the following quotes, which I think are from Wing-Tsit Chan's *A Source Book in Chinese Philosophy* (Princeton University Press, 1936), though I can't guarantee the reference:

Utopia is the worst thing for a man. He is old [or is that *dead?*] by thirty.

Conversation should not be used unless it is certain to improve the quality of silence.

We all must now shut up. Shush. Listen.

We are a Pleistocene people, born sometime during the last 600,000 years, an ice epoch; born of hunters, gatherers, warriors, and explorers. This place, Mongolia, was the home of the wildest, the farthest-roaming tribes, nomads whose restlessness was written in every lineament and whose undiluted, primal DNA still sparks and twines memories of dispersion in our collective unconscious.

Travelers of a hundred ages, nomads are a here-and-now people, explorers in the truest sense of the word. They start to go somewhere, to do something. And sometimes they do, sometimes they don't. They forget or don't care or something else of more interest turns up, and that new something is always primary. And just like that, everything changes. They see what they want and that's *all* they want now, and so they go straight for it, no detour necessary; the shortest distance between two points, between here and there, is the direction to go.

Nomad life is so unconditional. It all depends on the moment. It fits me. It seems only rational. Logical. The way of the universe, the way of poetry and the loony ones. The way of monks, nomads, outlaws; I love them—ineffable and evanescent, they are my brothers.

Stand on a high place and howl. Rip out your heart when you must. Never accept things as they are. We are not and should never become law-abiding citizens. Our primary duty is to be freedom fighters.

Or as Henry Miller—our gloriously subversive father—declared, doing his best to laugh the puritans into extinction: "I was a born anarchist . . . [believing] that my sense of freedom was particularly personal . . . that the very idea of discipline was abhorrent . . . I was a rebel and an outlaw, a spiritual freak."

Thank you, Master Miller. For that is the human imperative. The evolutionary imperative. Imperfection. To be human is to at every moment break some law, bend some rule—legal, spiritual, scientific, philosophical, creative. To run full and fast for as long as we can. To push the envelope. Because that's what is right and just and brilliant and beautiful and intoxicating. Because that is life-affirming. Because that is our job. Our sacred duty. The hope of humanity.

Just the other side of the airport, Clanton C. Black pointed at what passed in this part of the world for forested mountains. "Right there, that's the oldest national park in the world. So old they can't figure out themselves when it was set aside."

"Good luck," he said when we parted. His final words were, "And don't eat camel cheese. In my experience, I found it can induce projectile vomiting."

We shook hands. "Thanks. I'll remember."

First there was that sky again, luminescent, pearlized, higher and more piercing than any other place I'd been. Then distance like the ocean's, a claustrophobic's heaven, the horizon in every direction falling away in a long smooth curve. And again the wind, always the wind from the west in your face carrying a different kind of cold, a cold of air desiccated by the great High Asian deserts, the Taklamakan and the Gobi. A wind that felt colder than it was. A pallor of haze.

I had been referred to Christopher G., a German filmmaker and cashmere exporter, and his Mongolian wife, Enkhe, by Paul B., a Harvard-educated Buddhist scholar, theater aesthete, and producer. One of the best-informed people I know on just about everything, he has contacts everywhere, or so it seems: a bon vivant à la Henry Miller crossed with Sartre.

Christopher and Enkhe, friends of Paul's, spent springs and summers with Enkhe's family in Mongolia, their winters in balmy Katmandu. When I wrote to Christopher in advance of my trip, he sent the following reply:

Sorry I didn't respond immediately. Unfortunately, we left
Mongolia last week and have packed up our summer camp. A
dear friend of ours, Jumaand, nomad, filmmaker, wild man,
and partner of mine in many projects, will meet you at the
airport. Regarding car and driver, insist Jumaand contact
Tooroo, Enkhe's uncle and our summer camp manager. He
speaks little English which he should improve. He has a Toyota
Land Cruiser and could be your driver.

> We wish you good luck
> in your work.

Looking around the airport for someone who might be Jumaand, I spotted a likely candidate: baggy wool sweater, quilted
pants, a sheepskin jacket with the patina of having been long lived
in, fancy tall Mongol boots—the kind with the turned-up toes
(Buddhist boots, I'd been told, made that way to avert, as much as
possible, the accidental murder of insects).

He spoke my name aloud several times, pronouncing each sylla-
ble separately. When I approached him, he put out his hand and I
shook it. It was like gripping a hunk of tree, still barked.

"Jumaand," he said. The name was Tibetan. It meant Graceful
Wind. A good sign, a very good sign, for wind was my alter ego,
my mantra.

"Glad to meet you," I said.

Jumaand was in his late forties but looked older, with stiff long
eyebrows, thick and fused together, a drooping mustache, washed
gray and sparsely whiskered, and a squinty, tight-skinned, leather-
colored face that was deeply furrowed. His nose was straight and
fine. He had a fighter's ears, small and close to his head. His bush of
hair—black, dusty, and unbrushable—cowlicked in three directions, though he occasionally tried to smooth it with the flat of his
hand. He stood erect, five-ten, a middle-weight-lean body, heavy

big-boned wrists, thick fingers. A ferocious mug with a nasty-looking razor scar that ran white, curving from beneath his hairline on the left side, across his cheekbone to the corner of his mouth. A knowing half smile that said, It couldn't matter less what you think of me. A cigarette dangling. Just another tough, if you missed the softness, the melancholy intelligence about the narrow hooded eyes—moody, cynical, egotistical, defiant, angry, but above all emanating the sense that here was a man who understood the joys and sorrows of life, who lived hard but well—to be alive was enough. It was clear. He loved women. Women loved him.

"Do you like coffee? Espresso?" he asked, grabbing my pack.

He smiled at my expression. I'd prepared myself for salt tea. Packed a two-month supply of caffeine tablets to ease my addiction.

"Espresso. Please. Lead the way."

Millie's Espresso, a light-filled room with Gobi Desert photographs on the walls, sleek wood tables and chairs, and a stainless Italian espresso machine, a Rancilio, was on the second floor above the Internet café, just off the main drag. It was the favored meeting place and hangout among the sizable consulate, UN, NGO, and expat community in Ulaanbaatar. At Millie's, not only could you get a decent cup of espresso—I've tasted worse in Paris—but information, rumors, and a damn good plate of huevos rancheros from a menu that offered an odd mix of American, Mexican, and Cuban food.

The café's proprietor, namesake, and social director was the elegant Million Skoda, whose circuitous route to Ulaanbaatar began in 1964 when she left Ethiopia to study in the United States. There she married an American and had two children. In 1997, her husband, a water and sanitation engineer, was stationed in Mongolia to work on a UN project. When Million arrived, there was no good coffee, just instant, and so she, looking for something to do, opened her café.

Jumaand ordered two for each of us to start. "I don't like to wait for coffee," he said.

"I know how you feel. I don't like to wait for anything. I've the patience of a flea."

Rising from the chair, Jumaand saluted me with his cup. "Good," he said. "In life we have no time for waiting. That is the artist's life. No time. You are an artist. Me too. Christopher told you. I am a filmmaker. I studied in Moscow. At the school for film. I learned to speak Russian. Still I hate Russian. I hate Moscow." Jumaand hesitated and his face turned momentarily dark. I could almost feel him force the smile that then creased his face.

"Now already I have made three films: *Stranger, Water Rings,* and *Heaven's Will*; the last one I made in 1992."

He didn't want to talk about them. The first two were lost, he said. Destroyed, something—he was vague.

"Always about nomad people, our stories," Jumaand said, after a long brooding pause to think things over. I'd asked him what the movies were about.

"And also I am a black belt," he added, returning to his bio. "Kendo. A stunt man for the movies. First Mongol. I am very proud of that. You know, because I was a horserace rider, one of the best in Mongolia. Very proud."

Jumaand was a man of absolute self-confidence, but without any sense of braggadocio.

"Paris film critics voted *Heaven's Will* one of the ten best films of the year. So I went to Paris, but I didn't like the food. Very hard for me."

"In Paris? You didn't like the food?"

"Not enough meat for a Mongol. I just want to eat meat. I don't like sauce. I don't eat vegetable. I'm not a horse."

He drained his cup. "*Fire on the Water* is the new one," he said. "The one I am writing. The one I want to make next. But now it is hard. No money in Mongolia for movies."

"Do you have *Heaven's Will* on tape? Can I get a copy?"

"Of course. I'll give it to you. Wait here." Then he stood abruptly and walked out of Millie's.

Three espressos later Jumaand was back. He removed his jacket, dropped it carelessly on the floor next to his chair, and sat. He leaned forward on his elbows. His mouth was close to me, his breath foul. And then, true to his word—*no time for wait*—he handed me the tape, as if it was the most natural thing in the world. And for him it was; it was, as I learned, the Mongol way of focus. There is no distance between what Mongols want to do and doing it, between deciding to move on and going. If you see a friend across the street, make a U-turn; forget the traffic. If you've got a destination, go until you get there. If you have a tape to give, give it. *Wait? No time.* He said nothing more about it, seemed to show no more interest in the topic at all. He motioned for another coffee.

There was a handwritten label pasted on the tape below the brand name. It read: *Kyyióap. Heaven's Will.* Unfortunately, I've never been able to watch it; all that shows is noise.

Still leaning, close enough now for me to see every broken blood vessel in the purple pouch beneath his eyes, the pores of his nose, he said, "You are tired. It is written on your face. Clear."

"As bad as that?"

"That bad."

I leaned back in my chair to escape his breath. "It's true I'm beat," I said. "It was long flight and a late night in Seoul."

"Korea?"

"Yes."

"And here, in Ulaanbaatar, where will you stay?"

"Zaya Guest House. Do you know it?"

His mouth tightened. He looked through the confusion of cigarette smoke and steam rising from his cup. He shook his head. "I don't know."

There followed then a long silence until, shuffling through my notebook, I found the address: Zaya Guest House and Backpack Co. Ltd. on Peace Avenue 63 10 12, Sukhbaatar District. Zaya, Director.

"Very close," he said and held up two fingers. "Only two minutes. We can go now. You rest. I have something I must do tomorrow and the next day. I can meet you here at nine. The morning. The day after tomorrow. Then we can talk. Make arrangements. Christopher told me you want to travel into the Gobi. Do you really want to go?"

"Yes."

"Good. In three days then."

"Millie's at nine. Three days. Perfect. That gives me time to get grounded, get over my jet lag. Look around. Find someone I want to meet. A Buddhist nun. Her name is Ani Jinpa. She takes care of children. Do you know her?"

Jumaand finished his coffee in a single gulp, and stood. His manner was distant. Cool. "No. I don't know of her. But I can take you to Zaya."

I paid. He hoisted my pack.

Zaya's was on the first floor of a four-story building. It was a depressing place, Chinese, dating from perhaps the early 1950s, its dank hallways set with broken tiles and cracking concrete that echoed every footstep and guaranteed perpetual darkness. I felt my way along a wall, up four stairs to a metal door on the right, and knocked.

At three-thirty on the next to the last afternoon in September I found myself alone in a room at Zaya Guest House, single occupancy, seven bucks U.S. a night, ground floor in the rear, ten-by-fifteen, barred windows looking out over a garden of rubble, back streets, and a pool hall—the Royal Snooker Club. Everything was the color of sand except a wedge of fierce blue sky. The room had two single iron bedsteads, pushed together side by side, concrete walls. Bare floors, if I remember right, linoleum. A chipped oval mirror flaking flyspecks of silvering. It was clean, had the faint smell of disinfectant and laundry soap. Some old cooking smells I didn't recognize. Tobacco and all the rest. A chair, a table, a pressed-board armoire that I wouldn't use: I would live out of my pack as always. Not bad. But hot. Too hot to breathe. Hot even with the window open. But with the curtains drawn, gloomy, and not too hot to sleep. My body, limp with fatigue—in a fog of semi-consciousness—was living in yesterday's time zone, where, on the other side of the world, it was still last night and something with yellow eyes was watching the stars take their turn through the universe.

Earlier that September, three weeks before leaving New York, I received a letter from Mongolia by way of London that had been forwarded by my British publisher. It was dated May 12, 2001. Written in purple ink on graph paper, in a careful hand, it had been in transit for just under two and a half years.

A picture was enclosed—a Western Buddhist nun with one baby hanging around her neck and shoulders, another curled in her arms, and twenty more surrounding her. Wiry and trim. Steel-gray hair cropped to a short crew cut. A brilliant smile. Ani Jinpa's eyes, even off the photo, sparked joy. An ecstasy that saints can find even in suffering. And she had read my book *Bones,* she wrote. This on a week when things were not going well. On a day that I felt like grade-A shit. A fraud. It seemed odd. Out of context. I thought, old

Barnum had it right. You can fool some of the people all of the time and most of the people some of the time. But the Venerable Thubten Jinpa?

In other news . . . lies are the truth of the human soul.

Ani Jinpa had included an e-mail address. I immediately sent off a reply, telling her when I was due to arrive in Ulaanbaatar and explaining why my response was so late in coming. My e-mail came back as *address unknown.* The only other address in the letter was PO Box 219 in Ulaanbaatar.

Dear George Crane:

I am an Australian Tibetan Buddhist nun working in Mongolia. (Outer.) In fact I think I'm the only Western TBN in Mongolia. We work here with homeless and abandoned babies and children.

With the thought to buy a gift for the only Australian Buddhist monk in Mongolia, I went to the nearby secondhand bookshop and found a perfect copy of your book which I restrained myself from reading first.

Now I have just regretfully turned the last page. I did not want to leave the wonderful Tsung Tsai or your lovely prose.

Thank you for such a beautiful book about enduring faith in people and a monk's profound faith in the Buddha's teachings.

Are you coming back . . .

Will you write more . . .

Yes [ ] Yes [ ]

Please tick both boxes

. . . bearing Buddha
constantly in mind
I gave up grief
and illusion . . .

A perfect teaching—I have it on my wall. Thank you for it.
Much love,
Ani

Ani was easy to find. I asked Millie, who seemed to know every foreigner in the country. "Ask him," she said, pointing to a very tall fellow leaning over a plate of eggs.

I asked. He knew. John, a Brit working for one of the NGOs operating in-country, knew her. Had helped her raise money.

"I just talked to her this morning," he said.

He gave me her number. I called.

"Ani Jinpa?"

"Speaking."

"Ani, it's George Crane; I got your number from John. You wrote me . . ."

"George Crane? The writer? *Bones of the Master* Georgie?"

"One and the same." I laughed. "I'm in Ulaanbaatar. I'd love to meet you. To talk to you."

"Oh yes. We must. What about tomorrow? Lunch? Join the children and me for soup at the nunnery. We begin serving at two. Come early. I've so much to ask you. How's Tsung Tsai? No, wait—" She stopped herself, her voice girlish and excited. "*Tomorrow*. Before lunch. After lunch. Tomorrow we can talk. Tomorrow is soon enough."

I got directions. "Tomorrow then," I said. "I'll come around noon. I look forward to it."

"Yes," she said. "Just wonderful. The conditions are ripening."

Thubten Jinpa's Dolma Ling Nunnery and Mahayana Buddhist Center, formerly the Chinese monastery Dari-ekh, was located on the city's edge, hidden deep within a maze of narrow squalid alleys that were the nomad slums. These walled-off shanty communities were an anomalous collection of ragged, out-of-context *gers* and squalid shacks cobbled together from the capital's garbage, from industrial remnants of every conceivable sort, from burnt-out buses to rotting boilers and oil tankers.

The elegant utility of the *ger* was lost in these asylums for the outcasts, the dispossessed, the homeless; the now useless, the weary and broken; the burnt out and drugged out; the sick and the dying—the hopeless, vacant of everything except despair and insanity. For a nomad imprisoned in this place and time, where every social and cultural contract has been destroyed, to be untouched by madness would in itself be madness. Delusional. Catatonic.

I'd arrived by taxi early, first having to bribe the driver with an extra bill to drive me into those back-alley slums. Ani Jinpa, looking just as she had in the photo she'd sent, was waiting at the gate. She was tall and slim, with crew-cut steel-gray hair. She radiated energy—a dervish spinning, a force of nature. She was one of those people who are bigger than life; she filled space. She was in control, on a mission, whether serving soup, tending children (she was a nurse before she took her vows), raising money, or battling bureaucracy.

Dari-ekh Monastery was abandoned early in the Soviet occupation and was a near ruin when Ani came to Ulaanbaatar for a short visit. She saw need and stayed. In the decade since, Ani has carved out of that dilapidation a temple, nuns' housing, classrooms, graveled pathways, and a courtyard with scraggly young trees.

"In time . . . ," she said, looking with eyes that saw what remained to be done. Saw how it would be. In time.

Her pride and joy was the new one-story 1,500-square-foot white stucco community center with its red-tiled roof. "This is what I really want to show you . . . just finished last month . . . the dining room, kitchen, and infirmary."

She opened the door to warmth. The new coal furnace and boiler had been fired up for the first time that morning and were still being tinkered with when I arrived.

"Ah, we have heat." She shivered and rubbed her hands together. "Hot water to wash the children. They have to wash before lunch. Dysentery is such a problem. The biggest killer, particularly among the very young. They eat garbage, you know. They hide it in their pockets, under their clothes; I try to keep them from adding it to the soup."

Ani slept in a small whitewashed room behind the kitchen which also served as the infirmary. There were cabinets for medical supplies, an examining table, a window looking out across the courtyard through newly planted twigs of trees to the restored temple. The only signs that she lived there were a metal military-issue footlocker, a backpack leaning against the wall, a chair by the window in which to sit and read or rock children, and a narrow, thin futon mattress on the floor. Drawings by and Polaroids of her children were taped to the wall. These were, I guessed, the sum total of her possessions.

Across the hall, she pointed, there was a bathroom: a sink, a bath for the babies and for younger children, showers.

"This little one," she pulled one of the photos off the wall. It was a classic: a picture of just a dynamite little kid mugging, full of herself, teasing, wagging her tongue at the camera—her eyes are fearless. "Dolma we call her, was found wandering alone, almost two years ago now. She was, best guess, about four years old. Coal black. Obviously had never had a bath, clothes so filthy they stuck to her—she probably had never been out of them—we just cut them off. Her hair also. The last layer of rags, practically fused to her skin, had to be soaked off, peeled away in the bath. The first four soaks the water turned mud. Her skin was pocked with sores and cankers. How she survived, I can't imagine. But look at her now."

The white-tiled kitchen was equipped with two four-burner stoves, a refrigerator, an incongruous restaurant sprayer over a stainless double sink, preparation tables. An alcove opened onto a bright and airy dining room where eight wooden tables and benches could seat thirty-two children for soup with meat and vegetables, bread, and milk tea.

"I officially feed fifty children a day, but most days it's closer to sixty."

"What's your budget?"

Ani Jinpa took a breath to calculate. "Five thousand U.S. a year," she said at last. "Sometimes a bit less."

I did a little calculating myself. "Less than fifteen bucks a day? For sixty? How?"

"I have suppliers . . . connections," she said with a conspiratorial wink and a twinkle that indicated she said less than she knew. "But corruption is almost universal; corruption and despair are choking this country," she continued. "Every year we have to make an appearance before some bureaucrat, some committee head, some secretary of something or other, and justify what we're doing here. Which means they want to know what's in it for *them*. How much can *they* get?"

It was just twelve-thirty, and already the children, plus a few pregnant and nursing mothers (whom Ani also feeds and cares for), had begun to gather, huddling together at the nunnery's gate, along with an old man, a tough-looking pug with a battered and broken face. Ani pointed in his direction. "That one's spent most of his life in prison. For murder. He told me he killed someone in a fight. He's seventy and takes care of two young children. His wife is eighteen."

Ani sighed as she took in the scene. "Look at them," she said, again pointing out the window overlooking the street and speaking in such a low voice that it was difficult to make out her words. Her voice changed now, its tones and cadence more suitable for speaking to a young child. "They come early. Always so early. *So* early. And they have such patience. Such grit. They're so stoic. Quiet. Never complaining." She crossed her arms, hugging herself and rocking from side to side as if comforting a baby. "But the wind . . . it's so cold. In rain, snow. I thought if they at least had a place to stand out of the weather."

She stomped her foot and turned away from the window. "I'm going to build a waiting room. We must begin tomorrow. The carpenter has already drawn up the plans. *Tomorrow,*" she said sharply, determined. "Tomorrow, without delay. The money will." She nodded to herself, to the beneficent universe, and there was no contradicting her passion, her certainty. "The money will just have to . . . I'll *get* it. Somehow."

Ani Jinpa circled the table with one of her Mongolian workers, who held the big dented pot as Ani ladled. Another followed, pouring tea and serving bread, two slices each. They all waited. Their washed hands folded. Quiet. Not one of them moved until their bowls were filled—and not paper bowls and plastic spoons either, but crockery and stainless. That's Ani's idea. She wants them to feel as good as possible about themselves, permanent and important. They eat quickly. Nothing is wasted. Not a drop. The bowls are licked clean. Filled with milk tea and licked again.

"How's the soup?" Ani asked.

"Good but a bit salty," I said, trying for politeness.

Ani closed her eyes and leaned her head forward, chin on chest. "I know," she said, sighing. "I know. I'm working on the cooks. Trying to get them to use less salt. It's better now. But still . . . they use so much salt. If I put salt on the table they'd use more. Mongols love salt. High blood pressure and kidney failure are endemic here."

"It seems the least of their problems."

"It is."

The need in Mongolia is overwhelming. Easy to see. The number of homeless children is unknown, but it's in the many, many tens of thousands. In a country with a total population of 2.3 million, there are an estimated 200,000 malnourished children. "An optimistic number," says Ani, shaking her head sadly. "A very optimistic number."

The official population of Ulaanbaatar is 820,000. The actual population may be closer to twice that number, if one counts the uncounted homeless, the nomads forced off the steppe by poverty's push. They've sold everything, finally even their *ger,* to survive. In the short time I walked the streets, I was most often followed by clouds of street kids begging or selling small bags of sunflower seeds to scatter to the wind and the pigeons—offerings, gifts for the Buddha. Some so young they fried the soul, stripped away the opaque membrane that stands between us and compassion. Because what I saw there of the human condition was too raw, too hard, too horrifying for us to justify our lives of comfort and possessive greed, too terrible to let us continue to think that we are *good* people, a noble species. We are, all of us, damaged goods.

Here homeless, parentless children as young as four years wandered the streets, babies cradling even younger babes in their arms. They crawled up in the morning from the underground, the network of heating tunnels beneath the street where they slept, huddled like moles in the dark, hibernating against the long freezing winters. One thing you quickly learn in Ulaanbaatar is to watch your step, look down always, for there is not a manhole cover left in place on the sidewalks and streets of the capital. They have all been removed for ease, for quick escape, coming and going. Children, occasionally whole families, crawl out from the underground with morning, continuing their hunt for scraps of garbage, for handouts—for survival and hope. And of course there *is* almost no hope for these children. Most of them, still babies, will die; they will die of every ill known to humankind—of malnutrition, of pneumonia, of influenza, of colds, of dysentery, of infection, of neglect.

They will die as native peoples have always died. Of genocide. Of cultural mass murder, pushed off their land and out of history by progress, by humanity's inexhaustible hunger for power, for land, for more stuff. They have died and will continue to die. Indians, Africans, Tibetans, nomads—it doesn't matter the country or tribe or race; they will die.

It is Darwinism carried to its logical extreme. The survival of the fittest—that is, survival of the most powerful. It is humanity's repulsive underbelly—prejudiced, superstitious, oppressive, caste-ridden, corrupted by wealth and political power. That we are collectively guilty of murder is the truth; that we are nothing but barbarians, all of us unfit to be called civilized, that too is the truth. Our civility is but a thin façade covering the absolute cruelty of a demented, cannibalistic species—that is nature's truth. We've got the ideas, the ethics all right, but our minds can't control our nature, what's written in the primitive code of life: *Win. Survive at all costs. Damn the consequences.*

China will continue to do to Tibet what America did to *her* native cultures, what the Europeans did to the Africans, what Russia did to the Mongolians, and what the new Mongolia continues to do to its remaining nomad peoples. What the powerful do to the weak. Period. Etcetera. There is no hope.

But then there is Thubten Jinpa. Ani, who seems unexhausted by the miseries of human life: war, disease, decay, filth, poverty, starvation; the continual, insistent demand for sympathy and personal concern that would harden all but a saint's supply of compassion.

Mostly I don't like saints. Or trust them. They are the same as we are. Barbarians. Sinners also. In the end everything will be found to be true of everybody. Saint and villain are one.

But then there is Ani Jinpa. She is a saint beyond my understanding.

25

Thursday, October 2: as promised, I would meet Jumaand, but not at Millie's, and not in the morning. He'd called and left a message—he would, he told Zaya, pick me up at the guesthouse that evening at eight. The arched doorway to the restaurant was lit by the dimmest red flashing bulb. Its signage was lettered not in plodding ugly Cyrillic, but in the elegant and flowing Mongol characters from the golden age of calligraphy—a script that was now almost extinct, having been outlawed by the monster, Stalin. The sign painted in black over the green recycled remains of another advertisement was wrinkled, faded, almost lost to time and weather. The letters of this older signage showed: *Camels.*

The place was empty of customers. There was a tiny bar near the door; there was sand on the floor and a jukebox for music. There were six tables. We took the one closest to the bar. I stared out past the grimy window into the dust and noisy dark. Gray. A dirty sprinkle of snow and dust silted in on the wind—gritty on the teeth, salty on the tongue—from the shabby monolithic streets of Ulaanbaatar, a city that is 360 years old but has no history but the recent, the crap designed and built by Stalinists and Maoist mentalities—classic despot architecture, designed to dull the senses and kill the soul, dedicated not to the perfectibility of humanity, but to our domination, our enslavement.

A tiny child beggar, six years old or younger—wretched with dirt, snot, lice—opened the door of the restaurant and peered in; she was looking for someone who was not there. The blinking red light above the entrance beat on her face, her pitiful expression: sullen, apathetic. With tiny fingers she pointed anxiously into her mouth. Running her was one of the most pitiful human beings I'd ever seen, a humpback with the twiggy, bandy legs of a newborn. I'd seen them together on the street, not far from the restaurant. His face was stiff and stupid, and when he sniffed gasoline, which he did constantly from a rag tucked beneath his chin, he got enormous erections. He was nothing but sagging skin and bone, but somehow he threw himself forward with impossibly mighty thrusts of his twisted stick crutches. The child had just enough time to make that terrible sign of hunger before she was shooed out by a shout from a dimly seen man standing at the rear of the restaurant, where the darkness was almost complete. I got up to follow her out into the street, but Jumaand grabbed me by the shoulder. He was silent for a moment, thinking through the possibilities.

"There is nothing you can do," he said.

"I know. I know," I repeated in shame under my breath as I sat.

Our waiter—he was ageless, with spiked punk hair and no neck, a small perfectly round head supported on massive shoulders—came with a tray that held a bottle of vodka (the best Genghis Khan brand), two glasses, an ashtray, and a rag. He began drying the table with the rag, the same one he would use to fastidiously dry the glasses, holding each one up to the light before slapping it on the table. The same with the ashtray. As soon as he'd finished, he left without a word. Jumaand stubbed out his cigarette, poured two vodkas and raised his glass in a silent toast. He was a drinker, hard and fast. I would try to keep up.

Not without suffering or desire but without illusion.

Jumaand had warned that a Mongol meal would be huge, and I was glad I'd eaten nothing that morning because my stomach had yet to catch up with the time change, and had skipped lunch (same reason) except for two cups of espresso at Millie's. To begin there was corn tea and soup that looked in the bowl like steaming puddles of congealing blood—I didn't ask, I didn't want to know.

There was mutton of course, which Jumaand cut—or rather, *hacked*—into hunks with a heavy hunting knife pulled from a leather sheath strapped to his calf and concealed beneath his pant leg.

"Spanish steel," he said, holding the heavy curved ten-inch blade up to the light after licking the grease first from it and then, one by one, from his fingers.

There were shoulder blades severed and served separate, the choicest of Mongol treats, bone spoons layered an inch thick with pure fat to suck up in one fell *slurp*. The nauseatingly sweet, oily smell hung like humidity in the air, a smoky haze as the evening wore on, draping purple shapes in failing light.

There were plates of pork with pickles, and fried meat patties drizzled with what looked like diesel oil. And the vodka went on and on, and then the bitter coffee, and when that ran out, the salty milk tea. And *still* more vodka.

Finally Jumaand pushed his plate aside, sighed, thumbed his lighter and lit his cigarette and my cigar. Without saying another word he leaned back in his chair, clasped his hands behind his head, closed his eyes, contented and concentrating. He smoked without taking the cigarette from between his lips, burning it to the nub, the ashes trickling down the front of his jacket, then flipped it onto the plate. He immediately lit another. I waved him off when he offered me one. He rested his elbows on the table, covered by a flowered oilcloth—tiny cabbage roses in a jungle of vines on a yellowed cream field—that was faded and cracking. He leaned forward, squinting into the smoke rising from the cigarette centered in the middle of his lips, and began without segue to question me about everything (or so it seemed) he thought important.

"What do you think about globalization?"

"It works for the rich."

"And integrity?"

"It's flexible. Depends on who defines it. And cultural."

"Do you like to hunt?"

"I don't know. I've never been hunting. I know I don't like being hunted."

He paused, waiting for the whine of an overworked engine passing on the street outside to fade away before beginning again.

"Do you think the blind see in dreams?"

"Yes. They must; language, words are also visions."

"Life is good for you?"

"A little good. A little bad. Spectacular sometimes, a kick in the ass from nowhere. Love might help. Might not. The usual. I want more. I always want more."

"How much do you believe in intuition?"

"One hundred percent. It's *all* I believe in. Except for imagination."

He took a deep breath. Another. Then, "I always get into trouble when I don't live by this quality. I become afraid when I think. Do you?"

"Yes." I paused and laughed. "But then, I get into trouble either way. But intuition trouble is better trouble."

He grinned all over his face, showing large yellow teeth, and let out an understanding grunt. He grabbed my head in both hands and, leaning across the table, kissed me three hard smacks between the eyes. "Good. Life is better through the feeling." He was moved near to tears. His tiny eyes and thin lips at first glance made him look hard and bitter, disappointed by what life had brought, disappointed by the ugliness he had seen. But when he smiled it was clear that bitterness and disappointment were just a small piece of the story. His whole being shouted a celebration of life. "I am alive. Alive. Alive." Here was man in touch with his female side, rooted in home and people. He knew what he needed. He knew what was needed.

"Mongol mentality prefers wisdom that comes through the heart. So now we are brothers. And now we can travel together. We can take a taxi to the moon."

I raised my glass. "To the moon."

"What kind of woman do you like?" he asked, his voice trailing away in a sigh.

"The female kind."

Jumaand's eyes twitched at the corners. He slapped me on the back. "Me too." He paused to laugh. "Sure. Sure. But wide or narrow?" For illustration, he curved shapes in the air with open hands, gesturing with such covetous sensuousness that for a moment I had trouble deciding.

Shall I describe for him, I wondered as she popped to mind, Ikana, honeyed-black as spades, the long-limbed Nigerian beauty who sold gently worn haute couture at number 10 Vlasská in the Malá Strana district of Prague? I pictured the beveled ceiling beams of her small shop, which were first stenciled with twining leaves in the seventeenth century; I saw the bared midriff that revealed the jagged scar of what must have been a terrible wound slashed diagonally across Ikana's belly.

Or perhaps I should tell him that Prague is the cleanest city, where not even a butt or a stray match stands much of a chance against the orange-vested legions of street-sweepers, a remnant of the Communist era before Havel's velvet revolution, who with their brooms, shovels, and handcarts clear the rubbish from this most literary of European cities.

Or say that language, the whirligig of words that is the holy force that drives the mind and makes books, is also rubbish. And "rubbish," said Ivan Klima, who in the bad old days was a Prague street-sweeper, "is immortal. Rubbish is like death. What else is so indestructible?"

But I said nothing and answered, "Narrow."

"Wide is also good," he said sotto voce—not with embarrassment, but lust.

"Do you know of a place called the lost temple?" I asked. It was a kind of throwaway, a balm to assuage my underactive writer's sense of honor for promising something I couldn't deliver—another serving of Tsung Tsai, the teacher who had given up on me, and a search Beyond the House of the False Lama, for a lost temple.

Jumaand surprised me. He blew out a puff of air. "Yes. Of course."

"You're joking," I said, thinking, Luck be a lady! Perfect. Just what I need, a lost temple—any lost temple will do.

"Got to be joking," I said, thinking aloud.

But Jumaand was dead serious. He got abruptly quiet and looked at me with a strange tight smile. It was the look of a man who, like all of his people, had been powerless in the face of oppression, but who had survived, whose life force was so strong that he would continue to survive, but would not forget or forgive or, about those times, joke. There were limits to sorrow, but there were also limits to laughter.

"It is no joke. It is a hopeless place. I've been there."

"I want to get there."

"I'll take you."

Jumaand leaned across the table. His black eyes narrowed and watered, and one nostril dripped onto his sparse mustache. "Tooroo is worried about money. But I told him you are an artist." He turned aside, worked a leaf of tobacco to the tip of his tongue, and spat.

Tooroo's prices had kept changing, an upward spiral. I was irritated, feeling that I was being played, but only said, "I can't afford more. I don't have it. I'm close to flat-out broke. Bankrupt. Do you know what I mean?"

Jumaand nodded that he understood and smiled honestly. "I know. Because also I am an artist. A filmmaker. Writer. Director. Camera. I do everything. I am a performer. But also like you I am no good at business. Nomad people are ashamed of money. I hate capitalism's way of thinking. But also I hate Communists. They are even bigger fucking pigs."

"I'm no good at money. I hate it. The utter banality of getting it flattens the mind, the imagination; kills the dreamer." I began my well-rehearsed and oft-repeated spiel, but before I could finish I began to laugh helplessly.

George, you are drunk. True. Very. *I'm painting myself into a corner here.*

"Sorry, but I'm drunk," I said. "You know, I never learned the simplest of economic lessons—not to spend more in a day than you have earned, for example—but then I've never earned enough to pay for what I need. For the necessities—family, books, music, travel, women, food, drink, drugs . . ." I was mumbling. Stuttering.

Jumaand was nodding and silent. His eyes were mere slits that I couldn't read. *A broke American? Just what I need. Unbelievable!* There was a long, uncomfortable pause.

"I do what I have to," I said. "I survive."

"How?"

"I hustle. I play the joker and the ace, the artist card. Understand what I'm talking about?"

He nodded slowly, almost imperceptibly. His face clouded. He drummed his fingers on the table.

I closed my eyes and drifted for I don't know how long. A minute, maybe more. Waiting. Thinking, Now you've blown it, George.

When I finally opened my eyes Jumaand was still nodding. A rueful smile. A flicker of disappointment. Resignation. A sigh. "Actually," he said, "how much do you have?"

I did a quick calculation. "$3,500. American," I said, keeping a secret five hundred bucks in the hole for emergencies.

The cloud passed. His voice softened. "We can try," he said.

"Good. Do the best you can."

He shook his fist next to his ear as if shaking the dice before a throw and thrust out his hand. I took it.

"Done," Jumaand said.

The going rate for a late-model Japanese SUV, with all the amenities that implied (including driver/guide), was fifty a day. Gas averaged fifty-five dollars per 250 kilometers. One of the Russian or Chinese army soft-tops was thirty-five dollars a day. To that we'd have to figure the extra cost in food and water for the driver. At that rate, I didn't have enough. There was no one left to borrow from. I owed everyone. It was too late in the game.

So it was decided: Jumaand would drive—no need for a guide— and we would use his truck, an eighties-model Nissan 4x4, a four-seater with a canvas-covered short-bed, a roll bar, and a roof rack. Once white with red lightning bolts on the hood, it had decals, curling at the edges, on the door panels:

WSPA

WORLD SOCIETY FOR PROTECTION OF ANIMALS

A rattletrap, but with plush faux-leopard-skin seatcovers front and back. The tires looked good, near new. I jumped on and off the front bumper. The springs were shot. "No problem." There were brackets for four spare gas cans riveted to the truck bed. "Cool." It had no muffler and was loud. The windshield was starred from stone throws. For a Mongol, a truck was just a horse with wheels, and obviously this one had been used hard and put away wet.

"Same age as my truck," I said after looking her over. Perhaps in better shape than old scout, my Cherokee; at least all her doors opened and closed. Regardless, I had a long-established love, an overflowing solicitude, for old trucks. And in them, I had an almost mystical faith; they'd always get you there and back before dying.

"Feels like home," I said, now giving those imaginary dice a shake for luck before letting them loose. *Lucky* seven. "Done."

Everything arranged, I handed Jumaand the thirty-five hundred, in hundreds. He would do the rest—figure supplies, do the buying, take what he needed. I didn't ask for an accounting.

"I know exactly what we need. Do you want something special?" he asked, almost as an afterthought.

We had talked and smoked and drunk enough so that, by midnight, I could care less where we were going and how and what we might take with us to get there.

I waved him on. "Whatever you think best."

"Good." He nodded appreciatively, relieved, and aloud to himself began his calculations. "One day and one night on the desert equals one bottle of vodka, one of whiskey, four gallons of water."

I gasped and then laughed. *This will be interesting.* "Sounds like a party," I said.

"For our good health," he said, beaming, pleased with the negotiations. Entirely nonchalant, he poured us both another glass.

"To friendship." He raised his glass, quaffed it in a gulp, and wiped his mouth with the back of his hand.

I followed. "To friendship."

Jumaand dropped me off at Zaya's, where tonight the street lamps were dark. He leaned out the window, pointing his first finger like a revolver. "Tomorrow morning," he said. "Early."

"I'll be here."

He drove off, disappearing immediately into darkness—either he hadn't turned on his lights or they didn't work—but for the unmuffled roar of the engine lingering back.

26

It had snowed lightly, off and on, that first week in October. In the gloom, through light dry snow that blew like dust, I stared out at the streets: slick and black, headlights and red blurs. I looked at my watch: 11:30 a.m. Paced the room. Settled down to wait, lying on the bed, hands laced behind my head. I dozed off and then awoke suddenly. Almost two hours had passed.

A knock on the door.

"George!"

"Yes?"

"Hello. It's Jumaand."

"Coming."

One last look around the room. I grabbed my pack. Put on my Levi's denim jacket, fleece vest, yellow parka, and black United Artists logo baseball cap.

"Jumaand," I saluted and looked beyond him toward the gear-filled truck. And looked again. Two women were sitting in back. One was narrow and the other wasn't. I gave the narrow one a closer look. She was slim, elegant with a sharp, high-arched nose and cheekbones, green-almond eyes. Her mouth was wide, generous, her lips always seeming just about to part into a smile. Not tall enough to be a runway model, but otherwise perfect, she sat straight and proud; she had hair the color of black olives with copper-colored high-lights—intoxicating—I could think of nothing else, no one lovelier, no one more exotic.

A serpentine red-sequined scarf was wound loosely around her neck, a close-fitting black sweater, faded—jeans, scuffed and down-at-the-heel boots.

"Uka is a student. A singer," Jumaand said, making the intro-ductions. "Mongol tradition. Songs of the nomads. A beautiful voice. She will be your friend, helper, and translator."

I offered her my hand and she took it and didn't let go. "Uka, Uka Uyanga," she said. "It means 'melody.'"

"George." I let my hand go limp in hers. "It means nothing."

"Nothing?"

"Yes. Nothing."

Probably picked out of a book, I thought. Names have no mean-ing in America. We are all new men. With no history. No an-tecedents. Free to reinvent ourselves, free to live lives based on self-selected fictions.

"Uka. Uka," I repeated slowly, elongating the melodic vowels.

A wonderful laugh, a slight overbite, a blinding smile. She gave up my hand a bit at a time. Hers was rough and made a sound like fine sandpaper as her fingers slipped across mine. She was small-breasted. Long-limbed. Fine-boned. Elegant. Mesmerizing. Abso-lutely stunning. Coltish. The kind of woman that turns girls into anorexics and keeps old men's dreams moist. I could see her wear-ing—at another time, in another place—a thin summer dress that floated as she walked and I watched, following her swinging skirt down rue Vieille du Temple perhaps until she turned a corner and disappeared, looking back over her shoulder. How old was she—twenty-four? Twenty-five? Five years older than my daughter, with long hair, like Siri's, braided into a thick tail that would bounce between her shoulder blades depending on how she moved. *And how she moved.*

But Uka looked older, much older, as if she had left girlhood behind so long ago that now it was only a faded vision, or more likely a time that never was. In her face was the record of a life that was too hard too soon. That certain smoky look. A bit worn. Ingeniously desirable. If asked what she was hoping for, what she was expecting, I thought she might have answered, like one of Anaïs Nin's sexual adventurers, "The marvelous."

It was hard to look away, but I turned now to the other girl. She was round-set and fleshy, with soft-soft breasts, heavy hips and thighs, wet pouchy eyes; her skin was blanched almost transparent, not white but the palest possible yellow, waxy; her face was pinched, lined by tragedy, tinged by a sad mothering tenderness. She had a faint mustache and lush lips. She wore crimson lipstick and a tight thin sweater. Something faintly awkward in the way she sat, held herself. She seemed to be waiting. She'd been to the wars. Carried battle scars.

"Her name is Tseegi," said Jumaand. "She lost both her girl children, two and four years, and also her husband, to winter, one year past. Pneumonia," he added, as if the word was strange to him. "I take care of her." He took a pack of cigarettes out of his jacket pocket, tapped the pack against the side of his hand so that two popped out, and held it out to me. I took one and he lit it and then his own with a brass lighter. He had the look of a man who needed to cry.

I mouthed the obligatory words. "I'm so sorry." I exhaled a sigh of smoke. "A nightmare. I have a daughter."

I flashed back to when Siri was two, in finally the quiet after bedtime, when the window reflected lamplight. The floor a mess of brightly colored toys, a rag Raggedy-Ann doll, a scattered pile of alphabet blocks: A for apple, B for bear, C for cow. The memories of her babyhood, my babycakes—the basics, like her fine long legs and fine big feet marching. Marching round the house in one bunny slipper singing, "One shoe on and one shoe off." So proud and happy. "Papa." Papa, I am called. "Papa, look at me. Look at me. Look at me."

And when she turned four, it was her birthday but my crown:

White felt,
decorated with blue roses;
sequin sparklers also.
Tied in back with a ribbon bow,
I wear my daughter's birthday crown.
Four years tomorrow,
four years . . .
four years are gone?
And oh my giggling girlie bows,
papa,
silly papa.
Yes your majesty.
Yes. Yes. Yes. Yes. Yes.

But two dead babies. One right after the other. It was much too painful to contemplate her horror. The terror of that loss. So Tseegi was hard to look at. Hers was a delicate, a fragile life; the finest crack could shatter it. A tear started at the corner of her eye and hung there. Once again in the face of overwhelming grief I felt stupid. "I'm sorry. Very," I mumbled. She looked away first, her mouth tight, curved down. A muscle in her cheek ticked. A single shake of her head, a philosopher's sigh that said everything and nothing. Hurry. Time is short. Life will be over soon. If you're not careful, paradise can go by in an instant when you're not looking. *Poof* and you've missed it.

The store was in a low, long, brick-built warehouse, hidden away in a narrow, filthy alley not far from the central market. Day was fading by the time we'd finishing buying and packing supplies—an odd assortment of preserved meats and sausage, a sack of wrinkled apples and one of oranges, bread and crackers, pickles, salt, six cartons of cigarettes—but mostly bottled water and, true to his word, vodka and whiskey by the case.

Even through the wind and diesel fumes I could smell the mutton, blood, and compost. The wind and a drift of soot-dusted snow blew sideways through the truck's cracked passenger-side window. Uka sat behind me. Not much room between us. The wind blew harder and I turned back to see how she was doing. She was holding her hair back from her face with a hand. Her other, holding to the seatback, brushed my shoulder.

I looked away. A child cradling a rag-swaddled baby sat on a rusted, upturned bucket beneath the comic hysteria of one of Ulaanbaatar's incomprehensible life-size plastic palm trees, complete with hanging coconut balloons in Day-Glo yellow, orange, and green. A crippled man leaned on a stick; blue snow was falling through the streetlamps. The traffic lights up and down the avenue were blinking sequentially without pause: red, yellow, green, yellow, red . . . It was 4:45.

Entering the tidal fearsome rush of madcap traffic, the anarchy that is the rule of the road in Ulaanbaatar, we drove south-southwest out of the city. Close to an hour later, at Songino Khairkhan, we stopped to make an offering, to ask the sacred mountain to bless our travels. A tin cup of vodka for the mountain and one for each of us.

"George, you will have much moonlight in your life," Jumaand said after breaking his silent meditation.

I held out my empty cup for a refill. "I'll drink to that. Moonlight and love."

There was light and then there was none. The sun fell off that ancient seabed as it did at sea. The Mongols call it sun-setting country. I turned and caught a last backward look at the city spread out below and to the northeast, with the beams of light from the Soviet-built coal-fired power plant caught in the great pall of smoke from its stacks reflecting red and drifting eastward. Over the crest of the hill ahead, nothing could be seen but the thick-starred western sky.

That first night Jumaand arranged for rooms and food at a hotel, an imposing three-story brick and concrete monstrosity located fifty kilometers or so west of the city, in a low mountainous ridge—elevation 4,634 feet—next to the Mongolian Galactic Observatory. Jumaand had thought we might look at the stars, get to know each other, and have a celebration of friendship before setting out into the Gobi.

But there would be no stargazing that night. The observatory was chained shut. It was a fine outcome, for Jumaand I knew would rather get right to partying without any delay for sightseeing. Life first. The cold dead universe would wait.

"Stars. Who cares." He smiled ruefully. "We can't touch, we can't kiss them. Come, let's eat. Drink. Talk. Sing."

The room was crowded with furniture. Heavy stuffed Chinese-red frayed chairs and a couch dominated. The low dining table set between them was liberally dusted with sand brought in by the wind. The rug on the floor was worn down to woof and warp. The rough plaster walls had once been painted perhaps baby blue. There was one north-facing window covered by bars and yellowed lace curtains. The radiator under the window was cold and hopeless. A bare fifteen-watt bulb hanging from the ceiling lit it all.

A knock at the door, and a young woman with one white eye entered with a tray—glasses, cups, two thermoses (one of hot water, one of milk tea) and a platter stacked high with dumplings. The smell of cabbage filled the room, rank as this extremely dry air could make it. We only picked at the dumplings, so rubbery and foul-looking that not even the Mongols would eat them. But we smoked, drank the tea, drank the vodka, drank the vodka; drank and talked—and the more we drank, the more we talked of love and art, of sex and death. And sex. And sex. The ladies took turns singing erotic Mongol songs of bed and lusty *ger*s. Jumaand recited poetry. There were no translations. None was necessary. Or I should say, only one: *shasha*.

"*Shasha,*" Uka said, "in Mongol, means 'fuck.'"

Mongolian is one of the three language groups in the Altaic family, closely related to Turkish, Uigur, Manchu, Daur, Ewenk, and Oroquen. I found it near to impossible to catch even the syntax. A single word was a victory. And what a word, the all-purpose beginning. But then, like a woman's body, language is best learned in bed.

"*Shasha,*" I repeated. "*Shasha. Shasha.*"

"Oh-hoo," Jumaand said, his mouth round and blowing air. He stood and crossed his arms across his chest. "What do you think?"

"*Shasha.*" I hissed the sibilant *sss*. *Shasha*.

Uka touched a finger to her lips. Tseegi actually giggled, hand over her mouth like a schoolgirl.

Uka took her finger from her lips and touched mine. "Now you. You must sing."

I had one of those blank moments. A combination of too much drink and that finger touching my lips. I was drunk and getting drunker. Not even the slightest recollection came to the surface of what can be facetiously referred to as my memory. A thousand years ago in courtly Japan social acceptability depended on one's ability to extemporize poetry, preferably in classical Chinese. Then as now I would have been a failure, a social liability. *Performance anxiety. Stage fright.* Perhaps just one more vodka (or is it one *less* vodka, when the room wouldn't have been spinning so?) and I would have taken off my clothes and danced on the table, improvising in a beat rush of eros. Instead I recited a poem that suddenly popped into consciousness, the incongruous to the moment and decidedly not erotic "Love Song of J. Alfred Prufrock," by the last of the Victorians, that prudish puritan T. S. Eliot, the most unlikely poet ever to sing to the soul of Mongol sensuality. Prufrock, who worries if he should eat a peach or wear his trousers rolled. Nevertheless, I was cornered. There was nothing to do but to plunge forward with an X-rated version. The honor of Western literary eros was at stake; and so, standing to recite, I began softly, hoarsely, my voice like a stage gangster's whisper in Uka's ear.

"Let us go then, you and I / When the evening is spread out against the sky / Like a patient etherized upon a table . . ." My voice was slurring, a seductive cajole. "Let us go through certain half-deserted streets, the muttering retreats / Of restless nights in one-night cheap hotels / And sawdust restaurants with oyster-shells / Yes yes Uka yes . . . of one-night stands in cheap hotels . . ." As memory failed my voice got lower, and acting out desire, I made vulturine bedroom eyes. "Uka, yes, let us go then you and I in cheap hotels / In cheap hotels. . . in cheap hotels. . . one night. . . a one-night stand. . . you and I in cheap hotels . . ." And then it came to me, a flash of Joycean inspired *yes!* And yes now I crooned, lowering my voice and leaning closer. "And yes she put her arms around him yes and drew him in so he could feel her breasts all perfume yes and his heart was going like mad and yes she said yes I will *yes*."

And after a suitable and interminable pause for effect, I bowed. From the waist. Deeply.

Applause. Tongue clicks. Finger whistles. Yodels and ululation. Kisses thrown. And for good measure, Jumaand grabbed my hand and gave it a vigorous shake. "Now we understand you. We understand you very well."

Jumaand took me aside and handed me three foil packs of condoms. "In Mongol this is called 'love without pain.'"

They lay in my hand like invitations to a beheading. "Impossible," I said.

Jumaand looked puzzled. He spread his arms, hands up. "You don't use them?"

"No. No." *Impossible? Really?* "It's not that. No . . . it's the name; love without pain. Never true. Should be 'love *with* pain.' You know, truth in advertising."

He was quiet for a moment. Surprised. "Yes. Must be pain." He suddenly got so very theatrically sad-looking it seemed as if he would actually cry." He rubbed his eyes that dripped only sarcasm. "Always hard," he said.

We laughed. I began it; then Jumaand joined in and did an Elvis pivot to boot. "Always hard." He wrapped his arms around me and laid his head on my shoulder. So amused was he with his humor, his stories, and life that his belly was still shaking against me when he kissed me three times on both cheeks, snorting.

"Uka likes you," he said. "She will share your bed."

Lifted out of time, I heard Frederica L. say, "I like you. You are closer to a Greek god archetype than any man I've ever been with."

Freddie was a Jungian, a postdoctoral student of Greek mythology, an utterly brilliant academic with a mop of kinky red curls, a woman of uncontrollable, omnivorous sexual appetite. Married to someone else. An adventurer in every sense of the word.

"You're Hermes," she said. "The god of the unexpected, of luck and synchronicity; the god of adventure and confusion. The most boyish man I've ever met. And also a major pain in the ass. Thief of hearts. Seducer. Wanderer."

"In Greek mythology cranes—distant relatives of mine, I'm sure— are given credit for having inspired Hermes to invent the alphabet. Writing. Yes. Call me Hermes."

She ignored me. "You were probably the first kid on the block to talk the neighbor girls out of their panties. I'll show you mine if you'll show me yours."

"You got me, kiddo. And don't forget the greatest of all the can't-lose con games: spin the bottle for two."

"You!" She sort of laughed. "Eternal emotional adolescent."

"Easy now."

She blew me a kiss. "Don't call again," she said, and wished me luck. Voice under control, but soft at the edges.

As Uka made the bed, a rat ran under it.

Uka pulled off her jeans and left the rest on—her sweater, long underwear, and socks. She crawled into bed, pulled the blanket up to her chin. I waited. She pulled back the blanket and smiled in that certain way that meant she was just as confused as I was. Like her, I took off just my jeans. And just stood there beating my arms for warmth. She kicked the blanket back further and patted the hard mattress, making room for me, turning onto her side, her knees pulled up, fetal position, facing the wall. I curled up next to her, into her; that was the only way, on that narrow creaky bed, for two to sleep—my knees in the crook of her knees, the belly of her bottom fit into the concavity of my hips, my nose in her hair, my

right arm across her shoulders, holding onto her arms folded across
her chest. The blanket rough against my neck.

We were cold and quiet. Then, as Jumaand had promised,
warm. There was a contest of silence. Uka ended it.

"What are you thinking?" she whispered.

I surprised myself, lying lamely. "That you are beautiful," I said,
groaning inwardly when the words hit the air. If I'd been alone I
would have knocked my knuckles hard several times against my temples and groaned, frustrated and embarrassed by my stupidity. *Stupid!*

Uka gave a brief dry laugh. "I'm not."

"You are." There was nothing else I could make myself say. But
what was left unsaid was clearly understood. I fell. I fell. I fell slowly
into a deep, intoxicated sleep. I woke once that night. We were tumbled up together. Carefully, so as not to wake her, I untangled my
arm to look at the luminous dial of my watch: 3:55. She had gotten
soft. While, against her, I had gotten hard. She might have been
awake, my platonic (or, more accurately, my un-*shasha'*d) lover.

Why did I hold back? For what reason? Why wait? Why hesi-
tate? We're all going to die; there's only tonight. I repeated once
again my mantra: Against the flood, the endless ocean of death,
each death including mine is a drop of water evaporating. Less. So
shut up. Go back to sleep. The point is to get up in the morning.
See what will happen. Good. Bad. Indifferent. Move on. One foot
in front of the other. Thumbs up or down. The verdict of the mob
or the emperor be damned.

Last night something, most likely the rat, ate a chunk out of the
leather sheath that held my Swiss Army knife. In the morning
there was a ragged hole and shredded bits of leather left.

That day, such a pretty day, breakfast was milk tea, bread, pickles, horsemeat sausage, blood sausage, potato soup with stringy

meat of unknown origin, rice noodles, enough salt to flavor an ocean. I had tea and bread.

Jumaand grabbed up a handful of sand, kissed the fist that held it, and opening his fingers, one by one, gave his sacred land back, scattering it like the ashes of a beloved to the wind.

"Earth, wind, and sky all have their honor, their riddles," he said.

His love of land, of country, was a connection, a passion I would never know, could never understand. I was from nowhere. Connected to no land. From no country. One of the rootless ones, a product of the diaspora, an immigrant, an exile whose past was a slate wiped clean by time, by loss; by pogroms and assimilation. I never really knew my parents or they me, never knew my home, never knew where I came from, never knew my history. All I had was a dream of Shambhala—that is, the search for the unknown place of peace and belonging; of steps and steps and steps and huge doors; locked, always closed. I was only who and what I had the nerve to pretend to be.

"I have no home," I said. "No place I feel about, in my heart, as you do for Mongolia."

He looked uncomprehending. Struck dumb. Surprised. "What? This is no good. Completely stupid."

"I'm not sure."

He thought for a moment, cocked a thumb dead center at his chest. "I *am* sure. It's why I am not afraid to lose my life. Wherever I am, if I'm in Europe or anywhere else, I say: I am Jumaand from Mongolia. What can *you* say?"

"I am George from earth."

He smoothed his mustache slowly and repeatedly, nodding while considering. A long brooding pause. "That works," he finally agreed. "I am Jumaand from earth," he said slowly, trying it on for

size. Chewing the words. "Jumaand from earth." He smiled reflec-
tively. "Yes, I like it. Jumaand from earth, from earth. From earth,"
he repeated softly, hugging me into one of his now-familiar bear
hugs, kissing me three times again.

"I am I," he announced to the known universe. "I am Jumaand
from earth."

A spectacular morning. Spectacular. And strangely warm. There was a slight breeze, but no sound came from the air. The road was deserted, scorching. There was no shade.

We drove south by southwest under a pitiless sky, the sun dazzling, crystalline, extraordinarily brilliant. It was a day that defined with razor sharpness, with the surreal chiaroscuro power of its revealing, every blade of grass, every stone and pebble, every grain of sand. A light that divided shadow from substance.

Grinding along in low, the jeep bounced, swaying musically in the rising dust, a metronomic cacophony of rattles. We followed tracks and trails, crisscrossing age lines that faded here and there to vague hints of passage; stone markers older than history. There was almost nothing of man here. A jumble of stone and shallow dun-colored soil. Blowing sand. No houses, gardens. No trees. Yet every inch, every foot of it had been walked and ridden and touched and grazed and birthed on, lived on and died on, though the signs, the marks of that life were few, almost nonexistent.

I watched a covey of desert finch, envying their flight, the way they capered, swooping and gliding effortlessly, sixty, a hundred yards at a pop.

As Jumaand drove, he sang, his mouth open wide, his voice and song growing stronger as the miles clicked off. It was his song for the road, his "long song." And without knowing the words, I understood it, understood its fierce, its ravenous, its ancient pulsing chant of freedom, its reverence for family and home and earth and sky and wind.

But I asked anyway, when he stopped for a smoke. "What is this song you sing?"

"Mongols sing in praise of the five senses, trying to give some kind of feeling to being alive, trying to answer the question of why we are human beings," he said. "Why we are nomads."

"Good question. What's the answer?" I said, largely to myself.

Jumaand smiled. He shrugged me off, said nothing but simply began again to sing. And of course, that was it; the answer was the song, the act of making music. We are human beings because we sing.

Jumaand was singing his world into existence. His voice was deep and booming. From the "songlines" of the Aboriginals to the tunes of the Okies on their way west, the road song—that traveler's connection to past and place—was universal. It's what we do. It's the human way. Our connection, our sacred geography.

When Jumaand finished, he turned to me. "Now you," he said.

I knew what was coming and was prepared. Something celebratory from another of the world's lost tribes. Something spiritual. Hebraic. Something with connection to the footprints of my ancestors. A scat version of "Hava Nagilah."

let us rejoice and be happy
awaken brothers and sisters
with a happy heart

That I didn't know any of the words was not a problem. I knew the melody. No need to worry about words. "I learned this one from my grandmother," I said and simply belted, jived, and improvised as the old Hassid jazzmen did, a wordless bim-bom melody, a language without meaning; the power of rhythm, of sound alone; the magic of understanding beyond words. The Aboriginals call it the "way of the law." It is the human way, the tracks of our dreams.

haaah-vaah naah giiii-laaah
haaah-vaah naah giiii-laaah
hey-schmay-re-nismecha
hey-schmay-ha-ra-nema
hey-vey-re-nismecha
haaah-vaah naah giiii-laaah
haaah-vaah naah giiii-laaah
u-ru, u-ru, u-ru a-him, u-ru a-him
hey nismecha

And so inspired, finished, I segued into a rousing rendition of a verse, a scrap of playground doggerel, that completely out of context popped suddenly into consciousness and out of mouth, in that marvelous abstract, expressionist way the mind functions, creating (besides mostly nonsense) occasional evolutionary leaps in that random sparking of neurons connecting.

all the girls in France
go to school without underpants

and the way they shake
is enough to kill a snake
when the snake is dead
they put roses in his head
when the roses die
they put tulips in his eye

A rhythmic clapping when I'd finished. Then, "George!" and Uka threw her arms around me.

Then Tseegi began. She sang from her heart of grief; she sang as she must have once crooned lullabies to her sleeping babies, her soft breasts rising and falling in a gentle swell. "We have such a huge country, so my children we must travel day and night through the endless world. Day and night my sweet little ones. Day and night."

The landscape was vacant. Its beauty was in that utter bleakness, that prodigious, mostly mineral solitude, where life, by tooth and claw, merely hangs on, where all distant things shimmer and fade to haze.

Crossing over a ridge we met a good wind, an echoing sky. The butter light of noon was cold and dry and still—as if all human life had fled. Which was happening, one way or the other. The Gobi was emptying out fast: the great Mongol tribes who had hunted and haunted the steppe were being forced off the land in ragged retreat from the big grass country to the corrosive, reservation-like squalor of Ulaanbaatar. Newly arrived off the steppe where they used to live as nomads, where they knew how to survive as fully functional human beings, where they understood and had purpose.

The last three winters had been terrible, with heavy snows and with animals and people—in unprecedented numbers—dying and abandoning winter pastures and territories that had been safe refuge since before the days of Genghis Khan. A third of Mongolia's herds had been lost, and much of what remained was weak, on the edge.

Jumaand was sure: "There will be another *zud*" (a long dry summer followed by an extreme winter), he said. "Three years in a row this has happened."

But the weather was really just another excuse. The nomads were being moved off the steppe by government policy, a strategy that began with the Soviet occupation and continues to the present. Now, in this newly independent Democratic Republic of Mongolia, they were being forced into the walled shantytowns growing up around Ulaanbaatar. Those empty corrals I'd seen from the air on our approach were corrals all right, but not for livestock; they were for nomads, were permanent *ger* reservations-in-waiting.

It's all about control. Nomads don't like being organized. They're wild cards. All governments fear the unpredictable, the independent thought; freedom is anathema and threatening to the greedy, the power-corrupted politicos, their dewlapped faces slobbering like pigs at the trough.

On the steppe there is something relentless and inextinguishable about the nomad, charged by the central Mongol belief that they are a people born to conquer the world. With their utter lust for life, the simple pleasure of it—in the sense that life is a song to be sung, not a condition to be endured—they have triumphed. Wanting only freedom, they ask not one more thing of the universe. Period. They make disastrous city dwellers; used to relying totally on themselves for everything, they now must rely on a system that gives them almost nothing when they need everything. They get lost. And so go mad.

A people who have had their ancient laws and customs taken away, whose language and history have been made to count for nothing, whose temples have all been destroyed, who have been shorn of culture and function, of their horses and animals and movement—such people are easily exhausted, demoralized. Easily controlled. Neglect will finish the job, with poverty, starvation, and disease taking their deadly, inexorable toll on this now-no-more-than-a-mob of homeless drunks, of glue- and gas-sniffing zombies. Tsung Tsai had warned of hungry ghosts: "You also need watch for hungry ghosts who look like people, exactly same as people, but not real people. They walk-walk-walk and talk-talk-talk, but never know life."

Such sadness. Such terrible sadness. And suffering. And suffering . . .

The days of the nomads are numbered. But for those free nomads remaining on the steppe, it is a talisman of their intrepidness, their courage in the face of assimilation, that even as they understand that they and their way of life are all but extinct, understand that now they are headed nowhere in history, they are still somehow happy en route. They care little about property; the land belongs to all and to no one, and owning more than one needs to survive, more than one can easily move, is a misery. They seem to be looking always at that place unseen, that invisible blank in the distance beyond the horizon. The direction they are heading. For, seen in the long light of time, only this earth will remain. *Take heart: only the earth survives.* This colorless, monotonous, austere, inhuman, magnificent country that stretches away, away in every direction. And the end is only where humanity leaves off—stops and lets the story continue in wordless silence.

The mountains started before they showed. Small ridges, jaggy bedrock spines, folds, and arroyos fissured the up-running plateau. Far off, that mountain range not yet truly visible loomed unsteadily, contorting liquidly in the dust-flowered air. Eight more hours brought us over the northern hills and into the central Gobi. Here be the resonance—the splendor, squalor, dementia, and accomplishments—of travel older than history.

Toward evening the sky of no color cleared, and that night the stars showed their best glitter when we came around a dogleg and spotted an abrupt stone wall. It sheltered a small encampment, a string of four horses, a couple of *ger*s. It was three a.m. There were no lights. Dogs barked and growled. "We can sleep a few hours here," Jumaand said, leaning on the horn.

Inside a *ger* a lantern was lit and the fire stoked. The teapot would be put to boil. Day or night, time-honored tradition required nomads to offer hospitality to strangers coming out of the steppe.

It was a bright night, extraordinarily brilliant, giving the air itself such an aura of desolate beauty and living, such a sense of timelessness, of universal oneness, that I was instantly and utterly without fear—fear of death, fear of failure, fear of the ordinary—struck instead by a feeling of absolute contentment and happiness. It was the ideal time for oblivion, then when all was perfect, when the darkness was lulled rather than disturbed by the distant clamor of dogs. I wrote in my notebook, propped on the still-warm hood of Jumaand's truck. Watch the pen move; round black cursive letters, the mystery of words.

The moment slipped away. As always. And I returned to chaos. To curiosity, thank god. To the insane, the glorious rashness of the living; this wild rush through obscurity.

I was surrounded by the generous and friendly vibes of a nomad family—father, mother, a baby, and one in the oven. "America," the father said, his big head nodding up and down. It wasn't a question but an exclamation. He said it as if it were a magic word, a spell promising power and privilege, money—*gimme all that stuff; there must be more stuff*—all the goodies.

I wondered if I should tell him that it was a hoax, unsatisfying, intolerably venal. That the only thing important in America was fame. People killed for it. Themselves or others or both—it didn't matter. It was the real prize, the gold ring; the stuff was just the gravy.

Still, I kept my gravy. I tracked our progress via the $250 GPS—a Garmin eTrex Summit—in my pocket and kicked sand over my $200 Technica Kevlar hiking boots. Just that stuff alone and what it was costing me to wander loose in the world added up to more money than our host would make in a year. A lifetime. Power and privilege equals freedom. It was true. I had it. Wanted it. Wanted to keep it. I was always, one way or the other, even when flat broke and without reasonable prospects, able to find the money I needed—by hook or by crook, as they say. Altruism be damned. Freedom and survival. You must survive. You must survive. You must. You! It's a perversion, of course, a perversion that only the best of us can resist. And I'm not one of them. I am not a moral man. I have no principles except survival.

28

With the headlights fingering a tunnel of blankness into the darkness, up through the beams, weaving and twisting, the day birds flushed and rose squawking from their roosts.

The sky looked like oil. Hallucinations, quick antic shapes, appeared and leaped back from where they came.

There was the dark of dawn, the paling stars, and then a silvered floating world. A faint edge of moon that barely showed over the horizon. The briefest dawn, and then it was day. As the coldest air came, we took a side track down a narrow incline; to the left the fractured-up face of a bald knoll, limestone falling in a pale swath. On a broken stretch where the track and the truck barely clung to the earth above a gorge, where the shadows were dark and sharp, a stiff updraft whined.

Turning out toward a pan-land plateau—hoary in the hazy cold—we came upon, leaning into the neck of a shaggy smallish roan, a weathered herder, his face like a dried apricot, watching the first morning sun, blinding as it topped the mountain.

Jumaand rolled to a stop and climbed quietly out of the truck, closing the door softly. Idly stroking the horse's neck, he offered its rider a cigarette and asked a question I couldn't hear. The old man listened, thought for a moment, said something, and pointed vaguely at the horizon. Sitting deep and solid in the saddle, a cigarette dangling from his lips, he lifted his hand once in parting, turned back to the day, and rode slowly toward it.

Jumaand seemed satisfied. "Close," he said on returning to the truck.

"How long?" I asked, though I knew better and got the answer I expected. We were on nomad time, horizon-to-horizon vision. Just on the move.

He grimaced and shrugged. "Close," he repeated.

We came into a sparse furred country, naked riprap, bare freezing sand, cutting sand, and thorny bramble. There were boulders close ahead, and then we were among them, winding around ancient rockfalls up through dust plumes. I had no reasonable conjecture about how that boulder- and shattered-stone-strewn field, a rough circle of maybe five acres, had come to be sitting in the midst of a featureless prairie grassland that stretched, otherwise uninterrupted, as far as the eye could see in every direction.

Off to the right, dun-colored from its shroud of sand, but mostly hide and bone, was the carcass of a horse that had died screaming, the longing patience of vultures not far off. Dead horse, dead children, dead parents; just garbage, so much trash, after all.

Under a sky cloudless to the horizon, snow flurries blew in from who knows how far to the west. A narrow line of birds, high and remote, flew east-southeast. The winter grass, the shoe-top veldt, hissed; underfoot or underwheel, it crunched and shattered into ankle-high clouds of dust. Out on the periphery of my field of vision something gray loped the ridgeline and was gone. A desperate beauty.

On and on we drove, worming slowly south by southwest for the rest of this day and one more after it, until on the afternoon of the second day we veered right, at the place where the westward terminus of some ancient washout bumped into the plain. We picked a track through a flood of stone-strewn outwash and oddly blackened bunchgrass arrayed like armies of Orcs on the march through Middle Earth.

Another hour and we were, without warning, there. Elevation 4,650 feet. Here, marked by one low flat cloud, was Jumaand's lost temple. So this was it? All there was after a year of planning and weeks of travel? Yes and no. It wasn't Tsung Tsai's lost temple, intact and flourishing—that dream remained hidden some 2,000 kilometers or so to the south and west, in the Wolf Mountains of China's Inner Mongolia. What I'd found was a poor substitute; a memory, a pile of rubble.

There were ten thousand monasteries in Mongolia before the Soviet conquest. The orgy of destruction that began in the late thirties left none standing. They are all lost temples—not lost in time but lost to man's cannibalistic madness, standing now only as a stark indictment of yet another evil, banal ideology. The Mongols call them the *unstii khiid,* the temples of ashes, a fitting reminder of loss, of man's inhumanity. Perhaps only the lost temple at Two Wolf Mountain remains whole and complete, still undiscovered, a mystery. There would be no Shambhala. Perhaps it exists, but only in dreams, the hope of a better, more enlightened humanity.

"Well, did you find it? Did you find Shambhala?" they would ask when I returned.

"No," I would say. "I found what in this world is truer."

"And what's that?" they might ask. "What's truer than Shambhala?"

And I would answer, "Its opposite."

The slow warmth of the midafternoon sun bathed the marshy swale and waist-high yellowed grass. There were clumps of reeds and bulrushes, geese in surprising numbers honking into the air. The still-water pond held their reflections and those of the cloud bellies passing, a patch of blue shine. Thin sheets of ice floated near the shore; no more than an occasional eddy moved the thin, clear water as the sun beat down.

Where the water had retreated there was a flat, sour sward of mud crosshatched by animal tracks.

All that remained of the lost temple was a roofless cadaverous ruin; the walls were rounded and insubstantial, like the remains of sandcastles at low tide, worn grain by slow grain, fissure by slow fissure. And these, like a wind player's reed, vibed the west-slope downdrafts into a soulful wailing, running molten over the rubble, the visible bones, the blackened stone shaped in ripples and flutes.

"We should pray," Jumaand said.

We should ask why human beings are capable of such shit.

We made our prayers and an offering to the gods on an *ovoo,* an altar, built from the ruins. Both traveler's cairn and shrine, it was made of roughly piled stone, broken glass, and sraps of blue prayer flags. It was topped by a twiggy branch from who knows where, as there wasn't a tree or bush to be found for hundreds of kilometers in any direction. At an *ovoo,* in a tradition predating Buddhism, it is strictly forbidden to dig soil, move rocks, disturb vegetation, or hunt. Jumaand sprinkled the vodka, first to the four directions and then onto the stones, an offering for the wind and the beloved earth. Then he poured triple-shooters, one for each of us. I pressed my fingers against my eyelids until vermilion constellations exploded behind my eyes and blessed all that had been lost in the drift of time.

"The stupid Communists destroyed everything. I hate them. I just want to kill. So much. I pray for their death. The shit-fuckers," Jumaand said, hawking up a blob of pure bile and kicking up a clod of tan bunchgrass. With a sense of desolation and fury, his jaw clenched on his words, he added, "With my bare hands." His face twisted into a sneer. His voice was pure contempt. His hands, miming unconsciously, seemed to be slowly wringing a Commie's neck as he might a chicken's. There lived in Jumaand's soul a whole range of beliefs that had nothing to do with his lamist pieties.

"I tell people you can't know love until you know hate. George, do you know hate?" It was clear that, when pushed, he would have a terrible, a violent temper.

"Do you know the stone writing of Mongolia's warrior poet, Prince Tsogt?" Jumaand asked.

"No."

"Tsogt Taij carved poems into stone—in the desert you can still find them, warnings to invaders. Leave this land or die, he wrote, or he—Tsogt Taij himself—would kill them. All of them."

"A simple idea," I said. "Perhaps even a good one. Though he couldn't have. It can't be done. As the Native Americans discovered, the invaders are too many. And they keep coming. They want everything."

Jumaand nodded slowly. Sadly. "Yes."

I'd like to save the world, I thought, but I can't. I can't even kill the bastards that need killing. The ones that the world needs to be without. But who are they? There are a lot of them. Perhaps the whole damn species is contaminated beyond saving. Bring on the flood. Forget the ark.

"I've considered murder. And suicide," I said. "And once almost succeeded."

Jumaand lowered his voice and leaned closer, his expression confidential. "Suicide? You tried to kill yourself?" he asked with a wink of amused interest.

"No. Murder," I said. "When I was ten I tried to kill a man. Revenge. That he didn't die was luck. I waited in ambush on a rooftop and dropped a brick on his head. A few days earlier, when I'd run across his crummy patch of grass, he slapped me across the back with a rake handle, raising a diagonal welt that leaked blood from right shoulder to left hip. And I got him back. The brick hit his head square on with a *thunk* like a melon bursting."

Jumaand tilted his head back and blew a long, meditative plume of smoke over the water toward the ruins. "Suicide and murder, both are important to know," he said. "Also revenge."

An involuntary electric shiver ran down my spine. Toasting all the gods, spirits, and hungry ghosts of place, I slugged down my triple in a gulp. "Live large and enjoy"—not prayer but advice; to myself, to all who love and are loved. For the rest, the stone-assed carnivorous killers—for those bastards there's no help. Let them die and to hell with them. Let someone else forgive. Let the saints, let Tsung Tsai, let Ani Jinpa forgive. I won't. Can't. Like Jumaand, I know hate. I know love and play also. The antidote.

Life ends in death. Together with us, even our sins will fade away; death itself is illusion. That's the way things are, wrote Ikkyu:

All is vain!
This morning,
a healthy friend;
this evening,
a wisp of cremation smoke.

Things change and the stars move. There's always hope in the new, and I wanted done with this deluded present tense, now and forever. So when Jumaand poured another, I drank, this time toasting our better natures—to a saner future, to change, which sense tells us is the only constant in the universe.

But here's the rub. Relativity and Zen suggest that even change is an illusion. According to Einstein, things do not become; they have not been, and they will not be: they simply *are,* and (take a deep breath now) we reach the future by displacing ourselves in time. Ipso facto, and here's where it gets interesting, we do not bring things into being—and if nothing is brought into being, there is no change. The distinction between the past, the present, and the future is only an illusion. Brother Einstein, meet Father Buddha.

Still, without regard to the surety that all is illusion, just fantasy, I drank, and will drink again, raising my cup to hope, which neither Buddha nor Einstein can refute. To hope. To love. To falling in love again. Yes, again. And again. Mad. Obsessive. Over the top, to die for, better than nirvana, lusting, monomaniacal love. Falling once again for Faulkner's dopey Nobel sentimentalism: "Man will not only prevail, he will endure." So here's to a better future.

Should auld acquaintance be forgot
and never brought to mind . . .
we'll drink a cup of kindness now
for auld lang syne;
for old long-since times gone by
for auld lang syne my dear
for auld lang syne.

The gentle pressure of Uka's hand on the small of my back pulled me back. She stroked my hair back from my forehead.

"Do you know how to skip stones?" I asked her, bending down to pick up a perfect skipper, flat and round, at my feet.

She looked confused.

"Watch. I'm a pro," I said.

And I was. Holding the stone resting lightly on my forefinger and against the curve of my first finger with my thumb, I snapped my wrist with an easy sidearm motion, sending the skipper on a fast, low trajectory over the water. When it hit, it bounced, skipping a dozen or more times over the surface before sinking. We watched until the circles marking its fall died.

A sudden remote howl. And then with no warning, the first serious chill of winter whipped in, a foretaste of the bullying times ahead. With that wind a Chicago Bulls cap came tumbling in out of the steppe. The prince of hoops' number, Michael Jordan's 23, was emblazoned on the brim. This perfectly ridiculous oddity rolled to a stop not five feet from me, a cosmic joke and mockery. The gods had spoken. I picked it up and hung it from the branch topping the *ovoo*. It looked good hanging there, an ornament. It lifted my mood. Everything—hope and hopelessness, all tragedy—eventually dilutes to insignificance, to farce and laughter.

That was how winter came to Mongolia. A winter that would never end. I turned the page of my journal and began writing, without rhyme or reason. I wrote about another time, an opposite place.

"Why do you write so much in your book?" Jumaand asked.

"I'm afraid of forgetting," I told him. "Afraid of not finding my way back to where I've been. But mostly it's for the simple pleasure of discovering what I've been thinking."

There was a long silence, a reluctant nod. "Yes, but for example," he said, "what do you think about now?"

"Doughnuts and philosophy." I was pleased to be able to say this with a straight face. "Do you know what a doughnut is?"

He hesitated, unsure that I wasn't joking. "Of course." He made a circle with his thumb and first finger. "I've been to Paris."

I'd all but forgotten. "Yes, I remember. For your film. Except for the food, did you like it?"

He was very quiet. I could hear his breathing, feel his mind wandering back to the city of lights. He was less than enthusiastic. "In Paris I could count the stars. The sky became small and boring. Of no use." I could smell the vodka on his breath. "Doughnuts and philosophy," he repeated. "I don't understand."

"I was wondering what you, what Jumaand, what Mongol philosophy would make of Western cosmology's latest idea, a theory speculating a universe that's doughnut-shaped. A universe that, given enough time and speed, we could sail around, coming back to where we started from, but from the other direction. I was considering the confusing hole in the middle of this universe, which like the center of the doughnut is an emptiness beyond understanding, a place we can never get to, a place beyond knowledge. And, like the hole in the doughnut, it's something we can never eat, never taste."

"I don't care about this hole. I don't care about what I can't eat or taste. Why bother?" Jumaand reached down between his boots and scooped up a handful of dirt, squeezing it tight between his fingers before offering it to me. "Smell this," he said. "All the universe is in it. All the bones. All the ghosts. The shit. Everything. Your cosmology is stupid. Silly business. And not Mongol thinking. I have no interest in emptiness. I prefer wisdom that comes from the heart. I prefer life. Very big. Very crowded. Full."

I zipped my jacket up tighter around my neck and stuck my hands deep into my pockets. I found a cigar stub there and held it between my fingers without lighting it.

"You're right, of course. I like your dirt-based physics. Full. Yes, the fuller the better. Life is everything. All we are. All we will ever be. The body draws six to seven hundred million breaths in a lifetime. And I want all of them. Every one."

"All. All. All," Jumaand was chanting. "Yes. Yes. Yes. Life. Crazy against crazy. This is the Mongol way. The hard life is the good life."

"It better be. Hard is the only life we get. And not for sissies."

Jumaand squinted, his forehead rolling into a landscape of furrows. "I don't know the *sissy* word."

"It means like a coward. Almost the same. But more like without courage."

He hummed a guttural acknowledgment and rubbed his palms together, a sound like sand running on wood. "Nothing is made for the sissy. The universe, life for him is closed."

"Do you know George Bernard Shaw, the English playwright and philosopher?" I asked.

Two geese flew by, one following the other, with screaming honks.

Jumaand followed them with his eyes before turning back to me and shrugging. "I don't know him. Never read."

"Shaw said, 'If you don't get what you like you'd better like what you get.'"

"He thinks like a Mongol," Jumaand said, raising the bottle in salute. "To real thinking," he toasted, and then handed it to me. He laughed, omniscient and amused.

"To real thinking," I repeated and raised the bottle back to him. Whoa! Vodka straight. Incredible. Feel it washing over your heart.

"The Mongol thinks different," he said. "Western man loves in the head. Eastern man loves in the stomach. But Mongolian man loves in the liver."

The *liver?* I thought but didn't ask. Yes it's elemental. It must be the bile. Glandular and bitter to the taste. Cirrhotic.

Suddenly I recognized this man, Jumaand. I knew him. He was Rog Rogoway. Portnoy. Jimmy Walker. Mister Movie Picture. W. W. Storm, Jr. Joe. Tsung Tsai. Henry Miller. Jack Kerouac.

Gary Snyder. Jackson Pollock. Jim Harrison. Tu Fu. Lao Tzu. Ikkyu. Buddha. Zen beatifics all—nomads, wanderers, pure land souls, lovers of the lunatic experience. The human adventure. This fellahin feeling about life, this timelessness. This gaiety. This moment. This now.

"Drink more," he said, handing me the fat, perspiring hunk of horsemeat sausage he'd been waving for emphasis. "And eat." He didn't bother to lick the grease off his fingers before reaching out to squeeze Uka into an all-enveloping bear hug, grinning with his yellow teeth, grabbing her ass. "Look at this woman!" he shouted into the wind.

Marvelously luminous cirrus flowed from the northwest. I was fiddling with my GPS as we left the lost temple, about to mark another waypoint tracking our meanderings since leaving Ulaanbaatar.

"Where are we?" Jumaand asked with more than a touch of sarcasm. "This machine can tell? It can tell you where to go?"

I turned the damned thing off. I couldn't care less where I came from, where I was, or where I was going. I knew the long devious route by which I had come to this place. I knew approximately how and where we would begin tomorrow, and today—well, that was good enough.

"No. It doesn't work," I said. "Maybe another time."

He grunted with satisfaction. "Doesn't matter. Jumaand always knows where he is."

Last night I'd been lost. I'd found myself running through a dream of sand. In it there was the rushing passage of time—old age and its concurrent, most unimaginable horror—its mutilations, inevitable decay.

"Good," I said.

A slow tide of sheep rose above a hillock, their pale shapes rivering past. On the move, they threw their heads back, contentedly working their jaws, or stretched their necks out and pulled clumps of grass into their mouths.

Suddenly around and between a dip in the hills something fast flashed silver in the blue air, and the wind from Siberia fluttered the manes of a line of five tethered mares, but the dusty bitch lying at their feet never moved—lay so still, in fact, that I thought she was dead until I saw an ear flick.

"*Airakh.* Fresh." Jumaand pounded my back as the jeep pulled to a stop in a rising plume of sand. "First we must buy *airakh.*" He had an empty fifteen-liter water jug just waiting for the opportunity. He was enchanted. Excited. "Fresh, it is my favorite food. Food of the gods."

The encampment, three *gers*, made a silhouette of low black domes against the landscape. A toddler peeked out the door of one, hair falling around her eyes, her mouth gaping with wonder. When we got out of the truck, she bounced back into the *ger* and out again with her mother in tow. Bouncing, bouncing. No one at home but the women and an old grandfather. The rest of the family, men and boys, were somewhere, away. They wouldn't return tonight, Jumaand told me. But the nomads were without fear and we were surrounded only by curiosity, generous and friendly.

Jumaand offered apples to the little one and a cup of vodka to the old man. I had a tin of Altoids, the curiously strong English peppermints favored by potheads, in the pocket of my anorak, and I offered them to the girl. She took one, gave it a tentative lick and then another. A huge smile and a tittering laugh. She ran unsteadily to her mother. A lick. Another laugh. And then to grandfather. A lick. A grunt of delighted recognition as he dropped the mint into his cup of vodka, stirring it in with his index finger. I gave them the tin.

The fresh *airakh,* fermented mare's milk, was stored and brewed in sweating horsehide bags that were hung from the curving walls of the *ger.* It was stirred frequently with a twisted wooden paddle to promote fermentation, then stirred again before serving. Jumaand's goal was to stop at every *ger* that had a string of mares tethered outside, a sure sign of fresh juice, so as to keep our jug always full. With the jug tied securely to the roof rack, the bounce and sway of the truck was all that was necessary to ensure perfect fermentation.

"Always ready for us." Jumaand luxuriously rubbed his hands. I understood exactly how he felt. Our pantry full. The comfort of a secure stash.

"The first time you drink *airakh* it will clean you out. Puke, shit, piss. Everything. That is healthy, really good for your body. But after that one time, no problem. Then it is just beautiful. Beautiful," Jumaand said, repeating *beautiful* several more times, each time with passionate emphasis as if to seal the deal with me. "Beautiful."

No damning with faint praise here. And no need to convince. I couldn't wait to give *airakh,* the nomad's drug of choice, a spin, to experience yet another doorway into one of man's oldest preoccupations: altered states. "Sounds promising," I said, lifting my cup.

It wasn't bad. In fact, it was good and getting better the more I drank. Mild-tasting, like watery yogurt. A very slight fizz. Good nose. Nice bouquet. An overtone perhaps of horse piss.

"Delicious," I said as I emptied my water bottle and filled it with *airakh.* I walked off to be alone, finding a bare flat rock, confortable in the sun, to sit and gnaw on a hunk of horsemeat sausage between swigs of *airakh,* health food, loaded with vitamins and protein. A flat shadow undulated over the spine of a nearby ridge. Light bent the landscape and, defying description, bounced in dizzying wavers, hazy and tinted by tawny hues. A linear purple chirographic stroke, north-by-northwest on the horizon, was the summit of a mountain not on my map—one whose beauty I remember but whose name I asked and was told but forgot to note and lost.

And though I never got to experience, as Jumaand had warned, that good-for-my-body clean-out, the food of the gods was, as advertised, one of the world's sweet highs; mildly hallucinogenic, it was also an aphrodisiac. Uplifting. Piercing. And glorious, with the day and I both growing huge and warming together. Swimming in wet fire. Floating. Ah woman, girly woman, this morning, such a pretty morning, I was dreaming of all things Uka: her dusty boots to untie, those little red socks to pull off, her ankles with those bony hollows, the arch of her foot. And what is that place behind knees and elbows called, the crook where skin is softest?

When I returned from Airakhland, where I'd been in imagination, Jumaand began where we'd left off. With introductions. "That man there knows the wisdom of nomad life. Knows the language of the wind and bird," he said, pointing at the old man, that otherworldly grandfather, now dropping another mint into another cup of vodka.

Out of *Road Warrior* bizarre, Grandfather looked as if the language of wind and bird barely scratched the surface of his knowing. On the other hand, it could be that he was just another stoned drunk (though one doesn't negate the other). He had a way of staring directly and sizing up instantly, but with no sense of challenge or fear. A certain silent solemnity, despite the fact that he had a dust-fuzzed, grease-blackened Lincolnesque stovepipe hat stuck squarely and firmly atop his head. A blue scarf, tied round its brim, hung down between his shoulder blades like a coon's tail. His skin and teeth, coming out of a wide smile, were the same shade of mahogany. His face was emaciated, with cheekbones like ridge lines outlining the craters that flesh should have filled. More like a magnificent bird of prey, a cross between a falcon and a vulture, a lammergeier; high-browed, with a chiseled beak of a nose; eyes all pupil, narrow black beads, reflecting all light; thin lips. Magnificently handsome, with a dark, almost cruel look, except when he smiled (which he did most of the time). Seven gold rings asymmetrically pierced his left ear. Beneath his battered sheepskin coat, which was ornamented with small silver bells and tied loosely at the waist with a red sash, a fashion T-shirt showed:

KENZO
Haute Couture

Grandfather never once said a word, just stared into the distance, smiling, nodding as if he saw exactly where he was going and everything along the way also, and approved.

"His name is Dashka. He doesn't speak," Jumaand said. "He lost the way."

"But he can talk with birds? Understand the wind?"

Jumaand clasped his hands, and staring past me seemed to reflect for a moment. He shrugged. "There is *true*. And then there is *truth*. Everything has truth in it."

"Sounds like philosophy, and true," I said. "But it's a language I'd like to learn."

He handed me a dented tin camp cup and looked as if he was about to smile. "Okay. Maybe then you need to drink more."

"It would be a help." I drank. "I've had conversations with dogs and spoken the language of a black cat named Crow who didn't live long but lived fast and full. But the language of the wind—that would be another dimension, completely other, a revelation."

I handed the cup back to Jumaand, who poured one for himself and then another for Dashka.

After he'd finished, Dashka took out a cracked, fire-smoked wood flute mended with string. "Listen," Jumaand said. "His breathing is very special. Like wind." Dashka played, producing pure and lovely tones that sounded something like a variation on a classic Chinese theme, imagery sweetening the dry air. A breeze blows. The bamboo rustles. Water falls. A temple bell rings. The breeze becomes wind and whistles.

"*Bunyanaanim*" ("May you add to your merit"), I said after he had finished, but I could see from the blank look on his face that he had not the slightest idea what I was trying to say. Instead I tried a bit of sign language, an on-the-spot improvised attempt at courtesy. I bowed, not as gracefully as I remembered Peter O'Toole doing in *Lawrence of Arabia* when he first met the sheik, Omar Sharif— much of what I know I learned at the movies—but doing my best, touching, in turn, with a flowery flourish my mouth, forehead, and heart.

He seemed impressed by my performance, for he nodded vigorously.

So I handed him my water bottle, filled with the food of the gods, our Lady *Airakh*. Very healthy indeed.

Squatted down on haunches, I felt the ligaments in my knees begin to squawk when Dashka passed me the pipe he had been puffing. I inhaled deeply, hoping for a shot at transhuman language abilities. I coughed. It wasn't tobacco. It wasn't hash or opium. It wasn't smooth. I wasn't enlightened. Overhead two hawks flashed, shrilling. Sharers, with Dashka, of the mystery: the idiom of birds and wind. I took another puff. The smoke standing in the air above my head, very blue.

I moved to hand the pipe back, but Dashka waved me off.

"Trade. For your water bottle," Jumaand said.

It didn't seem a fair trade, this ancient, blackened brass pipe smooth with touch and inlaid with the worn remains of some golden ornamentation—lotus flowers incised around the bowl—in exchange for a shatterproof climber's water bottle.

I loved the pipe, so I started again my O'Toole imitation, but I was already embarrassed by the time my hand reached my mouth, and instead turned to Jumaand for help. "Tell him that when I smoke I will remember him. It will help me remember all."

Sunset came down gorgeous and awesome, with great towering clouds of crimson and orange on the purple horizon. Every day now the sun seemed to set distinctly earlier, as if the process toward the solstice had somehow gotten faster and faster, leaving darkness and a vaster array of stars.

In the *ger* where Uka and I were to spend the night the air was choking, a sickly sweet combo of rancid mutton fat, sour milk, and barnyard combustion. Uka lit a candle, which though it sputtered and played weakly revealed a *barazza* of stuff, hovering like apparitions out of the gloom. Besides numerous indescribable objects of unknown origin and function, there were: an iron bedstead and mattress, baskets, boxes, a Chinese chest, unwashed clothing and rags, potatoes, strips of dried meat, a bowl of black curled fungus (used to make a tea, Jumaand said, that can induce abortion) and another of hard pebbly camel cheese, a sheaf of grasses bundled together with a rawhide tie, a good-sized sack of dried dung for the fire, slender sticks of thorn brush, hemp rope, bridles, plastic water bottles all strung together, a dented brass teapot, the ruins of two chairs, a ladle. Life was as cramped, as circumscribed inside, as life outside was unbounded.

The night began calm; nothing sounded but the piercing mooncries of the she-wolves and the grass's thin rustle. Again I thought I saw something lean and low slip from shadow to shadow.

Be alert. Millisecond by millisecond life is conspiring to kill you. There are billions and billions of ways. These stones, for example, that breathe and shake with disembodied energy.

The wind started hard, rattling the door. The wolves began again and stopped. The dogs answered and stopped. I howled. They answered. Uka laughed. We didn't talk. The fire crumpled at the core in a flash of flying sparks; a jet of blue flame hissed momentarily, glittering on her bronze earrings. All seemed flirtatious; the frail flames of a small dung fire were enough.

Our silence seemed at first a kind of wariness. It didn't last long. Suddenly off to the right, from Jumaand's *ger,* there came wicked laughter and then nothing until, as I lay wide awake, listening to Uka breathe, there came a lover's cry of full-blooded pleasure, sounding like something between a nightmare and ecstasy. Wild and long, falling away to a roar of silence that blotted out indifference. Then the scuffles and the murmurs and the kisses brushed and breathed upon. Naked and raw.

Still uncertainty followed. There were questions and no answers but one. I wanted her, wanted with Uka to turn what slight degree of warmth there was to comforting heat.

I've always had a reason to jump on experience. Or should I say an *excuse*. Perhaps this time I would play my neo-Confucianist card: that Everyman should work to fulfill his potential through self-cultivation and investigation of experience.

I wet my lips as best I could with a dry-mouthed tongue. My heart beat so hard that I could hear it. Yes. It had happened again. I traced the curve of her, from knee to belly, up and back. Her breasts. All that was true and fine and still is—the lover, the night visitor appeared. Invisible libido licked. Mincing beneath the blankets, the girl beside me, smelling of mutton and goat milk curd, reached out. She whispered, "George."

name the parts and sniff them.
it's pussy.
it's cock.
it's life.
and it stinks.
it stinks so good.

There was nothing to think about. This was an offering. Not a sacrifice, but a privilege. Clear. Plainchant. Concupiscent.

Still, I felt . . . not guilt but the need to explain, to justify. It wasn't easy, simple now as it was when I was younger, when flesh always insinuated magma, lucidity, and a wedge against ice. Sexual elegance was the classic aesthetic, visually and philosophically. Now simple is never easy. I'm not loose enough. Maybe I think too much. *Don't think!* Maybe there's a lack of pure *do* in my endless cognition. Before we had a thumb and then some—all that intellectual analysis—we only *did*. We had no principles except spreading the DNA. The dragon core beneath all that gray matter only *needs*—like our notochordate and chordate ancestors, like the giant saurians we have left behind—only *wants*. More. The dragon, my primitive backbone, needs neither reason nor excuse. Yes, automatic lust. For decoding indivisible genes, we are, some of us, by right of atavistic understanding, lechers and lovers both.

Colder. Immediately cold when the fire collapsed. The ashes glowed red, but fast cooled, as dung fires do, from orange to heatless gray, too cold for these thin blankets to warm. "A girl in your bed is warmer than a dung fire," Jumaand had said. The after-midnight hours found us curled around each other, her bottom warm against my stomach, entwined, hugging like long-lost lovers, spooned at the hips, riding each other for warmth through the long night, holding on to whatever we could grab on to. In a dream made of flesh, I loved, and left the rest to the gods. There was silence then and a sky full of winter stars.

I would wake four times that night—once to a voice whispering my name, three times to piss. I came back to a bed always warm with her warmth. She was a virtual heat generator, that one—so much warmer than I.

•　•　•

The word is *epigamic,* a zoological term used to describe behavior that attracts the opposite sex, such as large antlers or the bright colors of certain birds. It derives from the Greek *epigam(os),* "marriageable." What I am is an epigamic fool, strutting my stuff. Signifying. Proving what? That I can always play the game of seduction. Win. Get the choice piece at any age. Raise the flag. Dominate. The male imperative. Enough! Been there, done that. Enough; I say enough. But still there is that voice: *Listen. This is your dragon speaking.*

> *a woman's scream carrying distance*
> *a dog's bark*
> *the heaviness in my crotch*
> *everything else is rumor*

Only passivity seems like shame. And ennui, which in its ease can be a drug too seductive. The still life, which in French is *nature morte,* nature dead, the dead life.

Waking, I grabbed at the coming day, at the simple truth of still being alive, to that profound pleasure, to that ferocity of appetite for love, for an eternity of emotion, the hope that love with all its confusions and destructiveness can repair madness, weakness, aloneness. I pulled on my pants and boots. Her eyelids fluttered, her sleepy gaze. I stood and walked out into the desert, into the sand wind, into the faint, pale-silver luminosity appearing in the east, changing as I watched, moment to moment, to yellow. But when? At what moment? Thick with event, the moment continually sliding into memory. Memory that invades the present. Memory as insanely real as the moment being lost. There is no moment but movement. Everything is a continuum, a process. In that succession of events that is an experience, a life, there is no stasis. Nothing holds. Nothing waits. Nothing but this: at that moment, in that Gobi, in that cold yellow light, I was waiting to touch her again. Waiting on October 29, 2003, when the sun would rise at 6:15 and set at 4:59; when the high would be 41°F, the low −1°F. Wind gusting, twenty to twenty-five miles per hour.

I would wait no longer. I went back to bed; back to touch, back to passion's comforting heat—back to Uka.

Then it was morning. In the thin light before dawn, the first faint blur, the forerunner of sunrise showed when Jumaand stood framed in the *ger*'s open door rubbing the back of his neck. After we reluctantly crawled out of bed and pulled on our jeans, Jumaand came inside, hugged us both in turn, added dung, stoked the fire, and then stretched, groaned, and asked for aspirin and caffeine tablets. That he'd had little sleep that night was apparent in his epicanthic, heavy-lidded eyes, which sank and bagged. I dug through my kit and handed him both bottles. He took four of each, washing them down with half a jar of pickle juice and then a cup of tea into which he stirred two heaping spoonfuls of instant coffee and a splat of vodka. After a second cup and his first cigarette of the day, deeply inhaled and held long, he looked suddenly revived and none the worse for wear. Smoke curled up slowly from his nose; a passionate smoker, he squinted as it drifted into his eyes.

Around the fire stoked to blazing we stood scratching, swaying, tipsy still with drink and weariness, sipping milk tea and eating hunks of horsemeat sausage to which I added a supplement of vitamin pills and four aspirin, then added, in brotherhood, four more of caffeine. I was weak, dull with fatigue, my mouth and head filled with cotton fluff. The dung stove smoked, blackening the upper walls. Then the pills kicked in and my heart too began pumping.

"I'm back in business," I said aloud to myself. "Showtime and all that jazz."

Jumaand, who had been working hard over a bowl of water, now had the pink face of the just shaved, but with a dull blade—a fresh, rather large nick bled down the side of his jaw. I must have looked surprised, for he answered the question I never asked with barely a smile.

"I don't want to mark Tseegi," he said, making a toothpick and toothbrush from a match stick, sharpening the burnt end and splitting and raveling the other with his knife. Jumaand worked his teeth and gums in earnest with a paste of salt and saliva he'd mixed up in the palm of his hand. A vodka rinse.

"Aarrghh. Good night, hey," he said when he'd finished his toilette and, in a positively jaunty mood, leaned close and teased, like a Mongol Sinatra, with a song in his heart.

"The girl with jeans so close to me yet so far-aar . . . I give my tear-ears to her," Jumaand sang.

Uka took no notice. She was carefully adding water to whatever else was in the teapot and set it again on the stove. "More?"

Salty and weak, Mongol milk tea was an acquired taste I'd never acquired.

"No. Thank you. I've had enough."

"I love tea," she said, pushing her empty cup closer to the source.

There was also Mongol mutton soup for breakfast, boiling hot, globules of fat roiling. Jumaand quickly downed two still-steaming bowls, his and the one I'd refused, my stomach slowly turning. Too much reality. Not enough showtime and all that jazz.

"Mongols like to eat their food very hot and make a lot of noise." Jumaand slurped, making a lot of noise, and continued, "Young men would have"—he paused, looking for the word and slapping the table in frustration—"I don't know. Poor English, but they would make bets."

I gave him the word. "Contest," I said.

"Yes. thank you. Yes, a contest. And who could eat the hottest food fastest would win. The rest would pay. I never paid."

I smiled, remembering Tsung Tsai's boiling hot tea kung fu. Must be a High Asian, a northern latitudes tradition. A way to get warm, be warm, stay warm. Boil the innards. But my stomach, led by my nose, refused. I hate fat and meat in general for breakfast. Mutton in particular. I hate the smell of mutton, rank and greasy. The cuisine of Mongolia, ghastly.

The origin of the Mongol nation can be traced back to the T'ang dynasty and the Meng-ku tribe, which by the end of the eleventh century had emerged in what is now eastern Mongolia as a nation known as Mangqol or Mongqol, Menggu in Chinese. Of Turkic and Mongol-Tungusic origin, the Mongols themselves, up to the time of Genghis Khan, still described themselves as Tatars, a label derived from Ta-ta, the collective name for all the tribes and races of Central Asia. In the early T'ang dynasty (about 700 BCE), this consisted of only some 70,000 households—perhaps a total population of 350,000.

In the thirteenth century, an Italian merchant, one Plano Caprini, aghast with Western snootiness and hysteria, wrote:

They [Mongols] are not fastidious in their dietary habits, consuming everything that can be eaten—dogs, wolves, foxes, horses and in emergency human flesh. They also eat the afterbirth of mares, we even saw them eating lice; and with our own eyes we saw them consume mice.

A century or so earlier, and no less hysterical, Li Xinchuan, a Chinese traveler, reported:

The Menggu are rapacious and bloodthirsty. They have no rulers or chiefs. They have no agriculture, no fixed home, but migrate following the seasonal supplies of water and pasture. Their land has no iron. They fashion arrowheads from bone and make armor from fish scales. They can see in the dark and are eight feet tall. They drink mare's milk and eat the flesh of wild deer which they do not cook.

Rashid ad-Din, a thirteenth-century Persian historian, in his *Chronicles* said prophetically of the Mongols, before the rise of Genghis Khan, that had they been united, no race—not even the Chinese—could have withstood them.

Before the rise of Genghis Khan, it was said, stars fell from the heavens and the earth and its crust heaved. It was a time of poverty, misery, and death. Rather than rest or sleep, Mongols fought each other. There was only war; no affection, only rape and slaughter.

Genghis: the word has been variously interpreted as *firm, strong, righteous, loyal, hard,* or *cruel,* depending on the meaning given to *chinggis* by different Mongol tribes. All seem to fit the ruthless conqueror known as Genghis Khan, depending, it would seem, only on perspective, experience. Those that surrendered to his armies were treated with clemency and favor; those that resisted were, without exception, annihilated.

Eight centuries later the legend remains. And also, in the collective unconscious, the fear.

I'd choose mouse or deer Ta-ta over mutton fat anytime, I thought, as the steam rising from the soup fogged my glasses and I went outside to clear my head and settle my stomach with cold air. Slivers of ice had replaced the grass.

My bedwarmer, nursemaid, and bodyguard—my lover Uka—

followed me out. My curiosity about her was as great, I was sure, as hers was about me. But neither of us asked questions. Sweethearts? Wives? Husbands? Family? Everything outside the bubble of these few short weeks would remain unknown. There would now and forever be only this moment. Nothing before. Nothing after. It was absolutely faithful, true to what it was, what it could be. I would thank her. We would kiss.

There was a shadow on her cheek, a half smile. Her tumbled rat's-nest hair like a sleeping child's. Slim and long with youth; hair, arms, fingers, legs—straight and lithe, either walking or riding—and now stinky, sticky, half-drunk, with breath like a goat, still she fitted her body like a cat, never off balance.

"Don't like Mongol soup? Maybe you have stomach problems?" she asked.

My shoulders ached. I'd woken stiff and cold, and still was. Now a face numbed by the wind. "I'm okay. Not hungry." I touched her cheek. "It's cold, but you're warm."

She touched her lips with her tongue. "Mongol blood," she said, her mouth close to my neck. "Your hand is also warm."

I slapped my chest three times over my heart. It made a hollow sound. "Me too," I said. "Mongol blood."

"You make peepee three times in the night," she said.

"Two times," I protested.

"No. Three," she said. She counted silently, her fingers popping up in quick succession just inches from the tip of my nose. One. Two. Three. There could be no doubt. "It was three," she added conclusively with an imperious flip of the hand.

"You're probably right. The *airakh* made me do it," I said, defending the machismo of my sorry bladder, which it seems had become a topic of lively conversation among the nomads. They are not a private people, but straightforward and completely immodest.

As if to prove the truth of that unspoken claim, Uka walked perhaps fifteen feet north, put her back to the wind, unbuttoned her
jeans, and tugged. Down came her long underwear, and tatty lace
thong all at once, revealing her smooth coltish thighs and, bare
pubescent pubes. She stood languorous for a moment—naked from
waist to knee and gilded in absurdly brilliant easterning light—
then squatted. I turned away.

She came back to me, laughing. "Okay," she whispered, leaning
against me heavy and soft. The same insouciant hand that had
flipped me now circled my shoulders. Irreverent to play with, like a
kitten, she then bit me on the neck. I would carry the mark of her
teeth still the next morning and a few mornings after.

"White man's blood," I whispered.

Laughing harder, she hugged me and ruffled my hair. "Okay."

"Okay." I laughed with her and, remembering last night, could
only shake my head and laugh harder in amazement at what life
offered, the surprises life gave.

That her nipples were always hard. Erect. That between her
parted lips, her tongue showed very red.

We were singing.

"Always I am singing the feeling of life," Jumaand said. "Always with my heart beating stronger for all the memories to come."

For all the memories to come, I thought, when he'd finished and I began. I too loved to sing as I drove, and like Jumaand's, my heart was beginning to beat stronger now. And so I sang as an offering and a contribution to nomad ambience, to wandering, to memories new and old, a favored medley of "Buddhist pop standards." Tunes that, like Jumaand's songs, had been learned in childhood.

Grab your coat and grab your hat, yeah!
leave your troubles on the door step, yeah!
just direct your feet to the sunny side of the street.

And then, with no noticeable segue:

Ol' Man River, he just keeps rollin',
he can't stop rollin',

that Ol' Man River, he just keeps rolling,
he won't stop rollin' along.

"And this one," I told them, "is my favorite. Sigrid, my wife, and I sang it while driving to the hospital, waiting for our daughter to be born."

Row-row-row your boat gently down the stream;
merrily-merrily-merrily-merrily life is but a dream.
Row-row-row your boat gently down the stream;
merrily-merrily-merrily-merrily
life-is-but-a-dream-life-is-but-a-dream-life-is-but-a . . .

After about eighty kilometers of emptiness—a scattered flock of horses, a golden eagle perched on a low black granite outcrop—we came upon a *ger* sporting a satellite dish. We didn't stop. Jumaand said nothing but seemed offended.

The weather turned miserable, for though the blow was moderate, it had an ominous chill and a sinister tinge. Blowing sand. The wind Tsung Tsai had called the Yellow Flower. Tawny clouds sailing. And yet it felt regular and right, proper. The air was rarely still here, and when it was, it felt bad, wrong, dangerous. It was visceral: to live in this wind was to recapture the wonder of childhood, to be absolutely alive to the elemental pleasures. What I dreamed the night before I don't know, at least not the details; but whatever it was, it happened in the wind and I woke happy. In dreams I have no past, no future. And now again I was windward.

It would be three days before the wind softened. The sun was dim, the sky mustard-colored, and that evening there would be a luridly rayed sunset, pea green and orange. It had heavy weather potential. The nomads all knew the color of the sky. And from that and the wind, the phase of the moon, the light at sunrise and sunset, the smell and the feel of air, knew the weather to come. It looked apocalyptic. But then, I knew nothing. The mountains to the west showed suddenly as flat and sharply outlined as black paper cutouts. The pricking stars.

Jumaand was in a shitty mood. He stood in the doorway of the *ger* and fluttered his eyes against the grit. The first sign of day was becoming flush: a delicate pink and silver. With sunup came a dun-colored haze, a fine dust that gritted between teeth and irritated eyes, an odd sudden rise in temperature and then, just as sudden, with the freshening wind, an even more precipitous drop, with all warmth seemingly sucked out of the air. The sky was dark as lapis in the west.

I heard an arid retching, reminiscent of scraping the blackened crust from burnt toast. Jumaand's tobacco cough.

"I hate this moon," Jumaand said to no one in particular.

The previous evening the season had turned under the influence of a lopsided moon. Two days from full, it was for Jumaand a haunted and unlucky moon. But it was magnificent even if a bit feral. It dominated the senses, huge and clearly domed, undimmed by even the flimsiest veil of humidity, beaming and brilliant, casting cool blue light from horizon to horizon. It was like looking out over the vast inland sea that this land had once been; I could almost hear ripples of waves sucking the shore.

In spring this place would go green, billowing against the brilliant blue. It would come on like consciousness. One morning there would be nothing and then, the next, there would be everything.

"You must return in June, when wildflowers cover my country." Jumaand turned a slow 360, his right hand like a compass needle pointing: north, west, south, east, and finally to the center, the earth beneath his feet. He put his thumb and forefinger to his nostrils and with closed eyes took a long slow sniff, held and then exhaled: sweet sibilance.

October 31: a Friday, I think. I've lost track of the days. It snowed once last week. Today it is cloudless. Yesterday and the day before yesterday the sky was the same; painfully so. Jumaand's forecast is not more of the same. Today there was full sun early, the light oblique and brilliant, though the wind, as in older memories, had bite and rattle. High, 34°F. Low, 3°F. The desert's edge. Sniff it. This thin, cold Gobi air, like premonitions, was scentless. And hold the winter, please. The wind had begun to hurt.

Jumaand coaxed the truck forward, the clutch slipping *ka-thunk*, the shifter cranky, gears winding. Average speed twenty kilometers per hour. Money and supplies running low.

Beyond a small rise we dropped into a colder hollow. It had gotten progressively colder, and as the day went on it darkened so that when night came it would be hard to know exactly when it had happened. A strange soft gloom. The windshield wipers whacked as they swept back the sand from the scratch-smeared glass. The truck's heater was almost okay, but we were leaking most of its warmth through the gaps and cracks in the canvas top. Uka tapped me on the shoulder and handed me a Mongol sheepskin hat. It was greasy and stank, but nothing seemed to be living in it so I put it on, and it was warm.

"Mongol clothes are best for the Gobi," Jumaand said. "Uka is worried for you."

The steady beat of the engine. I'd traded seats with Tseegi and was dozing on the border of consciousness, my head on Uka's shoulder; every pore, every hair follicle an erogenous zone, the cup of my jeans like her hand.

• • •

November 4. Pressure falling. Random clouds. Overcast. High, 24°F. Low, −2°F. Gunning along the narrow track, faster than I thought possible, to make it up the steepest sonofabitch grade, the truck bouncing so hard I felt it from tailbone to blink. Rattling over the crest, Jumaand, his face yellow and concentrated in the glow of the speedometer's light, rode the brakes and a rooster of dust down the other side, the steeper downward slope. Sand and gravel peening the undercarriage, we rolled to a burnt-rubber-and-asbestos-stinking stop. But this was it for wheels. From here to where the wolves were, it would be hooves. Jumaand had borrowed the horses from a nomad family we'd stayed with the previous night.

'Can you ride a horse?" Jumaand asked.

I blew into my cupped hands and took a moment too long in giving an answer. "Not exactly. I have. But only once. A long time ago. More than thirty years past. But . . . why not? Of course. I'll ride."

A sympathizing sigh. A rueful smile. A bit of amiable contempt, perhaps. "Don't worry," Jumaand said.

I must admit I took no comfort from this. I worried. The ground was hard-packed, unforgiving as concrete. Paralyzed for life. A quadriplegic. I hated looking the fool. Not cool. Rather die. So I said, as I always say in like situations, the macho mantra. "Not worried. No problem. I'm cool. Easy."

It was an idiotic stance, but one that I've held on to, without change, throughout the days and years of my extended childhood—since grade school, when I was slow to grow, the smallest in my class. A skinny marine, always ready for fight—to scratch, bite, use a rock, a stick; do anything to even the odds, do damage. It worked. I got the reputation: "Crazy little fuck. Leave him alone, he ain't worth the trouble."

Survival techniques that work, stick: become immutable. Never admit. Never show weakness. Machismo, that sham. The stupidity of hormones running riot. Foolish. And there is nothing as foolish as a man acting still like a boy. Cock-a-doodle-doo.

Roosters,
for all their crow,
can't fly far.

Mongols are the most elegant of horsemen, the aristocrats of the steppe. Practically born on horseback, they and their horse seem almost one: one creature, one mind.

"I was a very famous rider. For seven years I rode in the long race. I rode for my people. I won many times. I won. I won. I am very proud for that," Jumaand said, absentmindedly stoking the neck of his horse with the same tenderness I imagined him stroking a woman.

As for me, all I knew of riding was the memory of a sore ass and thighs chaffed raw. Everything else was fantasy, what I'd learned again at the movies, from the oaters—Hollywood westerns—at Saturday afternoon matinees, from John and Clint and Roy and Hopalong. The nomads had laughed when I'd asked for a soft saddle but kindly gave me the smallest, and probably the oldest, horse in Mongolia. A skittish chestnut mare. Climbing into the saddle was easy enough, but inside I was whoa-ing and holding on with my knees, alert to every change in temper, every move and signal. But on the outside I sat imitating a nomad, back straight as I could manage, arms loose at the shoulders, reins loose in curled fingers, feet centered in stirrups, trying to time the bounce and keep my ass in the air. Not too bad. I wasn't too miserable.

The horses followed each other single file and catlike, their breaths rushing out into the silence. Climbing, we passed on the right, close enough so that I could reach out and touch the past, touch six hundred million years ago, a high bluff patterned with Paleozoic fossils—trilobites and the shells of petrified crustaceans from the ancient sea that was once the Gobi.

In less than an hour, perhaps a thousand feet higher, a light snow began to fall. My tailbone already tormented, my thighs chafing, I wrapped myself inside my Arc'teryx parka, pulled up the hood, and stared ahead into the white vagueness, through the snowflakes melting on my glasses. Saddles creaked. Stirrups rattled. And hooves rang (they actually do).

We were some 540 kilometers south-southwest of Ulaanbaatar in *Ömnögovi Aimag* (South Gobi Province), near the western border of the *Oyu Tolgoi* (Turquoise Hill) concession of Ivanhoe Mines, where huge deposits of both gold and copper have been reported, and where the Canadian company controls exploration rights to over 100,000 square kilometers. Also, just ten kilometers to the northwest is yet another operation, the *Shivee Tolgoi* (Lookout Hill) exploration of Entrée Resources, whose three contiguous concessions occupy an area of close to a half million acres.

The rush is on. The game is afoot. Better hurry. Get in early. Buy stock. Shares are trading higher. Up-up and away. Hoo-rah-rah. Goodbye nomads. Goodbye wilderness. Hello industrial waste. Welcome to the future.

Meanwhile, before the new order, the new world deluge, we were on our way up to the summit of Javhalaut Mountain to look for a Bronze Age petroglyph which I had been told was there by a young Mongolian guide I'd met at Millie's the day before we left Ulaanbaatar for the desert.

The café was jammed that day. Every table occupied, I'd thought to wait when I made eye contact with a young Mongol who was worrying at the dirt under his fingernails with a toothpick he stuck back between his teeth before rising from his chair. Tolgoi L. Erdenebulgan was about twenty-five. He was lean and muscular, with long shaggy hair falling to heavy brows over eyes impenetrably dark, incongruous in a gentle moon face; the corners of his mouth turned up into an infectious smile as he waved me over, pointing to the empty place at his table.

He spoke in a run-on rush of energy. "Please . . . you are very welcome to sit . . . they call me Buugi . . . I have learning English . . . I like to practice . . . you are American . . . yes . . . where are you from . . . why do you come to my country . . ." He stopped himself with a laugh and offered his hand. "Sorry . . . very excited today for meeting you."

"George," I said, taking his hand. "Nice meeting you."

"Nice meeting you," he repeated slowly. "Nice meeting you, Mister George."

"Just George," I said.

Buugi slowly nodded his understanding. "Mister Just George," he said. "Very good."

"George Crane."

He closed his eyes and tapped his index finger rapidly against his forehead. "Okay. Now I can remember very well."

The waitress appeared. "Can I get you anything?" I asked Buugi.

"Coffee would be kind. Thank you."

"Two espressos," I said, holding up two fingers. "And the huevos rancheros for me." I pointed at the menu to make sure I didn't get something else.

"Mister Just George Crane," Buugi repeated.

"Call me George. My friends call me George."

"Okay. Mister Just George."

I gave up. "Your English is good. Where did you learn?"

"I teach myself. From dictionary. Okay not so bad."

Over coffee, Buugi, a nomad from South Gobi, told me that he worked as a guide for Ivanhoe Mines and also, "in summer season," for Mongolia's most famous archaeologist, a Mr. Garamjav, who was also a geologist for the company.

It was from Buugi that I'd learned of the mysterious direction markers, of the stone-slab cists and grave markers dating from the late Stone Age (around the fourth century BCE), located in the central and southern Gobi, of the Neolithic stone tools found at Zurch Uul and Ulaan Uul, and of the petroglyphs on the summit of Javhalaut Mountain.

He had to return to the Gobi, he told me, and I was leaving the next day. We exchanged e-mail addresses. I asked him for photographs of the places he'd described, but he was vague. He nodded and smiled at me, a thin-lipped smile, and then turned away. He shuffled his feet. He half rose before sitting again. We shook hands and said goodbye. It was as simple as that. An accidental meeting. Passing ships in the night and all that. I never expected to see or hear from him again.

But shortly after I returned to the United States from Mongolia I would receive a note from him.

Subject: Hi?

Mister Just George Crane:

I am still in the Gobi since I came here from UB next to the day when you left. I am sorry that I cannot send you pictures. One thing I would like you to know is that we do not take pictures of fossils, ancient graves, and caves or something like that. But nothing that had life spirit in it. Only of cold things, gold and copper and of things like that can we take pictures. So

I cannot but it is ok. I can show you things. I hope that you will come back and visit my home which is in the countryside. Come in spring in summer.

Your Mongolian brother Buugi

First the shadow, then the light. The sun was in my eyes. I blinked blindness. There was only wind and space. The little horse to trust.

Two hours later, in a white turning wind, near the western border of Oyu Tolgoi concession, on the summit of Javhalaut Mountain, amid a tumble of fine-grained black basalt, I stood next to an early Bronze Age petroglyph: wolves forever frozen in their run.

We needed supplies. Petrol. Water. Vodka. Food. Probably in that order. We detoured north to a mud-brick town on the edge of the central Gobi. Its name nothing but a splot of ink in my notebook— Hujirt, I think it was. The town had a gas depot. A few shops. A municipal building. A hospital and school. A community well. A satellite dish. A dozen apartment blocks. These were all Soviet-era hovels, jerrybuilt in the late fifties and strewn about without plan. As usual unfinished. The speed of their decay outdistancing the speed of their construction. Instant ruins. Architectural progeria. Paint, plaster, and concrete peeling off in hunks; long cracks fissuring what remained. Sand creeping up west-facing walls. In streets and alleyways, deep-rutted and holed from the occasional rains and runoffs of spring, trash rolling with the wind like tumbleweed.

Two hundred or so inhabitants, give or take. More in the winter when some nomads use it as winter camp, living in the derelict buildings. The brightly painted doors of their dismantled *Gers*, leaning here and there against walls or on precariously out-of-plumb balconies, were the only spots of color in this otherwise gray place—the desert oasis, twenty-first-century style. Welcome to the future. The end of history. The apocalypse.

The filling station was empty, the gas pumps locked; the door on an empty shed next to the office clapping in the wind.

Jumaand leaned on the horn. In a few minutes a gaunt, dark-skinned woman tottered in from behind the office on high-heeled boots. A red sweater, skin-tight flowered bell-bottoms, and an over-sized Russian military greatcoat with officer's epaulets, worn like a cape, completed the ensemble.

"She says they have no gas," Jumaand reported after a brief exchange.

"No gas. Okay then, where can we go to get some?"

"No place. Every place is too far away."

"Okay. When will *this* place get gas?"

"She doesn't know. Nobody knows. Maybe one week. Maybe two."

"Shit. *Shasha,*" I said. "Fucked?"

"No. Because I am thinking there *is* gas. We just need to talk to the boss."

"Great. Where is he?"

"Not here."

"Not here. Where then?"

Jumaand shrugged. "She is the wife but doesn't know. He went away because he has no gas. We can wait."

"How long?"

Another shrug.

Like *Waiting for Godot,* I thought, beginning to feel as if we were caught in one of Beckett's conundrums.

Waiting for the boss. *Nothing to be done?*

A few hours later—a pack of cigarettes, five different sets of opinions, directions, and speculations—we found the boss and three of his friends squatting on a pile of brush in a hollow beneath the leeward prow of a huge dune, rising to a height of roughly one hundred feet. Here, sheltered from the incoming pall of a dust storm, a pale cold yellowing to the west, they celebrated this no-gas holiday, sharing some homebrewed hooch, a powerful vodka distilled from *airakh,* drinking it from the hollow of a recycled hubcap.

The boss was unshaven and haggard with red-rimmed eyes, but in seemingly good spirits after his sampling of the newly brewed vodka. And in the mood to talk. He struggled to his feet and, bending over stiff-kneed, comically at the waist, carefully and with singular concentration refilled the hubcap from a jar at his feet. He straightened, paused to get his bearings, and shuffled over to the truck, his ankles sticking out like withered sticks from beneath his too-short trousers. His friends followed, their eyes never leaving the prize. He leaned against the door and offered Jumaand the hubcap, which looked as if it had morphed directly from wheel to cup without any detour for cleaning, a faint hint of axle grease and brake dust flavoring the brew.

Even Jumaand, the always willing, held back, touching the middle finger of his right hand to the brew and then that wet finger to his forehead. The polite way of refusing among nomads.

Now it was my turn. The boss looked as if he might laugh, but wiped the incipient smile from his face. "Hello. Hello my friend," he said, offering me a spin on the hubcap as Jumaand passed it on.

I did the same as Jumaand, touching a drop to my forehead while thanking him profusely. The girls were ignored. After Jumaand and I had politely refused, the boss's three buddies cheered boisterously, nodding in unified relief at not having to share any of their precious and (from the look of their sobriety) rapidly dwindling supplies; their tongues swept their lower lips in anticipation. Beneath their skin, dry and papery as a roasted duck's, their Adam's apples rose and fell. No, no. Lucifer didn't shove that apple down Adam's throat. All he had to say was, Look at this. That's all it took. Free will. Desire. Gulp. Yum.

"This man once lived in the United States. He speaks English," Jumaand said.

"Chicago," the boss said, grinning. "I know Chicago. Five years I live there. I learn English there. I have cousin there. He is a car fixer. Me too. Mongolian very good at that."

And they *were* very good at it. Great natural mechanics. A genius for it. Nomad ingenuity—the father of invention and all that—was legendary. They could fix anything. Take it apart, figure it out, put it back together, and keep on keeping on. The horizon waits.

A few days ago we had come across a congress of six nomads working on an ancient Russian truck, a big GAZ-63, a flatbed 4x4 with a split windshield, flat square grill, pop-eyed headlights, soft rounded fenders, and skinny but aggressive knobby tires. Classic, from the look of her—fifty years old or more, perhaps of WWII vintage. A truckie's wet dream. She was weathered by life in the desert to an overall flat gunmetal gray. And clean, not a speck of rust.

Her six-cylinder engine had been disassembled, cleaned, and neatly laid out on blankets next to the nomads' tethered horses. Off to one side an old man carefully whittled a valve and stem out of a piece of fire-hardened wood.

I pointed this out to Jumaand, shaking my head. "That can't work?"

Jumaand asked. "Yes, they say it works," he reported. "Very well. He has done this before. Many times. Doesn't last many miles. But then he makes a new one. Very easy. Doesn't take long."

And now, several days later in metropolitan Hujirt, I was counting on the resourcefulness of yet another group of Mongols.

"Chicago!" I said. "You're joking. *I'm* from Chicago. I was born there."

"You!" he said with a histrionic start and grabbed my hand, pumping it vigorously up and down with genuine, unaffected pleasure. "Windy City," he shouted above the wind. "State Street. Dearborn Street. The Loop." He wiggled and wheezed a dry rattling laugh, slapping himself on the thigh and me on the back. Strangling back his laughter long enough to speak again. "A man's gotta do what a man's gotta do," he said, still wheezing and winking at Uka, impressed by his own drunken lecherous brilliance.

He spread his arms. I spread mine. We embraced, hugging like crabs. "Brothers," he said.

"Bothers," I agreed.

Disentangled, I offered him a cigarillo, a Cohiba, one of the mild-tasting, sweet-smelling Cubans I'd gotten addicted to in Paris. Useful when traveling, not only for breaking the ice, but for defeating rank odors, for fumigation, and for insect control.

He took one, smelled it. Licked it expertly and held it up for me to light.

"I don't even smoke cigars," said the boss of the fuel depot, exhaling grandly, "but it makes talking seem important, like . . . like . . . like . . ." He gestured at me with his hand, that universal *c'mon* signal of the pompous.

"Gentlemen," I said. "Like *gentlemen.*"

"Ahhhh, yes. Like gentlemen." He sighed and exhaled hugely, with much satisfaction.

Jumaand made a long speech in Mongolian, punctuating his oratory with big gestures—at the horizon, at himself, and finally at me.

The director's face got long and dour as the sky, and he sighed piteously. "I am ruined with devastation to have to tell you I have no gas. Nothing."

The fingers of god, alternate shafts of light and negative light beams, broke through the overcast and, with glow and shade, checkered the landscape: painter's clouds. A sign from heaven.

"Nothing," I said. "Not even for your Chicago brother?"

He lightened. "Perhaps though for my brother." He beamed, pleased with himself, with his power, his generosity, his beneficence. "There is a little something I can help, but I am sorry to reveal it will cost a little extra." He shivered and rubbed his hands. "Not too bad, though." He leaned closer to me, speaking confidentially. Man to man. "Just a little for my brother here from Chicago, my important friend from America."

"Of course. I understand." Now I grabbed his hand and pumped it. "Thank you, my brother. Thank you."

We resumed our slow perambulations, a creaky crablike trek (average speed, according to my Garmin GPS, eighteen miles an hour) over the steppe toward what goal I no longer knew or cared. I was carefree. Free. The happiest I'd been in now almost two years of being on the road, as it were—divorce, bankruptcy, a missed deadline for a book I hadn't yet found, agent and editor worried, my friends and even my old teacher tired of me, my daughter angry; the list long and getting longer.

But all that was behind me. Now it was slow going nowhere fast in this desert, so foreign yet so familiar that much of the time I felt intimately in touch, uniquely at home. There was nowhere to go but toward the horizon. I was loose. Lost. Long gone. In limbo. And Uka from behind with strong hands was squeezing my trapezius, neck, and shoulders. Heaven. Nothing could touch me but her hands.

"Could be vurse," as my great-grandmother Bubba Bailey, who knew from *oi-vey* experience, would have said. "*Al-vays*. Could be *vurse*. Much *vurse*. Let me tell you . . . "

Jumaand interrupted my reverie. "I would like to go to my home," he said. "The place where I, Jumaand, was born. What do you think?"

The midday sun was tempered by something *other* in the air. Some unsparing flow. I didn't care.

"Now?"

"Of course now."

"I'd like that."

"Good," he said.

"Yes, it is." I raised my hand. "Give me five."

"Five," he said and we slapped hands, giddy with brotherhood. And so we went.

Forty hours or so later, under the bowed shoulder of a ridge, lay a broad pitch of soft, sage-colored slope. Wheels crunching, the jeep rolled to a stop at its edge. "This is my country, Delgez Khaan, where I was born," Jumaand said. From the top of the ridge where the cliff edge fell precipitously and the sun ran red, a hawk folded its wings and plunged, calling *keer-eeee-reee*.

We'd refilled our water cans at his favorite watering hole: the Spring of the Water That Never Freezes. A purling spring. *Purling.* I love that sound. And also the word *purl,* one of the omnific words, onomatopoetic, a word having unlimited power to create, in its pronunciation, the very sound it describes—from the root *to purl* (*v.i.*): to flow with a soft murmuring sound, making gentle ripples (*literary,* refers to rivers and streams), or (*n.*) the soft sound and gentle movement of a river or stream. A susurrus—again you can hear it—*susurrus* (*n.*): a whispering, murmuring sound.

Mist rising above the spring, gathered in gullies and crevices. It was, as Jumaand had said, sweet, sacred, numbingly cold, but never frozen. No matter how cold the winter, he said, it flowed steadily from a cleft fracture at the base of a low granite outcrop, trickling down over the rocks and making a narrow black stripe, curling, eddying; purling beneath a scalloped lace of ice as it carved a slender rill, following the fall line to a small, perfectly clear pale arctic lake.

Susurrus.

"This water is medicine," Jumaand said with an amorphous wave of his hand out over the water. "Mongols come here to drink, to bathe."

"What does it cure?"

"Everything. It helps."

"Then by all means, let's drink a lot," I said, reaching down and, like the many millennia of travelers before me, splashing cupped handfuls onto my dusty face and hair; drinking. A frozen flash headache. A moan of pleasure and pain. A thank-you to the gods. An awakening.

"This is my home, my birthplace; when I return it gives me all the energy and sadness I need to go on. My mother, father, grandparents, great-grandparents, my family back into time: they all are buried here."

And by that he meant "buried" in the old Mongol way—that is, left out on the steppe in the open, left where they'd lived and loved being, not *under* the earth but *on* it, left for the vultures, for the wind and sand and air to take; leaving their spirits to wander.

"My mother and father died when I was very young. I can't remember them. I was raised by my grandmother. But her I remember. I smelled her three times before she died. That's a Mongol way to say goodbye. Now I have her here," Jumaand said, tapping his skull with his finger. "May the gods keep her memory fragrant."

I nodded. I knew this was the right, the primal path to remem-

bering, for of all things, scent cues memories best; it lingers longest
and truest in mind.

I remember the smell of my mother's cooking. She was a terrible
cook. The world's worst, except for a few odd ethnic dishes that she
made well—like chicken soup with matzo balls, and cinnamon O-
ring coffee cake. But her chop suey was ghastly, worst of all—and
the smell? Celery cooking still gags me every time. It's the smell
that won't let memory sleep. I hate it viscerally, though it brings
back those long-lost dinnertimes of close to five decades past, the
narrow little kitchen with black and white tiles on the floor, the
flowered paper lining the cabinets, my mother's ruthless cleanli-
ness, the chrome-legged, blue-swirl Formica kitchen table pushed
close against the window that overlooked an alleyway, the red
cracked-leatherette chairs. And where we sat: my father by the
back door; I across from him, the oldest son, squeezed between radiator and stove because I was the skinniest, the only one who'd fit.
Bob, my younger brother, in the middle, the favored spot. And
Mother, because the kitchen was so narrow that four chairs
couldn't fit, on a high stepstool behind my brother and close to the
stove, on guard, plate in lap.

Jumaand snuffed the air like a dog. "This is my home. This is
where I was born," he said again and, without warning, began to
run out onto the steppe, shedding his clothes as he ran. It was a
dancing kind of run; and he sang, and his song sounded wild and
alien, filled with both pleasure and grief in equal measure. He ran
alone, probably much as he had done when a boy, here on this his
unchanged stomping ground, running naked into the hazy sunset.
Suddenly he stopped, knelt, and fell forward, naked as when he
was born, his chest to the breast of the earth, the sacred earth of
Mongolia, his home. And he wept, shuddering violently, hugging

the earth, clutching, his hands trembling so that his fingers drummed the pan land beneath him.

Awed and silent, I followed him. And waited. Watching silently. After a very long time he got to his knees and turned to me.

"At this place was my family's *ger* on the day I was born." He slapped the earth with the flat of his hand. "Here on this spot, exactly here," he said, still slapping the earth to show me, "my mother birthed me—Jumaand, the nomad. And it is here I will come to die. And it is here," now pounding the ground with a fist, "*here* that I will stay forever."

But what was I doing here? Why had I come?

There are certain moments, always remembered. I too would have liked to dive naked onto the steppe, kissing the earth in thanks for being born. Giving thanks and love and homage to the place I was born. To my past. To my mother and father. To my forebears. To my father, who died while his eldest son played.

To my father.

Then without warning my father died, his final illness the result of stud poker. He'd lost again; most of his old friends, his younger brothers, had already dropped. He was worn out, his life grown tired, when he rolled his oxygen-tanked wheelchair off a handicapped-access ramp at the casino, breaking three ribs, puncturing a lung; drowning slowly. And the dying, that death that I missed almost three years ago, became real now, and I was overwhelmed by grief. Gooseflesh rose on my neck and arms. I felt airy and cold, no longer able to run from time, from loss. I couldn't stop myself. I cried. I sobbed.

Jumaand, standing naked at the place he'd been birthed, squinted and stared, confirming with his eyes the oddness that his ears had already told him: that I was standing there beside him crying like a baby.

"George? What's wrong? What happened?"

"My father died," I said, for in truth for me he had, just now, as now for the first time I acknowledged his death, admitted that he was no more. "He just died. He died as the sun was setting."

"Dead now?"

"Yes, dead."

"Oh no," Jumaand said. He put his hand gently on my shoulders. Solidarity. Empathy. No questions asked. Not an inkling of surprise that somehow I'd known instantly that my father, on the other side of the world, had died. Whatever he may have thought, he only accepted. That is the way of the nomads: to accept everything at face value. It must have seemed quite natural. Normal. Thoroughly unremarkable.

"That's terrible. George, I'm sorry," he said, continuing to hold me by the shoulders, both squeezing me and shaking me gently as he might a child. "Your father—terrible . . . terrible. I'm sorry for you. So very sorry."

"Thank you," I said, deciding not to explain, since no explanation was asked for, why I was suddenly mourning, crying now for my father. He'd died in Phoenix, asking, I was told, for his eldest son. I was in Manhattan at the time. I got the news from my brother, the good son, there by Dad's bedside, while I, the black sheep, the bad son, living up to the role thrust upon me so long ago I'd forgotten when or how, talked on my mobile as I walked past the Soho Grand, coming from a lunch meeting with my agent. It was midafternoon. The May sun was warm. The air female. Swishy.

"We must make an offering," Jumaand said, finally releasing my shoulders. "A blessing to free his spirit. Yes, we must do this. What was his name?"

"Albert . . . Albert."

Albert, who ran wild once, and who in old photos can be seen wearing a belted brief swimsuit and pencil-thin mustache while flexing his muscles like Charles Atlas, and who, in natty jodhpurs and knee-high riding boots, would ride his horse through the poor immigrant section of Chicago's South Side to ask permission to take my soon-to-be mother, then a raven-haired eighteen-year-old beauty, out on a date.

He was her prince. Except for bad teeth, he was a handsome young man; the fine small bones, the long fingers and expressive hands, the high cheekbones and aquiline nose, the cool of his pale gray eyes flecked with green. She'd thought he was her ticket out of poverty. That it didn't work out. That he was bad at business. That he went broke. That my mother's sister married well—that is, rich. That he had to work three jobs, day and night, to keep his young family fed and housed. That the cry of money—*there must be more money; there must be more money*—bounced and echoed off the walls, the ceiling, the threadbare carpeted floors of the tiny two-room apartment in the grungy, once-stately Montrose Hotel. *There must be more money. There must be more money. There must be more money.* That poverty's push took his manhood, sapped his wildness, his spirit; that it became the raison d'être, the failure that marked his life.

"Write his name on a piece of paper and give it to me," Jumaand said, holding my gaze. His eyes were wet and very still.

"To my father, whom I deserted at the moment of his greatest need," I wrote, then added a brief tribute.

And even as I ripped the sheet out of my notebook, my trusty Moleskine on which I had written my father's obit, Jumaand still did not look away. He was watching.

Albert S. Crane
born Chicago, 1913
son of David
firstborn of seven children
firstborn in the new world

ran wild once
wrestler
fighter
husband to Shirley,
father to George and Robert
hard worker
always faithful
fulfilled his responsibilities to the end
died in the loving presence of his eldest son
and was buried here under a mountain called Delgez Khaan,
Outer Mongolia
birthplace of the nomad Jumaand
November 7, 2003
RIP

I folded it in half and handed it to him. He folded it twice more and placed it beneath a convenient stone. To keep my father company, I buried there two of my travel charms, an 1881 Liberty dollar that my grandfather, *his* father, had given me, and a golden braided lock of hair from his only grandchild, my daughter. *Goodbye, Father. Goodbye.*

"Your father, Al-la-bert, his spirit can be free now. He can go," Jumaand said.

Better here, I thought, free in the air of the desert, free at Delgez Khaan, than stored as he was, his thin shrunken embalmed body in an underground concrete vault, next to my mother, in a cemetery in Scottsdale, Arizona. Like mummies. Perpetual care paid for and guaranteed.

"Thank you, Jumaand. Thank you."

He acknowledged my thanks with a subtle nod and thought for a time. "I think," he said quietly, as if to himself, "that in exchange for his death you will find success."

I was beginning to feel giddy enough to laugh, and would have except for the seriousness in Jumaand's face. Thinking he would misinterpret my sense of relief as a lack of gravitas.

"That would please my father," I said. "That would make him very happy." I could hear him talking to his poker buddies: "My eldest son, the poet, a success? Who would have thought? You know what I'm talking."

And I swear that just at that moment, as a cloud of yellow dust in a gust of crepuscular air passed between us, Jumaand coughed, turned, and hawked up a clot of ectoplasmic phlegm so that it arced and splattered on the ground close to my father's grave.

And still standing stark naked in the cold, in air that felt balmy now, he giggled and so did I, both of us ridiculous, but for the moment both free of grief and ghosts and guilt.

Later, back at the truck, we drank and offered another sacrifice of vodka, poured out onto the sacred earth, to charm the gods of the mountains and curry favor from the dwarf gods of bad luck and ill winds, imploring them to let the spirit of all our fathers go in peace.

Now, I am ignorant of spirits, of metaphysical, parapsychological, or psychological release, but I know that ever since that November burial, in the glow before dusk on the steppe, I haven't had another moment of shame or cried again for my father. He was dead. Done. *I* was dead. But now I was alive. And *not* done. Definitely not done. And human. Do you recognize me? A human being. Connected to you, my brothers and sisters. Connected. Intimately. For to be human is to be consciously aware of mortality; to have a living relationship with death and the dead. With the dead who must be honored. Burial marks the beginning and is the definition of humanity, as Giambattista Vico, an Italian philosopher of the Age of Reason, proposed in his essay "The New Science." He had it right, even its etymology:

Hu-man (*n.*): a human being, *humanitas* in Latin, from *humando,* to bury; derived from *dghem* in Sanskrit, which is also the root of the Greek *khton,* earth.

Let the good times roll. It was January 20, 1953, again. America had not yet lost its innocence. If you were watching television, the occasion was General Dwight D. Eisenhower's inauguration, and Ike, the newly elected leader of the Free World, was on parade, riding, top down, along Pennsylvania Avenue in the back seat of a hot new sporty Cadillac: the gorgeous original Eldorado.

My father was watching and fell instantly in love with the gilded one, America's premier luxury car and its most conspicuous status symbol. It must have been lust at first sight. He must have *needed* that car. Needed it to wash the taste of failure from his mouth.

I don't know how he managed, or where the money came from, for the walls still whispered and echoed, *More money, there must be more money; there must be more money, more money.* But still, by the summer of 1957, a secondhand '55—with rocketship fins, circular tail and rear directional lights, cut-down doors, EZ-Eye wraparound windshield, sweet wheel cutouts (the better to show off the flashy saber-spoke wire-rim wheels and fat whitewall tires), and a grille sporting the two enormous protruding chrome bullets that we called Dagmars, in honor of the busty actress—was parked in the alleyway behind our apartment on Haskins Street, the far North Side, Chicago, Illinois.

Sputnik was launched. The space race began. The first inklings that perhaps all was not right in the American paradise were emerging. Elvis Presley's "Jailhouse Rock" was number one on the hit parade. Frank "Ol' Blue Eyes" Sinatra was number two with "All the Way." My friends had not yet begun to die. My best friend at the time, at Chicago's Sullivan High, Howie L., had yet to be murdered, stabbed to death in Mexico. James Dean had been dead for almost two years. My jazz hero Chet Baker was blowing "Embraceable You." *On the Road* was published and I began to dream of beat glory.

to be . . .
an old man dancing
with a brush
a pot of ink
an artist
drunk with words
wandering
romance to romance
for loftier pursuits
unsuited
for the professions

My father's convertible had a white top and was painted metallic-flake candy-apple blue, with matching leather seats and power everything—brakes, seats, and windows. The big 331-cubic-inch, overhead-valve, dual four-barrel-inducted V-8 gave the Eldo a shot of adrenaline, a gutsy 270 horsepower, and a top speed of 117 miles an hour.

"And that spells F-A-S-T in any language," my father would say, running the shammy along that baby's gleaming length. "Fast!"

Go Daddy, go. Run Daddy, run. I can see him now, a big fat grin on his face. Rocketship fins flashing sun spirals. Pedal to the metal, throwing up rooster tails of Gobi sand, driving 117 miles an hour into heaven. Fast!

•   •   •

"Past the black stones here, past that blue mountain there, which is called Stone of the Big Land"—Jumaand was still talking when I returned to the world of now, pointing south-by-southwest, where nothing but distance could be seen—"past there, near the Stone of the Small Steppe, is a sacred place. It is the Wind Horse. The beginning of the wind."

The beginning of the wind. Bingo. Rainbow's end. I suddenly knew. I was sure. *That's* what I'd been looking for; I'd been trying to reach the beginning, that time before life got complicated. I was looking for what every nomad knows: that all desert roads end somewhere, but that every one of them is more a direction than a mere destination.

"Yes, that's it. That's where I want to go. Let's go that way. Let's go there."

I was happy, near to manic, hopping first on one foot and then the other, waving, pointing to the territory ahead. Forget lost temples. I had found my goal.

"We be travel," Tsung Tsai had once told me. *Yes, my old dear friend, we be. We be travel. We be.*

To the west, lightning, splitting the darkening sky with a fine broad slash. It was there.

"There!"

Widening his eyes to look at me, Jumaand, seemingly pleased by my mania, showed both rows of his yellowed, tobacco-mottled teeth and said, snorting, "Brother, you have a taste for trouble."

"A hunger," I said.

He climbed into the driver's seat and was still smiling hugely as he settled himself behind the wheel. Behind him sat Tseegi, as always with a deep sadness beneath her steely determination. I followed, sitting my usual shotgun. Uka, behind me, laughed. She was ready. A green girl. Always hot. She, like me, eschewed sense, logic, and future planning; opting for mystery, romance; the eternal now. *Go-go-go*.

"I am just a crazy old man. I cannot stop my heart. I am a candle. I burn. But what do I care? I like the light," Jumaand said.

"*Emet,*" I said. "Truth. Forward. Back is for the dead."

He turned the key in the ignition. Again. And again. The engine finally caught, sputtered, missed, turned over. He gave it a few minutes, shouting over the unmuffled roar, the grind of the tranny, the crunch of the wheels rolling slowly forward.

"It's close. We'll be there soon."

Paris, July 2004

a c k n o w l e d g m e n t s

I was helped enormously in writing of this book by Elaine. Its completion was in large part due to her generosity, her sanctuary. These words don't begin to account for all her contributions. She was essential in more ways than I can write here. I am humbled by her love and support of the work, and deeply grateful.

Thanks to Chris Lawrence, "English," Jeff Moran, Peter Cooper, and Arno Finkeldey, the one-eyed bhikku, and Lisa Fernow. You all know why.

To those I traveled with—Bananas, Jim, Ken, Ani Jinpa, Jumaand, Tseegi, and Uka—my debt is great.

And finally, to my editor Eric Brandt—I wish his like on all writers—thanks pal.